**Also by Stuart Albright**

*Blessed Returns* (2005)

# Sidelines

# Sidelines

## A North Carolina Story of Community, Race, and High School Football

### Stuart Albright

MCKINNON
PRESS

Durham, NC

MCKINNON PRESS
2704 Bexley Avenue
Durham, NC 27707
(919) 943-6501

Cover Photograph by Derek Anderson

ISBN 9780578024318

Special discounts are available on bulk orders of this book. To inquire, please write to Stuart Albright at the following address: McKinnon Press, 2704 Bexley Avenue, Durham, NC 27707; ph (919) 943-6501.

Please visit **www.stuartalbright.com** to learn more about *Sidelines* and the author himself. Copies of *Sidelines* can also be purchased from the website.

Dedicated to Bill Eccles

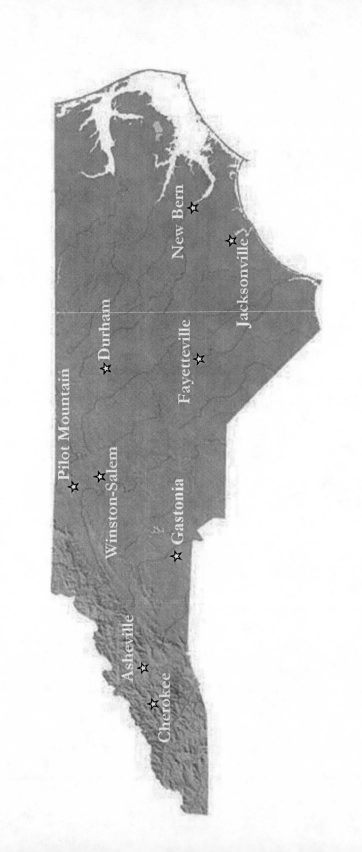

# Contents

Prologue: The Immaculate Reception     1

1. **Chapter One: Roll, Greenwave Roll**     11
   Gastonia

2. **Chapter Two: The Magnificent Golden Bull Machine**     45
   Fayetteville

3. **Chapter Three: The Fire Next Time**     65
   Jacksonville

4. **Chapter Four: Pigskins and Politics**     85
   Pilot Mountain

5. **Chapter Five: Castles on a Hill**     109
   Asheville

6. **Chapter Six: $100,000 Treasures**     135
   Winston-Salem

7. **Chapter Seven: *Eu-stugwoe***     149
   Cherokee

8. **Chapter Eight: Mecca of a Thousand Noble Aspirations**     179
   New Bern

9. **Chapter Nine: Bull City Lockdown**     207
   Durham

   **Epilogue**     239

   **Acknowledgements**     245

# PROLOGUE

## The Immaculate Reception

The metal bleachers on both sides of the field rumble like the onset of a summer storm. Only a minute left to go. Both teams are totally spent. Desperation is beginning to sink in. *It can't possibly happen. Not now, not here, after all this.*

A near interception. Another catch. *He was out of bounds! Stop the clock!* Seconds ticking. *Time out! Time out! Time out!*

We have one last chance. A ball wobbles high above the Raleigh skyline, almost end over end. It is an awful pass. *Too short!* The laces twist and turn against the backdrop of stadium lights and swarming moths. The ball sputters back to earth. A final gasp. Nothing more to give.

What happens next is impossible, really. Utterly impossible. I preserve the grainy videotape as a reminder, saving it like a priceless family heirloom.

From time to time I ask my football players to give their version of that October night. They are a little taller and stronger now, perhaps a bit more sure of themselves. Whenever I mention the Garner game, a knowing smile always crosses their faces and a glimmer strikes their eyes. Each of their narratives is slightly different – an intonation here, an exaggerated detail there. Perhaps they include a sprinkling of poetic license so that the listener can fully understand the magnificence of that game. The sounds and the smells. The unusually mild air for a late autumn night. But the basic story is always the same, with a climax so unlikely that I find myself retelling it again and again just to make it come true.

I remember driving one of our two activity buses out of Durham that afternoon. The details come to me in real time. The diesel engine hums monotonously, and gusts of air swirl through the open windows. Everything else is silence. It is a dense silence filled with the weight of anticipation and focus. Cars fly by us on Interstate 40 as the bus plods along at maximum speed. Through the rearview mirror I see heads nodding in rhythm to Lil Jon or Jay-Z as the beats pound steadily beneath headphones. Beyond the dust-covered windows, the sun begins to set over downtown Raleigh.

It has been a special season for us so far. Seven wins in seven tries. A tremendous amount of time and effort has gone into the past four months. I came to Jordan High School three years ago to coach jayvee football along with LaDwaun Harrison, Chris Starkey, and Tim Bumgarner. On the surface, we are very different men. But we love football, and we care deeply about kids. An unlikely family of brothers quickly developed. During the football season, I spend more time with these men than I do my own family.

Tonight's opponent is the mighty Trojans of Garner High School, one of the powerhouse programs in North Carolina. The Trojans are the only show in town. Even toddlers know all about Garner football. The peewee and middle school teams feed directly into Garner High School. They run the same offense, use the same drills, and learn the varsity's finely tuned system at an early age. Garner is part of a dying breed of schools. Redistricting has eliminated community allegiances in much of the state, and new building projects in East Raleigh ensure that Garner may not be far behind. For now, Garner fans cling to their football program with considerable fervor.

Garner's jayvee team has not lost a game in over five years. Fifty-five wins in a row. Most of them have been brutal, savage beatings over inferior foes. The Garner players are athletic and well-coached, and they are talented enough to hold their own against a number of varsity teams. In short, the Trojans are a machine.

On the very first play of the game, a 200 pound horse of a running back from Garner glides 70 yards passed our defenders for an easy touchdown. He hands the pigskin to the nearest referee with a nonchalance that indicates this is just another beating in the works. The man-child is but one of three powerful backs who will shred our normally stout defense to the tune of 350 yards. We bleed and we bruise and we bend our backs time and time again.

But we punch back as well. After another long Trojan touchdown run, there is a workmanlike drive of our own. A knockout blow from the 200 pound horse is followed by a long touchdown pass in return.

Renard Edwards is our field general. He is a gangly, athletic freshman with long cornrows and an awkward throwing motion that somehow gets the job done. Kids like Renard keep me coaching year after year. When Renard moved to Durham from Savannah, Georgia, at the beginning of the summer, his wariness masked a childlike innocence. Renard desperately wanted to be accepted by the team. Football was his salvation, and it was his only structure in a world filled with family drama and the ever-present temptations of gang life. When Renard became the starting quarterback two games ago, he gallantly took the reigns and kept us moving forward. Renard's talent is raw, but his fearless abandon serves us well on a night like this.

We wait patiently for the Trojans to make a mistake, and it finally comes in the form of an intercepted pass deep in Garner territory. Only three minutes remain in the game. Now it is our turn to do the pounding. Five plays later, a short touchdown run gives us our first lead at 33-28. All we have to do is stop the Trojan machine one more time.

The Jordan fans who made the one hour road trip are going ballistic. Fear is noticeable on the Garner sideline for the first time. We can sense it, like the smell of blood from a wounded prey. A deafening chorus comes from our sideline:

"Dog Pound!"

*"DEFENSE! "*

"Dog Pound!"

*"DEFENSE!"*

Sweat streams down my back as I shout instructions beside Coach Harrison. We chant and scream and grow hoarse. The whole world seems alive with noise and adrenaline and passion and focus.

Less than a minute to play.

The Garner quarterback takes a five step drop. His only option is to throw the ball. Time is running out.

"PASS!" shouts the entire eastern half of Wake County.

The pigskin floats beautifully in the air. Arthur Affleck, our diminutive defensive back, runs step for step with the much taller Trojan receiver. Art has played a brilliant game for us on both sides of the ball. He has thrown his body around with reckless abandon all night long. Art extends his arms to haul in the interception. A hush falls over the crowd. All eyes focus on Art's fingertips.

It is the one mistake Art makes all game. A mistimed leap. The Trojan receiver walks into the end zone with what appears to be the winning touchdown. Pandemonium erupts on the Garner sideline. A 450-pound ball boy joyfully waddles to the end zone, finds the prized football, and spikes it into the ground. Triumphant players in dark blue and gold shake their helmets in the air. It is the death knell for our gaping wound and the end of a glorious run. Garner 35, Jordan 33.

The remaining fifty seconds are a mere afterthought as our defense leaves the field dejectedly. We shout words of encouragement, but the words sound hollow. *It's not over yet. There's still time. Head up! Get your heads up! Let's go.*

Delson McAdams takes the Trojan kickoff to the Jordan 45 yard line. *A glimmer of hope?* An offside penalty. *Damnit. Keep your head! Listen for the count!* Clark Richards, our tight end, hauls in a graceful catch before getting drilled out of bounds at the Garner 44 yard line. But the referee sees things differently. He rotates his arm, and the clock continues to tick.

"Get to the line!" Coach Harrison and I scream to the offense.

Renard throws a deep ball to Delson, our playmaker. Incomplete.

Twelve seconds left.

Two more pass plays fail miserably. Fear and Regret unleash their deadly tentacles on the Falcon sideline. Coach Harrison calls our final timeout with only two seconds remaining.

In the huddle, all eleven helmets turn to Coach Harrison. It is a moment of clarity and calm. No one panics. No one says a word.

"This is what we're gonna do," Coach Harrison tells the offense. "We're gonna call this play and we're gonna score. I want Spread Left, with Antonio and Delson to the play side. Delson and Toni, you gotta go! Renard, throw it as far as you can. Line, you gotta block! You hear me? You gotta give us some time! It's *our* turn now. We got one shot."

Josh Dorfman, our stoic and steady center, eyes the rest of the line: "Nobody gets through. Just stick together and don't let anyone through."

It is a time for desperation, but with Delson and Antonio out there, anything can happen. As a running back, Delson McAdams has already rushed for well over 1000 yards on the season. He is cocky and confident on the field, with the invincible attitude of an undefeated prize fighter.

As a receiver, Antonio Smith has almost matched Delson's impressive yardage numbers. Antonio has matured considerably since I first met him as a freshman. When Antonio's mother dropped him off at the first day of practice last year, I could see the "Don't let anyone hurt my baby!" look on her worried face. Her concern was only slightly appeased by his play this year. Antonio is soft-spoken and intensely serious. He attaches a diligent "yes sir" to every comment he makes. But his confidence used to be shaky at best. Last season he was devastated by every dropped pass in a game, and I had to bench him for long stretches at a time. This year, Antonio's growing confidence has made him into a very talented receiver.

Coach Harrison returns to our sideline as the Garner fans dance and wave their hands in the air. Their singing grows louder and louder with every moment.

"Nah nah nah nah, nah nah nah nah, hey hey hey, goooooodbye!"

The referee finally signals for play to continue.

Four Trojan linemen charge hell-bent at Renard as the final horn sounds. The line weakens but stands firm in a solid wedge around Josh Dorfman. Renard heaves the ball high into the air as the Trojan defense flattens him. Everything goes silent. Renard's pass is a duck, and the wobbly ball descends far short of the end zone. Two Garner defenders lunge for the interception at the ten yard line. Delson hesitates, thinking the game is over. Clark Richards approaches from the right side to knock the ball loose as soon as it is intercepted. This seems to be the only remaining option. Antonio sprints past Delson to the left and converges on the Garner defenders.

I see the final moments in slow motion.

The two Trojan defenders collide as the ball arrives in their arms, jarring their bodies and sending a shoulder pad against the errant pass. The ball caroms backwards and upwards. Antonio sprints behind the defense and tenses his fingers. By some miracle from above, the ball lands in his waiting arms as he crosses the goal line. The head referee is too shocked to signal a touchdown at first, but his arms eventually rise into the glorious autumn air.

Game over. Jordan 39, Garner 35.

It is an impossible moment. Unreal. Euphoric. A collective pause grips our sideline before utter chaos reigns. The stories diverge from witness to witness at this point. As with any life-altering event, the moment takes on a very personal quality. I cling to this moment as my own, but it is Antonio's as well, for it is his first day as a hero, crushed beneath the weight of 55 ecstatic teammates. The moment also belongs to my wife and my brother as they hug each other in the stands. Antonio's mother laughs and cries and jumps up and down, screaming, "That's my baby! That's my baby! That's my baby!" I run to the end zone with Coach Harrison, who is pumping his arms in the air. Coach Starkey extends his hands as if he is about to fly off into the moonlight. Several of our players bend to the earth and pray. Others grab divots of the field and let the grass scatter across their sweat-drenched faces. The unfortunate defenders lie face down on the ten yard line in tears with their arms beating the ground in helpless frustration.

It is a moment that defines who I am as a coach while at the same time defining nothing at all about me. It is a miracle and a fluke. It is an aberration from the normal workings of the world. I don't know quite what it is, but it has a definite meaning. Flip to the ESPN highlights on any given night and the moment is there, just as spectacular and just as unreal. But it is not *my* moment. I could have witnessed this event anywhere. The world is full of such wonder and beauty, but our eyes are perpetually locked into the daily grind of work and pain and tedium. We react when we are shocked, and we are only shocked when the hot coal presses directly to our skin. We see life with detachment rather than fully feeling the world around us. Miracles are lost from our vocabulary. And ordinary miracles? They no longer exist.

The bus ride after the game is a snapshot of delirious and exhausted emotions.

It's growing late now, and I still have to get up at 5:00 a.m. to prepare for my English classes in the morning. We're in the middle of *Their Eyes Were Watching God*, Zora Neale Hurston's classic novel of the Harlem Renaissance. Thoughts of Janie Crawford and Tea Cake blend in with the block party behind me on the bus. Renard, our quarterback, sits with Coach Harrison to my right. He is exhausted and totally at peace with the world. I see Delson conducting our victory song through the rear view mirror. The song comes from *Remember the Titans*, but whenever I see the movie, I can only think of these young men and their triumphant call and response.

Delson: "Everywhere we goooooo…"

The masses: "EVERYWHERE WE GOOOOOO!"

"People wanna knowwwwww…"

"PEOPLE WANNA KNOWWWWWW!"

"Who we are…"

"WHO WE ARE!"

"So we tell them…"

"SO WE TELL THEM!"

Then Delson hits the high point of the song: "We are the *Fal-cons* …"

"WE ARE THE *FAL-CONS*!"

"The mighty, mighty Falcons…"

"THE MIGHTY, MIGHTY FALCONS. OOH AH, OH YEAH! OOH AH, OH YEAH!..."

As I drive back home to Durham, the bus shakes with the sounds of singing and clapping.

We watch the Garner game film after practice on Friday afternoon. The young men in the locker room slap each other on the back and exchange high fives. Spirits are still soaring. Everyone grows quiet as we admonish the defense for giving up 350 yards and critique the offense for penalties and missed opportunities. But as we approach the final play, the excitement builds yet again, and a smile plays across every face. Renard steps back, fires a wobbling pass, and Antonio snatches the miracle gift from the air. All 55 players break the silence with a deafening scream as they crush Antonio once more. The intensity of his face fades into a full-bodied laugh.

High school football is merely a game. At least that's what people on the outside might say. Football is certainly fun, and for that matter, our players perform at their peak when they love what they are doing. But athletics can evolve into something else entirely. When I think of my own education, the greatest learning experiences of my teenage years came from playing on a high school football team. Football can be a weapon against poverty and racism and broken homes and depression. It brings families together, and it provides fathers for kids who may not have a father anywhere else. It keeps students interested in school, and it opens doors to the intimidating world of higher education. Football can build men out of fragile and wary boys. They enter high school encased in eggshells and leave four years later with a durable exterior.

These are trying times. Throughout America, we are losing the hearts and minds of our youth. Many of our communities are slowly dying. Neighbors no longer feel connected to one another. The hopes and dreams of our recent past sometimes feel lost amid resegregation, home foreclosures, and the ever-present gap between the rich and the poor. The stakes grow higher with each passing year, and we repeatedly ask schools to solve the greatest ills of our society. Students feel marginalized and invisible within the ever-growing masses. We've entered a world of anonymity. But within this new world, there is still the audacity of hope – to borrow the words of Barack Obama – and coaches, teachers, and other local leaders stand on the front lines of the struggle. Children cling to hope when they find others who will participate in their journey. Hope originates when a community exists beyond the basic framework of a chalkboard or a classroom wall. It is this sense of community that drives much of the excellence we see in many schools. It can come from athletics, or it can come from something entirely different. There simply has to be a genesis. Community building starts with someone who is innovative and charismatic, someone who loves kids and believes in social justice. Coaches often fill this role.

So how does anyone ever change the world? Who are these coaches who engage in ordinary miracles? Where do they exist? What makes them successful? How do they shape the futures of so many young men? I long for the answers to these questions.

This book will be a pilgrimage of sorts, and North Carolina is as good a place as any to start. I like the dual nature of the state, where the New South and the Old South collide in a rollicking battle between liberal Chapel Hill and the conservative ideology of Jesse Helms. The rural tobacco culture of the east meets the burgeoning growth of cities such as Charlotte and Raleigh and Fayetteville. I find comfort in the ancient rolling hills of Appalachia and in the turbulent beauty of the Outer Banks. It is a land of both black and white. The dynamics are messy at times, but the contradictions are there for all to see. North Carolina is not a football-crazed state like Texas or Florida, but its character more aptly fits our national consciousness.

North Carolina is my home, but like most people, I bring a certain tunnel vision to my allegiances. I don't know what most of the towns in this state are really like. What lies behind the curtain of such far-flung places as Pilot Mountain and Jacksonville and Cherokee? What drives the pulse of these cities? Where does community building exist? I hope to answer some of these questions in the following pages. As the great Carolinian from Asheville (or Altamont) once put it, *"we are the sum of all the moments of our lives."* What clay will form from this pilgrimage? How will my own past color the new people I meet? Will this journey help me to create my own imprint on the world? Thomas Wolfe would surely ask me these questions. I accept the challenge with open arms and a ready pen.

On a hazy autumn night, a young man catches a touchdown pass along the outskirts of Raleigh, North Carolina. It is merely a junior varsity football game. There are no real stakes involved. The *Raleigh News and Observer* does not cover it. Nor does the *Durham Herald Sun*. The world is unaffected and unimpressed by these events, yet the moment matters to me and to hundreds more. I share it with my family - my brother and my wife, certainly, but I have a new family that transcends blood lines. We are a community. The moment is ours individually, but more importantly, it is ours collectively, and nothing can take that away. In the isolated, post-9/11 world we live in, such things really matter.

Every story must have a beginning, and mine does not originate on that October night. Antonio's catch is simply the pivot point for all that follows. Like so many things, the future is only as clear as the reflections of our past. My story begins with a shy, fifteen year old boy on a football team in the middle of June.

# 1

## Roll, Greenwave Roll
### Gastonia

The sound of hushed voices filled the Ashbrook High School gymnasium as seventy young men waited for six o'clock to arrive. Shoes squeaked on the polished court. Voices echoed across the varnished bleachers. All the while, I felt utterly alone.

It was June 13, the first day of summer practice. The veterans were easy to spot. They seemed relaxed and confident as they huddled in packs. They looked huge and otherworldly to me. I recognized Randy Rodriguez immediately. He was #11, the starting quarterback. Next to him was Cranston Johnson, #17, the smooth and sleek receiver whose moves I had imitated in backyard games for the past two years. I knew all of their mannerisms and all of their stats. I could recall the score of every game they played in. Like many kids growing up in Gastonia, I was raised on Greenwave football. These were my idols.

I sat uncomfortably beside the other newcomers. None of us spoke. It was like waiting in line at a doctor's office, not knowing quite what to expect, not wanting to talk to the patient next to you, only wanting to get the whole examination over with. I immediately thought back to the fifth grade, when a doctor first diagnosed me with scoliosis – a crooked back. *You'll never be very flexible, Stuart. Stick to low contact sports like track or baseball. Football's out of the question.* Perhaps I should have heeded the good doctor's advice. After all, I was 110 pounds on a good day. I wasn't fast. I wasn't very strong. As much as I loved the sport of football, I didn't even know how to strap up a helmet. I was an average athlete, but at least I was quick. That was my only real asset.

I scanned the room unsuccessfully for a familiar face. Almost every player had attended one of Ashbrook's two middle school feeders. They arrived with at least some basis of friendship. I was careful not to tell anyone about the little private school I had attended. Maybe the new kids from Grier would just assume I came from Holbrook, and vice versa. It seems insignificant now, but as a self-conscious teenager those things really mattered. I didn't want to be an outsider.

The comfortable chatter of the upperclassmen ceased as soon as the side door opened. Bill Eccles entered the room at a brisk pace, clipboard in hand, with curly hair poking around the edges of a solid green hat. His sharp eyes took in the room for a split second before he began to speak in a clipped accent that was equal parts Southern and Midwestern. Coach Eccles was not from Gastonia originally, but he was a coaching legend in this mid-sized city nestled to the west of Charlotte. His words were rapid and forceful, and it was obvious to everyone in the room that this was a man to be reckoned with. As Coach Eccles's voice echoed across the gym walls in staccato fashion, I knew that my life would never be the same.

Gastonia was the only world I had ever known.

G-Town. The Gas House. Tonytown. The nicknames were endless. To this day, people in my hometown refuse to think of Gastonia as a suburban outpost of Charlotte, and they do so with a stubborn pride that belies the city's rugged individuality. "Gritty" is a term often used to describe places like Gastonia. Outsiders use the word with a hint of derision, while Gastonians wear it as a badge of pride. Gastonia is an imperfect city, a very real place, a place not unlike the thousands of communities across America that have experienced a turbulent history of prosperity and destruction.

In the early 1920s, Gastonia had more textile mills than any other city in America. When the rural cotton farms of the South decided to send the majority of their wares to Gastonia, the struggling crossroads town transformed overnight. Stock prices for new textile companies in Gastonia grew from $100 to $200 a share before future mills were even built. Regal mansions sprouted up along Main Street and 2$^{nd}$ Avenue, with towering columns and carefully tended gardens on big downtown lots. Immigrants from Ireland and Scotland and Germany flooded the city. Laborers abandoned the cramped, urban lifestyle of Manhattan and Pittsburgh and Philadelphia in favor of Gastonia's open fields and new opportunities.

On the west side of Gastonia, the Loray Mill's massive, five story brick structure spanned two city blocks, and its castle-like watchtower and smokestack could be seen from as far away as the Appalachian foothills. Ramshackle bungalows and squat porches spread like weeds around the mills of Gastonia; the night air was filled with industrial haze and the steady music of freight trains. This benevolent, paternal culture thrived until 1929, when all hell broke lose in the city. A massive textile strike crippled the Loray Mill and brought national attention to Gastonia. Governor O. Max Gardner sent state militia to Gastonia as communist organizers stoked the flames of resentment within the city. The *Gastonia Gazette* warned of race mixing and revolution. Nationally prominent writers such as Theodore Dreiser and Sinclair Lewis came to Gastonia to write about the standoff. When all the dust settled, Gastonia Police Chief D. A. Aderholt had been shot and killed by union organizers. In no time, the labor movement's most effective worker, a woman by the name of Ella May Wiggins, was soon shot with a bullet through the chest. Her killers were never convicted.

Gastonia has done its best to move beyond the Loray Mill disaster, but the strike's reverberations continue to this day. Most of the textile jobs have gone overseas. The mills are empty now, their brick walls slowly crumbling into weed-scattered piles of rubble. The city has been left to reinvent itself. Somehow the tough, hardscrabble mentality remains. Gastonians are proud of their city. They defend it with great zeal. Try to call G-Town a mere suburb of Charlotte and you better get ready for a fight.

Gastonia High School took on the original Greenwave name during the peak of the textile movement. The school sat on a hilltop overlooking 2$^{nd}$ Avenue, and its shimmering white columns gave it a classical beauty. The columns stood three stories high, and there was a grand entryway with large windows and ornate brickwork. The textile boom funneled large amounts of money into the school system, and a new, Gothic high school was built south of downtown in 1925. Its impressive indoor swimming pool and $14,000 pipe organ in the auditorium made the school a perfect symbol of the booming, pre-Depression economy. Thirty years later, Gastonia High School changed its name to Frank L. Ashley High School in honor of its longtime principal. The Greenwave nickname stood until 1970, when integration brought the merger of Ashley and Holbrook High Schools in a new building outside of town. After a bitter fight between the two schools, Ashley and Holbrook students agreed to combine their names into "Ashbrook" and keep the Greenwave as the school's mascot.

My allegiance to the Greenwave runs thick. I love the sport of football for its contact and strategy and emphasis on team play. But my love for Ashbrook goes much deeper than sport. Robert Penn Warren once spoke of history as a giant spider web of events. If you touch one tiny fiber, the vibrations reach to the end of time. High school football profoundly altered the web of my life. These days, I see my past in many of the boys I coach. I see the same lack of confidence. The poor sense of self. The need for guidance. The web of my own life continually touches the lives of so many others.

I'm sure the heat was intense on that first day of practice, but I don't know for sure. I do remember feeling a sense of connectedness to the past as we clapped in unison and jogged through warm-ups. I didn't know the names of my teammates, but that would come with time. I couldn't allow myself to feel intimidated by them. I chose to be out here, after all; there was no turning back.

For the first time in my life, I was following directly in my father's footsteps. He'd gone through these drills and survived; so would I.

We raised our legs six inches off the dusty grass and held them, groaning, in place until the pain began to seep from my stomach muscles all the way up to my neck. My teammates were suffering as well. I could hear their anguished grunts, some greater than my own. I wasn't alone anymore. Dad would be proud.

I grew up idolizing my father, as many sons do. He was a good man and a well-respected leader in the Gastonia community. He often worked long hours, sometimes seven days a week, but for as long as I could remember, Friday nights in the fall were reserved for his two sons.

We never missed an Ashbrook football game, regardless of the weather or distance. I loved the set routine of game night. We always arrived at the games an hour early and bought hotdogs filled with chili to go along with the syrupy goodness of a Sun-Drop or Cheerwine. I carried seat cushions emblazoned with a giant green "A" while my brother, Rob, carried the food. The stands were usually empty as both teams warmed up below us. Dad quizzed us about Coach Eccles' strategy for victory. I loved the unique atmosphere of each stadium, and I welcomed the change from late summer humidity to the brisk winds of autumn. More than anything, I loved sharing all of this with my father. It was our time together. To this day, I cannot think of high school football without remembering the bond we created on those Friday nights long ago.

As humans, we live as we have been taught to live, and the ties that bind us into a family are filled with the imprints of the past. My dad lived by the same moral code as his own father. Dad loved to tell me about his own days as a Greenwave player.

"You know how many fans would travel with us?" Dad would ask me.

I knew the answer by heart, but I also knew that the repetition was essential.

"There'd be two fans, the bus driver and my father. Your grandfather. That was it."

I'd nod my head as if I was hearing him for the first time. That was my part in the play. Each time he told me this story, I picked up a new layer of its significance. And with each passing year, the meaning grew deeper and deeper.

"He was there for me. Just the bus driver and Daddy. You ever wanted someone in your corner, it was him."

I was seven when my grandfather died, and I have no recollection of his funeral. But I distinctly remember my confusion on that Friday. Ashbrook was deep into the playoffs, but Dad didn't take us to the stadium. Instead, we sat on his bed listening to the game on the radio. I remember feeling unsettled. I couldn't fully comprehend why my father looked so solemn and quiet. Death wasn't real to me then. I understood the ebb and flow of a football game, but human mortality was something distant and uncertain.

As I sat beside my father and listened to the distant hum of that playoff game on the radio, I wondered what he was thinking. In the years to come, Dad never missed one of my football games. Not even once. I'd see him in the empty stands during warm-ups with his hot dog, all the way with chili and slaw, just thinking about strategy and waiting for the game to begin. If I could go back in time, I'd like to talk to that seven year old boy about family and love, about the importance of having someone in your corner.

I loved the feel of the solid green uniform on my back. It was just a practice jersey, but the real thing would come soon enough. The first week of summer was just about over. As we finished our final wind sprints, I could see my father behind the fence with his sleeves rolled up and his collar unbuttoned.

On the ride home from practice, Dad told me the usual stories about former Greenwave players, people who had never registered in my consciousness until now. He was slowly creating a web of history that would forever bind me to the past.

Football was in my blood; it was impossible to avoid. Almost a century ago, a young man named Fred Wetzell coached the first high school football team in Gastonia. I see my own features in the faded pictures of this great-great uncle. Fred Wetzell had black hair and dark, serious eyes. His team bought their own uniforms, and they wore makeshift jerseys with high collars. Fred never had any kids, so it was up to his brother William, my great grandfather, to begin the family line that would one day produce me.

William had a son named Charles who was a lineman for Gastonia High. When I joined the Greenwave football team, Uncle Charles sent me all of his old news clippings, including one in which he enacted the ultimate dream of every lineman by stripping the ball and rumbling eighty yards for a game-winning touchdown. Uncle Charles was a decorated war veteran, and he often described this touchdown with the pride of someone who had just stormed Normandy. By simply wearing the Greenwave uniform, I'd joined a fraternity of men who were permanently shaped by leather helmets, makeshift uniforms, and the ecstatic joys of competition.

In the years after Charles returned from the war, William Wetzell continued to follow Greenwave football. He'd listen closely to the radio as Leonel Brunnemer, the "Voice of the Greenwave," described each play with infinite detail. As Leonel spoke to his radio audience, William would try to summon the atmosphere in his head.

"While we've got a break in the action, folks, I'd like to say that William Wetzell is listening with us this evening. He's the proud grandfather of the lovely Nancy Wetzell, who's down there with the rest of the cheerleaders right now. She's doing a fine job, William."

William Wetzell could picture his granddaughter, my mother, standing on the front ledge of the concrete bleachers. Her thick, black hair would be curled in the fashionable way, and she would be wearing a white sweater with a green, knee-length skirt. Nancy was smaller than the other cheerleaders, but she stood out nonetheless. At some point during that season, my father spotted her from across the stadium and decided that this was the woman he would marry one day. She was the prettiest girl in the stadium, William knew that for sure.

My web of history had become tangled and far-reaching, and there was nothing I could do to stop it. Southerners often bemoan the weight of the past. We see history as an immovable force that sticks to us like the humidity of a summer morning. Our identity is shaped by people we will never meet and by events that have come and gone before our time. Did I feel the gravity of Fred Wetzell when I signed up to play football? Probably not. But I have to believe that on some subconscious level he was passing the leather helmet to me, even if I didn't know how to strap the damn thing up.

All of that was about to change.

Two goals dominated my first season as a football player, and they were modest at best. First, I wanted to make the team; and second, I wanted to get into at least one game while the score was still in doubt. My aspirations were that simple.

I was anxious about attending a big public high school. To my private school friends, *public* was a dirty word. Public education was bad. Public school kids were mean and unruly. Perhaps the most shocking thought of all to the mind of a private school kid was that public schools had *black* students. Lots of them. It shames me to think back on my childhood misconceptions about race. Public school was my entry into the unknown.

I was greeted into this new world by Terry "T-Bone" Montgomery on the first full day of contact. T-Bone was only a sophomore, but he had the sharply defined features and 215 pound frame of a 30-year-old man. We were practicing on the baseball field next to the Ashbrook football stadium. The whole stadium is painted a deep green, with a Gumby-looking mascot stenciled below the press box. Spencer Mountain lies directly behind the concrete visitor stands, and the giant home side partially conceals the main school building. Ashbrook High School has very little esthetic value. It is a sprawling, vomit-colored brown, with concrete that has firmly stood the test of its 25 years. It is a world of concrete, concrete everywhere.

I adjusted the rib protector under my shoulder pads, which were already drenched from the July heat. We were in the midst of that most dreaded of all football experiences: two-a-days. This was only the morning session, but the 9:00 a.m. sun was already beaming down for the opening practice. During one of our drills, T-Bone took a handoff up the middle and plowed throw the defensive line, sending me airborne and sprawling on my back. Black spots danced before me as I struggled to regain my vision.

"Yo, you all right?" T-Bone shouted through the ringing in my ears. He picked me up and patted me on the butt. All of my body parts seemed to be intact.

The next time T-Bone came through the middle and plowed over me, I popped right back up. My ears were no longer ringing. T-Bone smiled as he ran back to the huddle, as if my initiation was complete. There were other beatings that summer, and sometimes I wondered why the hell I had even signed up for this gig. But my suffering was not unique. T-Bone was very generous in his poundings, and we all struggled through the stifling heat and the long hours of strain. A crumbling of the self was necessary for all of us to develop as a team. We were slowly being formed into young men. The change was gradual, but it happened nonetheless.

I was shocked to find myself starting on both offense and defense in the first game. T-Bone was the star, but at least I got to block for him as he scored touchdown after touchdown. I was a part of it all. The yelling, the high fives, the gang-tackles, the chanting. I was one among many, and the collective excitement was unlike anything I had ever experienced.

My teammates proved to be some of the most genuine people I had ever met, and this forced me to abandon all of my previous notions about race. They treated me like a friend and a confidant, even if their nicknames were exotic to me – T-Bone, Big Dookie, Q, Beast, Pooh Bear, Sack Happy, Sunshine…and Stu. I was one of them now. T-Bone may have been a tremendous runner, but he still needed my blocks. Football is the ultimate team game. It forces eleven different personalities to put aside their individual goals for the good of the team, because no part is greater than the whole.

Much of the strife in this country would be eliminated if our society truly bought into this idea.

Anything seemed possible now, and my confidence grew by leaps and bounds. I was part of something greater than myself, and this idea stuck in my head during the first few days of school. *If I can handle football, I can handle anything.* The loneliness that had filled so much of my middle school years was gone. I sat back and watched my classmates struggle through the time-honored rights of popularity and shifting cliques. None of that mattered to me. Life was far from perfect, but it held a richness that was foreign and exciting. Something was changing in the bottom of my core. T-Bone would see me walking down the hallway to lunch, and before I knew what was going on, I'd be tossed across his shoulders like a kid brother. Despite my outward protests, deep down I felt honored and proud.

Things could have happened very differently. I often wonder how these years would have played out if Bill Eccles hadn't been my football coach. Circumstance and history establish the paths we follow, and the people who guide us can build up or destroy the world we live in.

It would have been easy to destroy me. I was a fragile kid with minimal talent and very little self-esteem. I was not going to bring a state championship to Ashbrook with my abilities, but Coach Eccles treated all of us the same way. That's not to say he wasn't intimidating. Only a mere fool would take the man lightly, and if he did, he quickly regretted it. Coach Eccles could dismantle an ego quicker than anyone I had ever met. He was smart, too, and that played into the dismantling. Coach Eccles's mind was always two steps ahead of everyone else. His tongue lashings were a thing of beauty, and they were often hilarious – as long as you weren't the recipient of his wrath.

During my senior year, two of my best friends on the football team were twins by the name of Kevin and Eric Mullinax. They were big-boned boys with limited talent and hearts of gold. They wouldn't hurt a soul, which proved to be a problem on the football field. As hard as they tried, Kevin and Eric often struggled with aggression.

My teammates had it all worked out. On Mondays, Coach Eccles would scream at Kevin. On Tuesdays, it would be Eric. It must have been in the practice plans. Wednesdays were the wild card. Either twin could face the wrath of Coach Eccles on a Wednesday. Some of my teammates even drew up mock practice plans in the locker room:

*2:30-2:45 stretch*

*2:45-3:15 offensive individuals*

*3:15-3:20 scream at Eric*

*3:20-3:23 water break*

*3:23-3:26 scream at Eric some more*

"Damnit, Mulli!" Coach Eccles would yell after another missed assignment on the line. That's how things usually got started.

"Who do you block on 47?" Coach Eccles asked.

A look of confusion crossed the face of Eric Mullinax. "The tackle head up?"

"Did you block the tackle head up?"

Another look of confusion on Eric's face. "Yes?"

Coach Eccles gestured to our dazed running back, who was slowly getting to his feet.

"Tetrice, did Mulli block the tackle head up?"

A barely audible "no" came from the wobbling Tetrice.

"So why do you think Tetrice is picking grass out of his teeth right now?"

More confusion from Eric. "Because I took the defensive end instead?"

"Right, Mulli! Now we're talking." Coach Eccles gestured to the sideline. "Other Mulli, get in here and take your brother's place. We're gonna be here 'til it's done right."

*Pro Right 47 on one.* Tetrice took the handoff and was immediately thrown to the ground again.

"Damnit, Mulli!" Coach Eccles screamed as he grabbed Kevin Mullinax by the helmet. "Pro Right 47. What's your job?"

A look of confusion was on the face of Kevin Mullinax this time. It was a Wednesday. Time for both twins to face the music.

"Spit it out, Mulli! What's your job on 47?"

Still more confusion from Kevin. "I take the tackle head up?"

"Brilliant," Coach Eccles said sarcastically. "But who did you block?"

"The defensive end?" Eric offered from the sideline.

"Yes!" Coach Eccles screamed. "So who should you block on 47?"

"The tackle head up," Kevin said with slightly more confidence.

"Absolutely amazing!" Coach Eccles said as he shook Kevin by the shoulder pads. "Other Mulli, get back in here so we can go home."

It was dusk now, and the exhausted athletes on both sides of the ball began to blend in with the dying grass. I watched the final play in silhouette from my distant post at wide receiver. *Pro Right 47 on one.* Tetrice took the handoff and barreled through the #7 hole. Eric fired off the line like a man possessed and drove the defensive tackle all the way to Bessemer City. The whole team cheered for the Mullinax twins and gathered around them in a circle. Coach Eccles reached up and grabbed Eric by the facemask. Everyone grew silent. Eric leaned forward and prepared for the worst, but Coach Eccles kissed him on the helmet instead. The whole team broke into laughter as Eric sighed with relief.

Eric Mullinax made the all-conference team that year, and he was voted the most improved player on our team. Like many of my teammates, Coach Eccles squeezed the maximum ability out of Eric. He really knew how to break a player down. Unfortunately, many coaches stop at this point. They humiliate without showing any kindness, and a kid's self confidence goes from fragile to nonexistent. Coach Eccles rode his players hard sometimes, myself included, but he never once forgot to build us back up with a pat on the back or a word of encouragement.

Or, on that rare occasion, with a kiss on the helmet.

I spend my days teaching kids how to write, and if you work at this job long enough, you begin to see your life in a narrative form. We're taught from an early age that good writing begins with the exposition and characterization before moving on to the rising action, the climax, and the resolution. The climax and resolution of my own life are at least a few decades away. That's my hope, at least. I see the world in stories and vignettes, and these stories make up the web of my history. Stories connect us from the past to the present. We live through these stories, and memories lend truth to our tales. As the novelist Tim O'Brien once wrote, "Stories are for eternity, when memory is erased, when there is nothing to remember except the story itself." This is truly a Southern phenomenon, and if you sit long enough on the front porch of any small North Carolina town you will learn the history of mankind.

Memory is a fragile thing, and a story's power lies in the way it is told. A memory may be hidden in the recesses of our mind for years at a time, lulling us into thinking it no longer exists. The memory appears to be forgotten. Lost forever. My first two years at Ashbrook are definitely hiding somewhere. I can vaguely recall the feeling that life was changing within and around me. I remember T-Bone, but I don't know what happened to him after that sophomore year. Did he drop out of school? Did he move away? I remember cramping up so bad after that first game against South Point that the Mullinax twins had to carry me back to the team bus. I remember a desperate longing to be in love with a girl, and I also remember the even greater fear of rejection that kept me from asking anyone out. All the girls seemed so beautiful at the time, but would I even remember their names if I happened to see them today?

Most of us hope that our life story will be interesting to other people. This is particularly true in sports, where competition and victory drive our definition of success. We add an extra touchdown to the margin of victory; we talk about the 6'8", 350 pound linemen we battled toe to toe; we fill the stands with thousands of screaming fans when only a few hundred were actually there. We don't want the listener to dismiss our accomplishments with the wave of a hand, so we sprinkle fairy dust on our ordinary lives.

A good example: at the end of my junior year, we were beating Harding High School 55-14 (score not embellished) when Coach Eccles put in his final reserves. One of my best friends on the team was Coach Eccles's son, Jake. Jake Eccles was an all-conference center, and it was his dream, like all linemen, to run the ball just one time before his career came to a close. Coach Eccles gave in at last, and Jake took the game's final handoff up the middle for a respectable four yard gain. Jake handled this accomplishment the way any lineman would. The four yard gain grew to five yards by the following year. Later on, Jake complained that his eight yard run would have gone farther if the line had blocked the way they were supposed to, and he should know, after all. Jake was a groomsman in my wedding, and even then, on the day before my vows, he boasted about that beautiful twelve yard run against Harding. He would have scored, but the linebacker grabbed his shoelaces as he hurtled high into the air. It was a cheap tackle, really. Pure luck on the linebacker's part.

We all exaggerate on occasion. If I was to write much more about those first two years as a football player, the story would most likely muddle the truth. But my senior year was different. To this day, I see it in vivid colors and sounds and smells. I can feel the marching band's bass drums rumbling in my chest as we push for another score. The stale aroma of the locker room also remains with me. When I eat a greasy breakfast, I often think back to two-a-days. Some idiot came to practice one morning with a china plate full of bacon and eggs and left every bit of it next to the water fountain after sprints. I still see the grit under my fingernails, and I can feel the aching in my shoulders after a long practice. I remember Coach Eccles's words of wisdom about life. I remember the feeling of despair when it was all over, even though I was exhausted from three straight years with little more than a week off. Each memory holds a story, and every story is permanently sealed by the imprint of my mind's eye.

I remember cracking down on an East Gaston linebacker and colliding facemask to facemask. I don't recall walking to the sidelines, but I can still see Coach Eccles screaming at me to get back in the game. Eventually he noticed the confused look and the dilated pupils. The memories faded away as I forgot who we were playing. I couldn't tell the trainer my own name. One of the Mullinax twins came over and asked me how many testicles I had. Why did he say this? I still don't know. But it scared me to death because how was I supposed to know how many testicles I had if I couldn't even remember my name? The haze began to lift in the third quarter. I knew that I'd been crying a little because my entire identity seemed to be gone. The trainer asked my dad to keep me from wandering off. Dad reassured me that all the memories would come back soon, and eventually he was right.

It was the year I fell in love for the first time. While I didn't shy away from these emotions, I sometimes felt like I was driving down a winding road at night without headlights. It was new and exciting and frightening, all at the same time. It shook my foundation, and like most teenagers in the midst of love, the outside world seemed trivial and unimportant. Football alone kept me from being completely self-absorbed with this relationship.

On the field, my accomplishments were few and far between. I caught a nice $3^{rd}$ down pass against South Mecklenburg before getting drilled to the ground. It was a big play, though, and it led to a game-winning score. I guess I was a decent blocker, because Coach Eccles kept playing me even though I was never going to blow past a defensive back for a long score. I remember catching two passes against West Charlotte, and one of them was a diving touchdown grab. But we were thoroughly pounded that night. Tommy Knotts was already a coaching giant at West Charlotte in the years leading up to his time at Independence. The Lions won a state championship in 1995 and were the favorites to repeat the following year. Parade All-Americans Keith Matkins and Steve Shipp led the squad at West Charlotte, and both players would eventually sign scholarships to the SEC. I was one of the team captains for Ashbrook, and when I shook Steve Shipp's hand before the coin toss, I knew that this talented receiver was in a whole different league from me. Shipp torched us for 155 yards that night.

And then there was Senior Night against our cross-town rival, Hunter Huss, the enemy of all enemies. It was always the last game of the regular season, and this year's bout would decide the conference championship.

*Hunter Huss.* You almost had to spit the name out when you said it. Any Greenwave fan could tell you that the Hunter Huss Huskies were the spawn of Satan. You wanted nothing more than to beat them senseless and to rub their faces in the dirt. You hated their damn puppy mascot and their powder blue uniforms and, perhaps most of all, you hated how they'd won the last two games in the rivalry. It was a tragedy beyond all tragedies, and it simply could not happen again.

Games against Hunter Huss were always frigidly cold, and they typically fell during the week of Halloween. It all seemed very appropriate, and the hatred between the two schools was mutual. The star player at Hunter Huss my senior year was a linebacker named Marcus Kisner. Two years earlier, Marcus had committed a sin far greater than homicide and more disgusting than incest: he transferred from Ashbrook to Hunter Huss. It was unforgivable, like stealing your brother's wife or taking ice cream from a little kid. It was unconscionable and inhumane. But it was typical of the rivalry.

Every year since 1964, the Greenwaves and Huskies have fought for bragging rights and the much desired victory bell. The bell remains at the winning school for the rest of the year, where it is spray-painted green or blue and treated with the reverence of an idol. Ashbrook holds a slight lead in the series, but the games are always epic in scope. Greenwave and Husky players attend the same elementary schools, they play football for the same middle school teams, and they often live in the same neighborhoods. Ashbrook alumni have children who go to Huss, and vice versa, which only serves to complicate the emotions of the rivalry. A losing season is salvaged with a victory in the "Battle for the Bell." A winning season is forever tarnished with a loss. The rivalry reached its peak in the 1980s, when all but one game was decided by less than a touchdown. Every game was filled with thousands of boisterous fans desperately wanting their team to win. Rumors of violence often persisted in the days leading up to the game, and students occasionally vandalized the enemy's playing field with slogans etched in gasoline.

It was below freezing yet again for the Hunter Huss game my senior year, and the wind chill cut right through my uniform. Up in the stands, scores of my classmates had painted their chests and faces green for the occasion. Bullhorns and chants filled the air, along with choruses of "On Gastonia," the school fight song taken from the original Gastonia High School. It's a song I've heard my whole life:

*On Gastonia, On Gastonia,*
*We are all for you.*
*We will fight for the Green and White*
*To you we will be true.*
*Rah, Rah, Rah!*
*We're behind you to remind you,*
*We must win this game,*
*Gastonia, how we love to praise your name!*
*ROLL, GREENWAVE ROLL!*

It was a hard-hitting contest from the start, but we quickly took the upper hand. Coach Eccles played a no-nonsense style of football. The objective was to pound the ball over and over again until the defense showed it could stop us. When the defense put everyone in the box, we surprised them with a hot pass to the tight end or a corner route to one of our wide receivers. The key to the Greenwave attack was a running back with power, and Ashbrook was rarely in short supply. From 1985-1987, Parade All-American Junior Hall started the trend of big, powerful backs who would rather plow through opposing defenses than juke from side to side. The trend continued my senior year, with running backs tipping the scales at 220, 205, and 233 pounds.

We scored first, and the concrete home stands shook with the rollicking joy of the Ashbrook faithful. But Hunter Huss returned the favor with a long drive of its own. The Husky fans gleefully taunted the home fans by ringing the Victory Bell, which was painted a sickening light blue. An inspired

Ashbrook offense took the field after the kickoff. The deafening crowd noise faded away. We were focused and determined, and Eric Mullinax had a field day creating holes for our backs. It was a methodical drive. Four yards, ten yards, a short gain, a personal foul penalty, another eight yard run up the middle. The focal point of our running attack was Jamie Burris, and he was having the game of his life. The collisions between Jamie Burris and Marcus Kisner were titanic. The two athletes went at it again and again, with Marcus making almost every tackle for the Huskies and Jamie repeatedly gaining four or more yards a carry. We were approaching half-time, and another score would give us some desperately needed momentum. This drive would make or break our season. Less than a minute to go. Clock ticking, ticking, ticking…

"Yo, Stu, can I get a ride home?" Jamie Burris said to me as we slowly walked out of the locker room. It was July, and my junior year was just around the corner.

"Where do you live?" I asked.

"Like two miles away. Up past Garrison Road."

"Two miles? That's on the other side of town."

"Yeah," Jamie said with an innocent smile.

"Alright," I said with a sigh. "Get in."

We were an unlikely pair, a skinny white guy and a bruising, 220 pound tailback. The Maxima rattled from side to side as Jamie sank into the passenger seat. I was fortunate enough to have a car, although the Maxima had seen better days. It was a rusted tan, with a sunroof that had to be propped open with a stick. The seat cushions were ripped and frayed, and the joystick cover was gone, revealing all the wiring and machinery underneath. As we made a right onto New Hope Road, I waited for the Maxima to shift into third gear. The speedometer was broken, and the gear shift told me when we had reached 40 mph.

I turned the radio to Power 98, the popular hip hop station out of Charlotte, and Jamie immediately began nodding to the pounding beats of Bone Thugs-N-Harmony.

"Meet me at the crossroads, crossroads, crossroads..." Jamie sang as he smiled in my direction. "...So you won't be lonely, so you won't be lonnnnnnelyyyyyyy... And I'm gonna miss everybody, I'm gonna miss everybody..."

I laughed out loud in spite of myself. Jamie was completely at ease in the seat beside me, and I did my best to look comfortable as well. I'd learned a great deal about race over the past year, but I still felt out of place in a setting like this.

What should I say to someone like Jamie? What did we have in common? If I sang along with Jamie, would that show him just how white I really was?

Jamie didn't seem to care one way or the other. His frame was similar to T-Bone's, but his features were not nearly as sharp. He reminded me of a life-sized teddy bear, albeit a teddy bear that could bench press 300 pounds and plow through a defensive line with ease. Jamie was soft spoken, and his eyes gave a perpetual sense of calm. He rarely spoke, but when he did, he flashed a warm smile behind a carefully cropped mustache and goatee. Everyone liked Jamie. School did not come easy to him, but he was a hard worker, and teachers loved his earnest demeanor. My teammates respected Jamie's abilities, but they also flocked to him because of his unassuming nature and the kindness he showed to everyone. Jamie truly epitomized the team concept that Coach Eccles kept pounding into our heads.

"I live up past the tracks," Jamie said as we made a left onto Franklin Boulevard and headed downtown.

Gastonia is split in half by a series of train tracks running between Franklin Boulevard to the south and Long Avenue to the north. It is an unspoken racial divide, with ramshackle homes dominating the landscape north of the tracks for several miles.

Before integration, the Highland Rams were the pride and joy of this area of Gastonia. The all-black high school opened its doors in 1930 and quickly became a perennial powerhouse in football. Under legendary coach Eugene Dunn, the Rams reached the state championship twice before defeating Raleigh's Washington High for the title in 1946. Robert Mason played left tackle on that squad, and he eventually became the final head coach at Highland before the school fell victim to the ugly racial politics of the day. The school's name and mascot were abandoned in 1965, when Highland's students moved to Ashbrook and Hunter Huss.

The closing of Highland High School forever altered the prep football landscape in Gastonia. The rivalry between Ashbrook and Hunter Huss grew even more heated as new district lines weaved through the neighborhoods north of Franklin Boulevard that once fed into Highland. Slowly over time, Gastonia's African American community shifted their allegiances to the Greenwaves or the Huskies. Gastonia avoided much of the incendiary racial violence that accompanied so many other Southern cities during integration, but self-segregation continued to be a significant problem. At both Ashbrook and Hunter Huss, football became a bridge across the city's racial divide.

I knew about these neighborhoods, but I'd never driven through them before. Jamie lived on a grassless ridge about three blocks beyond the dividing line of the train tracks. As I turned onto his street, an old man stumbled in front of my car. A paper bag dangled precariously in his left hand, and his eyes looked distant and unfocused. The old man saw Jamie and waved to him before weaving to the side of the road once again. Jamie's home looked tidy but spare, and it had a sagging gutter along the front with chipped paint across the exterior walls.

Jamie shook my hand and punched my shoulder playfully. "Lock your doors when you drive out of here," he said with a final wave.

A daily routine began to evolve. After a while, Jamie didn't have to ask me for a ride. It was simply understood. Several teammates lived near Jamie in these run-down neighborhoods, and as the weeks went by, the Maxima sank further to the ground with passengers. Jamie always sat up front, and a revolving circle of teammates took turns in the back. Other drivers gazed with amusement at my rusted car as it sputtered along Franklin Boulevard. As many as four or five large athletes would be packed shoulder to shoulder, with an out-of-place driver behind the wheel.

I began to learn the personalities of my teammates on these daily trips across town. Besides Jamie, there were several other regular passengers. One of them was John Butler. John was an athletic defensive back, and his 6'2", 175 pound frame made him an intimidating force in the secondary. But John was confused about what to do on the field half the time, causing him to face the wrath of Coach Eccles on many occasions. John was the unofficial barber on the team, and his skill in that area probably exceeded his football abilities. John also had the uncanny ability to impersonate almost anyone. Our favorite routine was his take on Coach Eccles.

"Damn it, John!" John would scream in a perfect rendition of our coach. "How many times are you gonna get beat on the streak before you bail out? What the hell are you thinking out there?"

The entire team would be in stitches, and even the coaching staff thought it was hilarious. John somehow found a way to replicate that clipped Southern/Midwestern accent that was distinctly Coach Eccles.

"...Bump the guy at the line of scrimmage, John! ... That's not the play, John! ... Damnit, John, you've got outside contain! ... Somebody get John. He's lost out there..."

My other regular passenger was Nick Sherrill. Nick was our starting linebacker, and he was probably the most intense player on the team. Nick came from a military family, and he carried himself in the fashion of a soldier. John constantly teased Nick for his extremely dark complexion and his rigid personality, but Nick didn't seem to mind. While John and Jamie often struggled in school, Nick was an exceptional student. He masked this intelligence by toning down his vocabulary when other teammates were in the car. But when the two of us were driving alone, I saw a different side to Nick. He'd move up to Jamie's vacated seat, and his guarded exterior fell away more and more each week.

At first, our conversations stuck to safe subjects such as football practice and the usual drama of school. But it wasn't long before we moved into greater depth. Nick was the first person I could talk to about race on any deep level. Our conversations were honest and blunt, and neither one of us held anything back. I started asking myself questions about class and segregation, and I began to develop a deep social consciousness for the first time. I realized that my initial fears about joining this team all boiled down to simple ignorance. This discovery opened a Pandora's Box of ideas that went far beyond race. When it came right down to it, what did I really know about anything? Nick forced me to question everything I believed, and I found myself longing for these philosophical moments at the end of each day.

It was dark by the time I dropped Nick at his house. Most of the homes in Nick's neighborhood were in the same general state of decay as Jamie's, with weeds sprouting across dirt yards and windows vibrating from the deep bass of passing cars. As I retraced my steps across the train tracks each night, I drove to my comfortable home deep in thought.

"It's on, fellas. I'm already getting hyped," John said to no one in particular. We'd just finished the last Thursday practice before the Huss game my senior year, and John was in rare form.

"Man, you gotta know your coverages if you want Coach to put you in."

John sucked his teeth in mock anger. "Shut up, Nick, you're too black. And let me trim you up before the game tomorrow. You're killing that hair."

Nick dismissed his seatmate with a wave of the hand.

Jamie looked out the passenger seat window and occasionally nodded his head to the beat of 2Pac's "California Love" on the radio. It had taken me a year and a half, but I finally knew the lyrics to some of these songs.

"You ready, Jamie?" I asked.

"Yeah," he said softly. "We gonna win. You do your thing, Nick does his thing. Yeah, we gonna win."

The stakes seemed higher this year than ever before. Ashbrook and Hunter Huss entered the game undefeated in conference play. The winner received a relatively easy home game in the first round of the playoffs. The loser faced a two-hour road trip up into the Blue Ridge Mountains.

John reached over and patted Jamie on the shoulders. "Long as you get those 20 to 25 touches, Marcus Kisner and those boys are done."

Since the mid-point in the season, Jamie Burris had carried our team on his broad shoulders. We had a five game winning streak, and the excitement was visceral. You could feel it in the air. It was finally our year to return the Bell to its proper place.

I shook hands with Jamie and John as I dropped them off at their homes. Nick took his usual place in the front seat and turned the radio down.

"What else you got today?" Nick asked me. His musical tastes were broad, and I was surprised to discover that he liked rock about as much as he liked hip hop. I kept my music hidden from the rest of the team.

"I just bought the new Counting Crows."

"That's good stuff," Nick said.

"What, Counting Crows?"

"Yeah, I got it at home. Nights like this before a game, I need something mellow to bring everything into focus. There's this one track, 'Goodnight Elizabeth.' Put that one on."

The mournful wail of Adam Duritz filled the air.

"Kind of a sad song," I said.

"Yeah, but I like it. Plus, when you got a girl with you, it's perfect. You play it for your girlfriend yet?"

"Sure."

"Real mellow and quiet. It's a nighttime song, you know? Something you play when you wanna let your mind wander from one thought to the next until everything falls into place."

I looked over at Nick to see if he was joking, but his intelligent eyes were fixed firmly on the road ahead.

"You're a true original, Nick."

"I just call it like I see it."

I turned onto Nick's street as the song came to a close.

"Let's get 'em tomorrow, Stu."

Nick shook my hand warmly and hopped out of the car. As I drove home, I hit repeat on the tape player and thought about the game that was less than 24 hours away.

The clock kept ticking in the final minute of the half. Ashbrook 7, Hunter Huss 7. Jamie Burris pounded his way deep into Husky territory with an eleven yard run that was pure willpower and brutal strength. It took four defenders to drag him out of bounds. We could sense fear in the enemy; they didn't seem to have any fight left. Hunter Huss jumped off sides on the next play. The crowd was so loud that the Huskies couldn't hear the snap count. They were guessing wildly. Another powerful run by Jamie to the 16 yard line. A fullback dive up the middle to the eight. It was time to put the final nail in the coffin.

Coach Eccles sent me into the game with the play. It was an off tackle run to the left, a play that had worked beautifully for us time and time again this half. Our quarterback took the snap, and I sprinted out of my stance to seal off the defensive back. I looked inside to see Jamie running through a gaping hole. He barreled over a linebacker to the five yard line, the four yard line, the three. Only a safety and a defensive back remained, and they dove down to trip Jamie at the goal line. It was a futile effort to stop the massive back as he rumbled onwards.

Suddenly, I heard a collective gasp from our sideline. Jamie's leg buckled as the Hunter Huss safety slammed headfirst into his knee. The ball popped loose at the one yard line, where three exhausted Huskies immediately fell on top of it. Jamie rolled into the end zone, grabbing his knee in pain.

Our season was over, just like that. A fluke hit and an awkward turn and three players carrying our beloved teammate off the field. We fought bravely in the second half, but the lifeblood wasn't there anymore. Nick Sherrill saved us time and time again with jarring tackles from his linebacker position, but the Huskies broke the 7-7 tie with a final touchdown run with two minutes remaining in the game. The heartbeat of our team was gone, and we couldn't mount a final comeback. The Hunter Huss fans rushed the field as they rang the Victory Bell again and again. Several Huskie students stood on the fifty yard line and waved green and white flags lit by kerosene. I had never felt so low in my entire life.

The 31-6 loss in the playoffs the following week seemed like an afterthought. I remember the biting mountain air and the feel of the ball against my frozen fingers. I remember Jamie leaning against his crutches on the sideline. His calm demeanor was replaced by a desperate longing to help his dejected teammates.

One other moment has stuck with me all these years. I remember standing by the goalpost after the game. Coach Eccles placed his arms around my shoulders, just as he had done so often to all of us that fall, and he thanked me for being a part of his life. I was already crying before he got the words out of his mouth, and when I buried my head into his chest, he was crying as well. It was the only way I knew how to tell him thanks.

When I started basketball practice the following week, I immediately knew that life would be different. Something had died within me. The camaraderie of the football locker room wasn't there, and basketball didn't give me the same sense of community. I felt guilty, like I was betraying football by moving on to something else so quickly. I never recaptured that sense of belonging. I missed my teammates, even though I saw them in the halls and hung out with them after school. We no longer had a collective goal in sight. But deep down, I knew I was a better person because of football. Despite the boundaries of race and class, we had created an authentic community. I was part of something greater than myself. I was accountable to others.

I don't even want to ponder where I might be without high school football. While numerous classmates squandered away their GPAs in college, the discipline I picked up from football gave me focus and an unwavering work ethic. I am a better teacher because of football, and I'm a better husband as well. I appreciate people so much more these days, and I try not to take the world's beauty for granted. I see how a community can transform a school by simply creating an extended family for its students. My story is far from unique.

I couldn't stay away from high school football for very long. College teaches us that the world is ours for the taking as long as we are willing to step into the unknown. We pay lip service to social justice, but when push comes to shove, very few people are willing to put themselves on the line and then stay on the line for the rest of their life. I had a choice to make: a career in the corporate world or a career as a public school teacher. Wealth versus reward; I couldn't do both.

My final decision was easy.

I stood behind a chain link fence surrounding the Ashbrook practice field and watched Bill Eccles lead his offense through a passing drill. Ten years had passed since I last walked across this field, and the years had been good to the Greenwave – a state championship in 2002, numerous deep runs into the playoffs, a large new weight room, a totally refurbished locker room, and record attendance at summer workouts. When Coach Eccles retired from his job as head football coach back in 2000, he'd become the winningest coach in Ashbrook history. But he wasn't quite ready to leave the football program. For the next six years, Coach Eccles worked as the offensive coordinator alongside Joe Shepherd, who succeeded Bill Eccles as head coach at Ashbrook. Coach Shepherd has since passed the torch to Mike Briggs, leaving three men with head coaching experience on the same staff.

As I watched Coach Eccles, I noticed a few more gray hairs, but otherwise, the past ten years had treated him well. The pace of the practice was quick, and Coach Eccles had the same fire and energy. It was early in June, and some of the players looked cautious and unsure of the offense. Coach Eccles instructed them when necessary, but he was also quick to single out his quarterback when he made a good read or shout encouragement to a receiver after running a solid route. It was the same musical cadence I remembered all so well from my high school years at Ashbrook.

I spotted Coach Eccles' son, Jake, and I ventured over to greet my good friend and former teammate beside the huddled players. Jake recently came back to Ashbrook to teach math and coach football and wrestling. He is the spitting image of his father, and their coaching styles are very similar. We traded stories of our days together on this practice field, and Jake introduced me to the new team.

The Eccles name has become synonymous with Ashbrook High School. Both Bill and Jake Eccles teach math at the school, and Bill's wife, Sharon, is a highly regarded English teacher there as well. The Ashbrook football field is now officially called "Eccles Field" in honor of Bill Eccles's 36 years as a coach and teacher. Below the press box, fans can see numerous rows of conference, regional, and state championships from the Eccles era at Ashbrook.

After practice, Bill Eccles took me on a tour of the new weight facilities and the remodeled locker room. Everything looked so different to me, yet familiar at the same time. A bold white *A* was emblazoned on each helmet, and the same deep green paint covered every wall. We entered a classroom off the main gym – I could still hear the squeaking shoes from that first meeting – and it took me a moment to realize we were in the old weight room from my playing days. It seemed like a fitting place to visit with my former coach.

Bill Eccles and I sat upon wooden desks as the air conditioning unit sputtered unevenly from a nearby window.

"What keeps you in coaching after all these years?" I asked him.

"I've been lucky with everything I've done. I've been lucky with my friends, and I've been lucky with my wife and my children, and I've been lucky with my job. I love the practice, I love the games, I love the meetings. You know, the most fun I have all year is when we do two-a-days."

Coach Eccles said this with a knowing smile. A memory flashed before me of T-Bone running over my helpless body.

"You get a lot of confidence from football," Coach Eccles continued. "You learn not to wilt or give up or quit every time the going gets rough. You learn to take criticism without folding up your tent and leaving. And you start to feel a little pride because you did something that not a lot of other people were able to do. You get a real value for work, and you start to see that you'll be successful if you put the time in."

Bill Eccles' own childhood was a testament to this. He originally moved to Gastonia from Indianapolis in the seventh grade, several years after his father died of tuberculosis. In Gastonia, his new stepfather was a strict and severe man. Football became both an outlet and a means of acceptance for Eccles. He eventually starred as an offensive lineman for the Ashley Greenwave football team, and it was here that he developed his lifelong interest in football.

After graduating from NC State with a degree in mathematics, Eccles began his teaching career at North Point Junior High School in Baltimore, Maryland. It was a rough, inner-city school nestled among the steel mills and industrial maze of the Baltimore harbor. The experience was eye-opening. North Point did not have a sports program at the time, and very few of his students felt tied to the school in any way. Eccles noticed a lack of self confidence among his male students, in particular. There was simply no sense of community within the school. Teaching in Baltimore gave Eccles a renewed understanding of the value of athletics, and he decided once and for all to become a coach.

Bill Eccles came back to his alma mater in 1972 to teach math and coach football. The school's name had changed from Ashley to Ashbrook, and it was now fully integrated. This new influx of athletes from the formerly all-black Highland High School played a large role in Ashbrook's state championship victory over Sanford Central in 1974. It was a playoff run filled with come-from-behind victories and close calls eerily reminiscent of Ashbrook's 2002 march to the state championship, when all five playoff games were decided on the final play from scrimmage, including a field goal as time expired in the championship win over Greensboro Dudley.

For years, Coach Eccles taught a full load of trigonometry, algebra and geometry while working late in the evening with the football program. As soon as the football season ended, he immediately switched gears to coach the wrestling team. Eccles became the school's winningest coach in this sport as well, and he coached both of his sons to all-conference seasons in football and wrestling. Eccles was a teacher *and* a coach, he liked to remind me. The two were inextricably linked.

"I enjoy the kids, but I also enjoy the game, the technique. I'm a math teacher. I like to take a guy who's not as good and find a way to beat somebody who's a lot better than we are. That's a real thrill for me. I'm an emotional person, and emotion is a big part of it. I really love the Xs and Os, but I've never had an X or an O play for me. They've always been people. You get to be so proud of them. Maybe you see a kid who sacrifices for the team – a talented athlete, someone who has a lot going for him – and yet he gives up some of the glory for the good of the team. I'm proud of that. You enjoy seeing kids make sacrifices and learn to be tough and grow up.

"Now you get ninth graders coming in, and they're just babies. They don't know anything. You hope when they leave four years later that they've grown up. And you get to watch that, and you get to watch it year after year. And every year is a new start, and you get a new crop of kids to work with. In all my years of coaching there have been very few kids I didn't like. I like almost all of them."

"How often do you think about retiring?" I asked.

"I'm not a very calculating person," he responded. "I'm who I am and that's the way it is. Other than wanting to be worth something as a role model, that's the only thing I really think about. I like to have a good time – you know, it *is* a game, and it's supposed to be fun. There's only one real reason to retire, and that's if you don't want to do it anymore. If you don't want to do it you need to retire that day. But if you want to do it, you shouldn't retire if you're fifty or sixty or seventy. If you enjoy it, and you still have something to offer, then you ought to keep doing it."

We began to discuss my own experiences as a coach. The concept of community kept bubbling to the surface, and I couldn't find the right words to describe it. Coach Eccles looked directly at me without blinking. He has the ability to penetrate right through to the core of who you are and what you believe. I saw it as a player, and I noticed it now as an adult.

After a thoughtful pause, Coach Eccles said, "For me, more than any one thing, you want to be a good person. You want to be there for kids as much as you can. Football provides a great opportunity to do that because of the close contact. There are some I'm sure we've helped, and unfortunately, some I'm sure we haven't helped, but like I said, for me it's the whole package.

"With football you share something. It's like being in the same foxhole. There's pressure on you when you play, and you've got a common enemy and a common goal and you have a closeness with individuals that is very hard to get otherwise. I think in the end, I like making those close attachments. I like being personal. I like putting my heart on the line and having other people do the same thing for me."

I sat back in the desk, deep in thought. Through the concrete walls, I could hear the faint muffle of lockers closing and players laughing.

"So what makes Ashbrook such a successful program?" I asked. "How does it succeed when others fail?"

"We've done a good job here of coaching every kid. We don't single out the ones who are more talented and spend most of our time with them, and maybe that's cost us some wins. All of our kids feel like they are a part of the team. When you get in a drill and you take the worst kid there and you spend as much time with him, and you make him do it over again just like you would that starter, I think that makes a big difference.

"We have a class outfit that's going to play hard and physical. We're gonna get everybody involved and use everyone's talents as much as we can. If you want a successful business you have to have people who are willing to share information and to work together as a team, and you have to have people who are willing to let others get the credit some of the time. If you get more out of everybody, then as a team you're gonna accomplish more."

Former Ashbrook players such as Darrell "Sky" Armstrong epitomize this team concept. In 1985, Armstrong was a kicker and 3$^{rd}$ string defensive back on the Greenwave football team. Armstrong was known for his positive attitude and strong work ethic in practice. These traits landed him the final spot on the Ashbrook basketball squad his senior year. Joe Shepherd was the head basketball coach at the time, and Coach Eccles had to convince Shepherd not to cut the lanky senior. Coach Eccles wasn't sure if Darrell could play basketball, but he knew that Darrell's positive attitude made him an asset for any team.

After high school, Darrell Armstrong joined the Fayetteville State football program as a kicker. Armstrong beat the odds once again by walking onto the basketball squad and averaging 14 points per game over the next four years. After several professional stints overseas, Armstrong returned to Ashbrook in 1993 to help Joe Shepherd with the basketball team. That was my first year as a student at Ashbrook, and I remember watching Darrell Armstrong run hundreds of wind sprints to stay in shape after our practices. He spent his days working at the Dixie Yarns textile mill, and he waited for a chance with the NBA. Armstrong's break finally came with the Orlando Magic, where he went on to earn both the Sixth Man Award and the Most Improved Player Award in the same season.

Darrell Armstrong was one obvious success story, but according to Coach Eccles, success can also be defined on a much smaller scale.

"I don't know if it's really fair to grade people or not. On a scale of one to ten, if someone comes in as a one and graduates as a six – no, he's not a ten, and none of us are probably tens – but you sure have made a lot of progress with that kid. We had one this year who was in trouble, couldn't stay in school, couldn't get along. He was a bully and he was mean and he was probably a racist. It was a long time, and it was a bumpy road, but he graduated in June. He was no trouble in school this year, and now he's pleasant in the hall to people, and he knows that people care for him, and that's changed his whole attitude about race to a certain degree. That's certainly a good feeling when you see them go on and do that."

Jeremy Dixon came to Ashbrook with similar disciplinary problems. He was a big, awkward lineman who'd been thrown off his 7th and 8th grade football teams. The struggles continued when he arrived at Ashbrook.

"It was tough to get Jeremy dressed and on the field sometimes," Coach Eccles said.

Teachers complained about his awful behavior in class, and Jeremy had a difficult time getting along with other players. But as he became part of the Greenwave family, his behavior dramatically changed.

"You wouldn't believe the progress Jeremy made, to the point now where you see a teacher and instead of going the other way, we've got teachers saying Jeremy is the best student they have."

Jeremy played a central role in Ashbrook's 2002 championship run, and he recently finished up his freshman season at Fayetteville State University. He's on a full scholarship, and his grades are solid – a far cry from that first year at Ashbrook four years ago. It makes me wonder what happens to the Jeremys of the world who don't get to be a part of a football team.

I decided to ask Coach Eccles about the infamous Hunter Huss game my senior year. A pained expression immediately crossed his face.

"Do we have to talk about that awful game?" he said with a sigh. "There's this saying, 'Experience is the toughest teacher. It gives you the test first and the lesson second.' If you don't learn from your losses, then you really have lost something. We wanted to beat Huss, thought we could have won, thought we *had* won."

Coach Eccles shook his head as he remembered the crushing sight of Jamie's knee buckling to the ground and the ball popping out on the Hunter Huss goal line. Then his eyes focused, and he grew philosophical once again.

"The other day, I was demonstrating to some kids, and I took 77 pennies, and I put them in a big stack. I told them, this is the average life expectancy for a male. Seventy seven years. Then I took out four pennies and made a stack. I told them, this is how long you get to play high school football. Four years. It's a short time, really, so you ought to enjoy it. Unless you're a coach, of course, and you get to do it year after year."

Coach Eccles smiled as he patted me on the back. I was part of the coaching fraternity now. It was a new role for me, but I liked it immensely. We walked across the practice fields, and I glanced at the imposing green concrete stadium one more time.

I wonder if Bill Eccles is part of a dying breed of coaches. In an era of soul-searching and competitive job markets and fluctuating identities, will the people of my generation ever make such a lasting impact on their community? Will Jake Eccles follow in his father's footsteps for the next 36 years at Ashbrook, and will I make a similar imprint on Durham? Are there fields to be named for our generation, or is it already too late?

Gastonia is not the only city pulling me onward with stories. I must leave the textile mills and the rolling green tide and the comforts of home yet again. It's time for me to journey east. There are more stories to tell and new people to meet.

Hopefully, I will find more men like Bill Eccles to answer my call.

# 2

# The Magnificent Golden Bull Machine
## Fayetteville

The sound was distant at first, like a faltering heartbeat. *Bum, bum, bum, bum.* Cymbals chimed in faintly. I tried to ignore it. We were in the second round of the playoffs, after all, and the opening kickoff was only minutes away. The volume gradually increased behind the visitor stands. The crowd from Fayetteville stirred in their seats. They knew what was coming.

I turned my attention to the football field and shouted encouragement to the offense. The rumbling of the bass drums grew louder. On the home side I could see my parents hidden beneath a mountain of blankets and steaming cups of hot chocolate. The wind chill had already dipped into the lower twenties. My mother was easy to spot. She was the only one wearing Ashbrook green in a sea of navy and red – she claimed my letter jacket when I graduated from Ashbrook. Mom and Dad still followed the Greenwave closely, and Mom wore the bulky jacket to every game.

Ashbrook had suffered a rare first round loss in the playoffs, so my parents made the two and a half hour drive to Durham to watch me coach. Seeing them up in the stands felt comforting and familiar, as if the past eight years had never really occurred. Another familiar face beside them put me on edge. It was Bill Eccles. He made the trip from Gastonia as well. As a player, I would do anything for Coach Eccles. I never wanted to let him down or disappoint him. This was my fourth year as a football coach, and I wanted Bill Eccles to know he had taught me well. My old competitiveness boiled to the surface.

I stole a glance to the other side of the field. Milton Butts, the E.E. Smith head coach, towered over his players as they simulated our defensive sets. The drum beat grew louder and louder behind him.

*BUM, BUM, BUM, BUM...*

One E.E. Smith player stood out above the rest: Carter Sharpe, #33. On film, he looked completely unstoppable. Sharpe was one of the premier running backs in the state. He was big, strong, and explosive; while grainy videotape often masks the power of great athletes, Carter Sharpe was obviously a freak of nature. Sharpe rushed for 2,823 yards as a sophomore last year, including a staggering 1,077 yards and 12 touchdowns in the state 4-A playoffs. This season, the 6-foot, 220 pound tailback had rushed for 1,995 yards and 25 touchdowns. Our game plan was simple: stop #33 and we win the game; let #33 run wild, and it was going to be a long, cold night.

The bass drums reached a crescendo as the E.E. Smith band, the Magnificent Marching Machine, arrived at the field. It was an awe-inspiring sight. The metal bleachers rattled and hummed as the E.E. Smith faithful swayed to the beat. The Jordan High School home side had no answer to this challenge. Our own marching band decided not to show up for this home playoff game, so the visitors took control. The Magnificent Marching Machine wore navy and gold uniforms, and their high, white hats bounced from left to right in perfect unison. They high-stepped in front of the visiting bleachers in an impressive display of choreography and skill. Even the trombonists got in on the act. They played while they marched, and the sound was part song and part guttural wail. I could feel the rumble beneath five layers of clothing and the numbness in my frozen toes.

The drum corps continued playing through the opening kickoff, but my eyes were focused on the task at hand. Everything beyond the frozen grass faded away. The music stopped. The crowds disappeared. All that mattered was stopping Carter Sharpe.

I thought back to that game as I drove down I-95 to Fayetteville the following summer. It was a desolate stretch of asphalt lined with massive billboards, scrub fields, and pine trees on either side. Bright yellow and red signs towered over the interstate.

*South of the Border Only 70 Miles Away! ... Cigarette Warehouse Next Exit! ... Topless! Topless! Topless!*

Eastern North Carolina was still foreign to me. I'd always thought of the east as one big truck stop on the way to the beach. It seemed like a garish outpost filled with the eyesores of modern excess. My biases were obvious, of course. The same criticisms could be leveled at Gastonia or Durham. As I cruised along at 70 mph, I tried to absorb the pine trees and the surrounding countryside with an open mind.

We were lucky to beat E.E. Smith that night back in November. Carter Sharpe wasn't himself, and a bone-crushing hit by one of our safeties sent him out of the game in the third quarter. Up to that point he had managed 155 yards and two touchdowns. The momentum shifted our way for good after an E.E. Smith tight end dropped a wide open touchdown pass. We went on to win the game, 31-12. Our elation stood in stark contrast to the dejected Golden Bull squad. The E. E. Smith seniors had never lost this early in the playoffs. Milton Butts shook our hands and wished us well in the third round. Coach Butts seemed like a class act, and his players were disciplined, athletic, and well-coached. We were a good team playing our best football of the year. And Carter Sharpe – well, if #33 had performed his usual magic, things might have been very different. To his own credit, Coach Butts hated excuses. Jordan won the game. E.E. Smith lost. The *shouldas*, *couldas* and *might have beens* didn't matter.

The deep bass of the Magnificent Marching Machine ran through my head as I drove through Lillington and the rest of Harnett County. I had a meeting planned with Coach Butts in a few hours. Rumors were flying around Fayetteville these days about Carter Sharpe. No one seemed to know the true story, but everyone agreed that Sharpe was not coming back to E.E. Smith for his senior year. I didn't feel comfortable bringing up the subject of Carter Sharpe in our meeting, but how could I not?

Pine trees and sand hills appeared more densely with each passing mile. The August heat registered 102 degrees on my thermometer. This was the kind of "temperate" climate that drew so many military personnel to Fayetteville and Fort Bragg.

To many North Carolinians, Fayetteville would always be known as "Fayettenam." Thousands of Fort Bragg soldiers fought in the Vietnam War, and the military base dominated every aspect of Fayetteville's economy and culture. Fort Bragg occupied the northwest corner of the city along a dry, flat expanse of land covering 250 square miles and 160,000 acres. It was an enormous base, serving 47,000 soldiers and 8,500 civilian personnel. Fort Bragg was the world's largest airborne facility, and the city of Fayetteville constantly whirred with the sounds of fighter jets from the 82$^{nd}$ Airborne Division. The "Golden Knights" of the U.S. Army parachute team performed over 100,000 parachute jumps at Fort Bragg each year. From ground level the crooked trails of parachutes seemed to hover delicately behind the massive aircrafts. These black dots were as much a part of the landscape as the cumulus clouds floating above the flat, sand-covered fields.

Fort Bragg was also home to the Army's Special Operations Command, originally known as the Psychological Warfare Center. The Special Forces trained some of the military's most elite squads – the Rangers, the Green Berets, the unorthodox-warfare units. Soldiers from Fort Bragg personified toughness. They were the stoic defenders of freedom in a world of religious radicalism and unrest in the Middle East. You didn't mess with a Fort Bragg soldier. He was your basic, full-blooded American. He was Everyman, defender of the faith, the heart and soul of democracy.

This sprawling military base was the driving engine of Fayetteville. Every weekend, thousands of soldiers flooded the streets of Bragg Boulevard and enveloped the city. Bragg Boulevard was a six-lane cinderblock strip of seedy bars, car shops, tattoo parlors, and every imaginable commercial enterprise. The journalist Tom Wolfe (no relation to Thomas Wolfe) once described this avenue as an "appalling fever-line of late-twentieth century instant gratification" that called to mind "the gaudy gullet of hell itself." Perhaps Wolfe was being too hard on the area, but Bragg Boulevard was certainly a land of excess.

Fort Bragg was almost entirely self-sufficient. The base had its own cinemas, golf courses, recreation centers, and public schools from Kindergarten through $8^{th}$ grade. Fort Bragg did not have a high school, so the Cumberland County public schools picked up the bill. Military families sent their kids to ten different high schools across the Fayetteville area. These students were often world-weary travelers in a strange, Southern landscape. The district recently built two new high schools to handle the demand. In 2005, the Senate's Base Relocation and Closure commission (BRAC) voted to close down several bases in Atlanta and move upwards of 4,000 additional military personnel to Fort Bragg, which will complicate matters in the Cumberland public schools for years to come.

Here's where high school football comes into play. According to Fred McDaniel, the director of athletics for Cumberland County, Fayetteville's football success through the years is heavily influenced by its military roots.

"Ever since the 1960s, teams have to come through Fayetteville to win the state championship."

As he spoke, Fred McDaniel stared at me with a stern face that demanded attention. For over 25 years, McDaniel had been a teacher, coach, and administrator in Cumberland County. He knew the Fayetteville athlete by heart, particularly the military athlete. Fayetteville athletes were disciplined, hard-nosed, strong, smart, and ruthless in their attention to detail. They were a coach's dream.

"Fayetteville sets the standard for competitiveness and sportsmanship," McDaniel said. "There's no doubt about it."

The Fayetteville schools also have a rich coaching pedigree. Bob Paroli dominated the coaching scene at Douglas Byrd High School for over twenty years on his way to becoming one of the winningest coaches in state history. Bobby Poss inherited a South View program with the longest losing streak in the state and turned the Tigers into a championship squad in less than three years. Men such as Dean Saffos, Gary Wheeler, Red Wilson (who went on to coach at Duke), and D. T. Carter brought lasting football success to the area. As competitive as they were during the season, these Fayetteville coaches also collaborated together on strategies and techniques in the off-season. It was a fraternity of men bound by a love for football and for teaching kids.

Fred McDaniel's rigid expression softened when I asked him about Milton Butts. When McDaniel was the athletic director at Westover High School, he hired Butts to be his head football coach.

"Nobody," McDaniel said, "does more to help his players than Milton Butts."

Coach Butts instituted a successful tutoring program at Westover, and the concept eventually spread to every high school in Fayetteville. He kept an academic progress book for every one of his players, and his teams routinely had the highest GPAs in the region.

"What Milton does, and what we all try to do here, is to develop more than just players. We want good citizens. Integrity, character, values – that's what matters most. Milton wants to win more than anybody, but those other things come first. He runs a tight, rigid program, but he has a heart of gold."

According to McDaniel, a good coach has a profound impact on the climate of a school. A football team sets the tone for the entire year. If you have a competitive football team with the right attitude, other students will follow suit. A team that doesn't win many games, or even a winning team with a lousy attitude, infects the rest of the student body for months to come. Football can be a school's most visible identity. Outside of the military, football *was* Fayetteville's identity.

After five years at Westover, Milton Butts carried his passion for academic and athletic success to E.E. Smith High School. He's been a Golden Bull ever since.

Like every district in the state, the Fayetteville schools were segregated well into the 1960s. For years, most of the city's African American students attended a modest two story brick school on Orange Street. In 1927, the school changed its name in honor of Dr. Ezekiel Ezra Smith, a former slave who was a prominent educator, statesman, and minister in Fayetteville. For 42 years, Dr. Smith presided over what is now called Fayetteville State University, the first black state-supported school in North Carolina. E.E. Smith High School made its final home along Seabrook Road in 1968.

There is nothing spectacular about the physical exterior of E.E. Smith. The track surrounding the football field consists of dry dirt, and the football team practices on the game field for much of the season. There isn't enough space for a larger practice facility. Modest ranch homes surround the school's sprawling, one-story exterior in a two-mile cluster of compact neighborhoods. The gates of Fayetteville State University are no more than a mile away.

In years past, E.E Smith prided itself on academic success. Part of the success came from a lack of turnover in its administration. Ernest Miller ran the school from 1940-1971, and John Griffin was principal for the next 20 years before being named superintendent of the Cumberland County Schools. Rene Corders has been in charge of E.E. Smith for the past seven years, earning recognition as 2003 Principal of the Year for North Carolina. During Homecoming each year, all four grades compete in a contest to see who knows the most E.E. Smith history, from the origins of Ezekiel Smith to the lyrics of the alma mater. Graduates of E.E. Smith are deeply attached to their school, and E.E. Smith was the first high school in the state to have a National Alumni Association. Former students often return to Seabrook Road to cheer on the Golden Bulls in football and basketball contests. There is a great sense of community pride, even while other schools in the district struggle to maintain their distinctive character.

Assistant Principal Mark Pepper greeted me at the front entrance to E.E. Smith. It was his first day back at work, and he was kind enough to show me around the school. Before he became an administrator, Pepper worked as an assistant coach under Milton Butts for three years. Like everyone else I met in Fayetteville, Pepper told me that no coach in the state worked harder to get his students into college than Milton Butts. It almost felt like a broken refrain. I had to see the man in person to believe it. A bulletin board next to the main office was filled with newspaper clippings about the school:

*Quiz Bowl Team Takes First Place...Show Choir Performs for Sold Out Hall...E.E. Smith Lineman wins full academic scholarship to Harvard...*

Harvard University? I paused over this last article from the *Fayetteville Observer*. The student was Jeremy Wall, an offensive lineman for Coach Butts this past season. Wall was one of only 1,200 freshman admitted to Harvard out of an applicant pool of 10,000. He was going to Harvard on a full scholarship. As the son of a single mom, Harvard would be out of the question without this financial assistance.

In the article, Wall credits the teachers at E.E. Smith for his academic success. *Observer* reporter Earl Vaughan writes, "It seems unlikely that a high school that's been making headlines lately for being low-performing would produce a Harvard student. But that's not the way Wall sees it...He's been in a lot of schools over the past 12 years, and Smith's as good, if not better, than any of them."

The article goes on to state that "academics have always been a point of emphasis for E.E. Smith football coach Milton Butts. Since his days as head coach at Westover, Butts has asked teachers to volunteer for after-school tutoring sessions with football team members during the season."

"The purpose is to give them the opportunity so they have no reason to fail," Butts says in the article. "I've never had a teacher say, 'I can't be here to work with the kids.'"

Articles such as these were in direct contrast to the school's recent public image. The situation was complicated, to be sure, but the basic problem was quite clear: the state planned to shut E.E. Smith down unless the school made some drastic changes. E.E. Smith was one of 44 schools across the state involved in an explosive court decision called the *Leandro* case. The eyes of the nation were on North Carolina right now, and the final outcome of this case would undoubtedly affect educational reform for years to come.

The firestorm began in 1994 when a group of ambitious lawyers decided that North Carolina was not doing an adequate job of educating all of its students, particularly students in low-income districts. The team of attorneys traveled to Hoke County to ask a bright, 15-year-old student named Robbie Leandro to be one of the plaintiffs in the case. Robbie didn't think much about it. He was a standout football player, and he thought the suit could help the school pay for some basic supplies or more uniforms. Cumberland County was one of several districts in the eastern half of the state to initially join the case. Before long, urban districts such as Durham, Charlotte-Mecklenburg, Wake, and Winston-Salem Forsyth also asked to be included in the *Leandro* lawsuit. These districts argued that the state's funding formula was not sufficient to adequately support their at-risk students.

In 1997, the North Carolina Supreme Court sided with the plaintiffs, ruling that the state's constitution guaranteed "every child of this state the opportunity to receive a sound basic education in our public schools." The ruling defined a sound education in broad terms such as "functioning in society" and "gaining the necessary skills for further employment." Nothing radical here. The 1997 ruling seemed to follow the same toothless rhetoric of previous educational reforms.

The turning point came when Supreme Court Judge Howard Manning took control of the *Leandro* case in 1999. He vowed to implement the court's ruling by any means necessary. Using Performance Composite data, Judge Manning accumulated a list of 44 high schools across North Carolina with less than 60% competency on state-mandated tests. By 2005, Manning narrowed the list to 18 schools. The outcry truly began at this point. Manning threatened to close each of these "failing" schools within two years if their scores did not increase sufficiently. It was the responsibility of each school district to come up with a plan for change. Principals and teachers were fired. Schools began to establish small learning communities and freshman academies. Administrators scrambled to find ways to stretch their budgets. The initial ruling provided some increased funding from the state, but for the most part, schools had to get by with the same limited resources. Everyone feared that insufficient efforts could lead to a school-wide shutdown.

E.E. Smith was one of the 18 schools under Judge Manning's microscope. The problems at E.E. Smith were complex and multi-layered. Every single school on Manning's list had a largely underserved population. E.E. Smith was the most segregated high school in Cumberland County, and over 55% of its students qualified for free or reduced lunch. In most cases, the wealthier schools had the higher test scores. This phenomenon existed everywhere, from the farming communities beyond the Piedmont to the urban districts across the state. For many schools, integration never really occurred in the first place.

The E.E. Smith community was well aware of these obstacles. When I first arrived at the visitor's bureau in Fayetteville, I met a tall, gracefully refined woman named Tamara Holmes. She was a 1995 graduate of E.E. Smith. After majoring in art at Hampton University, Holmes returned to Fayetteville to work as a sales manager. She was involved in the preservation efforts to save the old Orange Street School building a few miles from downtown. Holmes was proud to be a Golden Bull. Her parents went to Smith. So did her grandparents. All the negative publicity was deeply troubling to her.

"There are a number of factors for the low scores," she told me. "You've got two new high schools pulling good students away. And we're not getting as many of the Fort Bragg kids. I've got friends stationed in Germany who are told not to send their kids to Smith when they move back to Fort Bragg. It's just frustrating."

Holmes actively supported E.E. Smith through its National Alumni Association, and she attended as many school events as she could. She said the community has stepped up its efforts to provide tutoring, hall-monitors, and financial support to the school. Community leaders such as former NFL player and E.E. Smith alumnus Jimmy Raye returned to Fayetteville every summer to raise money for the school. At a recent event, Raye's youth foundation collected over $40,000 in scholarship donations for E.E. Smith's senior class.

No man epitomized these efforts quite like Milton Butts. After searching for Coach Butts all around Fayetteville in the stifling heat, I finally found him in the school's weight room, which was a high-ceilinged hanger with a large garage door leading out to the football stadium. The whole room was covered in stripes of white and gold, a shade called "old gold" for its classically refined look. On the far wall, I noticed a gigantic mural of a bull. The bull's eyes were narrow, and his left arm curled a massive barbell. This was the football team's wall of fame. Each concrete block surrounding the bull was reserved for an E.E. Smith player who had gone on to play college football. Butts started the tradition when he took over as head coach eleven years ago, and the wall was covered with colleges such as East Carolina, North Carolina A&T, West Point, Wake Forest, N.C. State, Catawba – the list seemed almost endless.

Coach Butts' office was next to the weight room. It was a typical coach's space: no windows, an exposed ceiling, team pictures on the wall, a stained carpet on top of a concrete floor, and an ancient air conditioning unit humming in the background with no cool air coming out. This didn't seem to bother Milton Butts. He was at his desk eating a large plate of barbecue. Even sitting down, the man had an imposing figure. Coach Butts wore an old gold E. E. Smith coach's shirt, and his dark eyes squinted at me beneath a full-brimmed straw hat. He shook my hand and asked me to pull up a chair. Coach Butts immediately put me at ease. He carried himself a lot like my old high school coach, Bill Eccles. His calm, personable demeanor invited openness and respect in equal measure. Perhaps it had something to do with his Midwestern roots. Coach Eccles and Coach Butts were both from Indiana, although the two men took very different paths to get to North Carolina.

Milton Butts grew up in South Bend, Indiana, home of the fighting Irish of Notre Dame. Butts was a teenage activist – at one point he even joined the Black Panthers – and he wanted to go to an all-black school for college. Almost every historically black college (HBC) was below the Mason-Dixon

Line. North Carolina, in particular, had a thriving HBC community. Schools such as North Carolina Central, North Carolina A&T, Fayetteville State, Winston-Salem State, and Elizabeth City State all played a prominent role in the Civil Rights movement, and those were just the public colleges. Butts had an uncle who worked at NCCU, so he decided to play college football in Durham.

"I went to school to learn how to teach and coach," Coach Butts said to me. "I knew exactly what program or path I was going to take. And it worked out that way. It's rare – this is what I always wanted to do. I always liked working with kids. I just loved football and the things it teaches. I think it's a great avenue for kids, especially for young, aggressive kids to be able to let their anger out and learn on top of all that."

Milton Butts's own aggressive style turned him into a standout offensive lineman at NCCU. He was drafted by the New Orleans Saints in 1976 and spent three years in the NFL before injuries forced him to retire. At that time, the NFL hadn't reached its upward trend of high salaries and long-term contracts. Most players worked in the off-season. Butts kept a residence in Durham, and after his injury he knew exactly what he wanted to do. Most of his teammates lived for the moment. When their football careers inevitably came to an end, they walked around in a fog for months on end. Pro football was their final goal. Few players thought about life after that.

After retiring from pro football, Milton Butts jumped into teaching and coaching at Hillside High School in Durham. He worked alongside Tony Ford, who eventually became one of my co-workers at Jordan High. Tony Ford and Milton Butts must have been an interesting pair. Coach Ford has an off-the-wall saying for every situation in life, and his irreverent humor probably gelled nicely with the down-home charm of Coach Butts.

Back then, Fayetteville was arguably the king of high school football in North Carolina. After two years at Hillside, Coach Butts took a job with a friend at Cape Fear High School before moving on to head coaching stints at Pender County, Westover, and E.E. Smith. People took their high school football seriously in Cumberland County. Butts was fired twice along the way after losing seasons. All it took sometimes was one down year. But over time, Butts made a name for himself on the football field and in the classroom. People across the region took notice. On two occasions, Butts was a finalist for the coaching staff at Fayetteville State University. But each time he returned to E.E. Smith.

His players desperately needed guidance. They came from broken and transient homes. There was so much work to be done. Many of the kids who played football for Coach Butts stood precariously between the paths of good and evil. They lived difficult lives, but Milton Butts held the transformative power of a team.

Butts believed that football serves many purposes. "It teaches toughness and working together for one common goal. The sweat, the hard work – all of that has a lasting impact on a kid, whether he plays after high school or not. You're gonna need that toughness in life when bad things happen to you."

"And that's translated into victories, right?" I asked. "Y'all seem to go deep into the playoffs almost every year."

"We've been fortunate enough to have some good athletes. Getting kids to buy into the system. Everything starts from the top. I always let my kids know that you mean what you say. We've been in situations where you don't have that discipline. We didn't have it last year the way I like it. In many cases, that was one of the reasons why we didn't do well. That goes along with those dropped passes, jumping off sides, cheap shots."

I noticed a large picture of Carter Sharpe on the wall above the half-eaten barbecue plate. My eyes kept returning to the picture, but I resisted the urge to bring up the subject of Sharpe.

Coach Butts took a long swig of sweat tea from a Styrofoam cup. "It gets touchy sometimes. My number one goal each year is to develop these young people. It's not about winning or losing. I see the places I can't do that. We're gonna give you chance after chance after chance, but with everything we're trying to do, if you're not getting it, then you can't be a part of the program, no matter how good you are. The Sharpe kid. That's why he's not with us anymore."

I seized on the opening. "Coach, when we saw him on film, I thought, *If we don't find a way to stop #33, there's no way in hell we're gonna win this game.* He just lit up the field."

Milton Butts shook his head slowly. "Carter's not a dumb kid at all. He *is* eligible to play next year. But Carter was making some bad choices, hanging around with the wrong people. If you've got a problem at home, you've got a problem with me. You represent me out here on this field. There's certain things you're gonna have to do or not do if you're gonna participate. And those buttons weren't being pushed right."

Coach Butts paused, and his eyes seemed to soften a little.

"I think I'm good at what I do, so I look at this situation as a failure on my part, because you ain't supposed to lose kids like that. You don't get many of those."

Butts let out a full-bodied laugh and shook his head slowly.

"I probably could have done something differently to keep that boy. I'm working on that as a person, as a coach." He paused again. "Carter is fortunate because he's so good. If he wasn't so good, he'd be through now."

"How did he react when you made the decision?" I asked.

"He didn't believe me. And I gave him an out. This happened in late January. I told him, 'You pick it up in that classroom and show me the things I know you can do, or at least try. We'll talk at the end of the year, and we'll go from there.' We didn't let him lift weights or anything that spring. Well, nothing really changed. He didn't believe me. It really started to sink in by the end of school."

Coach Butts talked to Sharpe's parents about his decision, and then he called up Hargrave Military Academy and several other prep schools. They came down to Fayetteville the very next day. Hargrave immediately offered Sharpe a full scholarship for their nationally ranked post-graduate team.

"We just hope everything goes better for him," Coach Butts said. "He'll have a different environment. All the kids around him now will be moving towards the same goals, and most of those goals are more positive than the types of things he was getting himself into around here."

The Fayetteville community was floored by the turn of events at E.E. Smith. In a *Fayetteville Observer* article announcing the transfer, Carter Sharpe's mother praised the selflessness of her son's coach.

"I can't express how much respect we have for Milton Butts, and the whole coaching staff at E.E. Smith," Natalie Sharpe said. "He has done tremendous things for Carter and that has been a tremendous relationship that we know will continue while he's at Hargrave. We go with his blessings. He's a great man and has a great coaching staff."

That seemed to be of little consolation to Milton Butts this afternoon.

"He was *the man* coming back," Butts said with his eyes squinting back at me beneath the straw hat. "He was the *only* man coming back this year."

"What do you want people around Fayetteville to take from all of this?" I asked.

"Oh God," he said with a pause. "That I cared for the kids, and my number one goal was to care for the kids. It was really tested this year with Sharpe." Coach Butts laughed yet again. "It was really tested, because I did not want to do that."

Despite his disappointment with the Carter Sharpe situation, Coach Butts knew he had made the right decision. Consistent discipline mattered most of all. Coach Butts's players knew he wasn't going to abandon his principles just to win a few more games. The Golden Bulls usually found a way to win anyway. Butts's teams averaged almost ten wins a year, and he worked tirelessly to send his kids to college. The first goal was to develop them into men. Winning came second.

"I'm not any more proud of one than the other," Coach Butts said. "Just cause someone might have played pro ball and been successful, that doesn't mean I'm more proud of him than somebody who never went to college but has a family now – someone who's working in the community, church-going, I'm just as proud of him as the others. I want you to be able to take care of yourself. And you gotta understand that it's what you do for folks that's about the most important thing. I want that for all of 'em. *Then* we're successful."

Each season, Milton Butts establishes a set of priorities for his football squad. He calls them the "Big Four," and his players pass by them every day on the way to practice. The first priority is *Faith*. According to Coach Butts, faith is simply the most important focus for a football player. The next priority is *Family*. After family comes *Finances*. Education is the key to a good job and a level of personal responsibility. It is the primary avenue to further success in life. All three of these priorities come before the final focus: *Football*. The Big Four are the building blocks in a young man's development, and Coach Butts stresses their importance every single day.

Butts focuses on the *Finance* section with particular intensity.

"We really stay on them academically. We send out progress reports, and the progress reports don't have anything about the grade on there. I want to know four basic things: Is he prepared to learn? Is he coming to class with paper, pencil, and books? How is his attitude? Does he participate? I don't want you just sitting there in the classroom. The last one is behavior. Is he acting like he's supposed to act? It's real simple. All the teacher has to do is check it and put it back in my box. We stay on that.

"We try to make sure they understand that school is the most important thing, so we're gonna look after that first. After school we have a study hall. We do that before practice. The kids don't get home before 9 or 9:30. Sometimes as late as ten. But when the parents get 'em, they've basically already got their work done."

After school, all E.E. Smith football players attend mandatory tutoring sessions with their academic teachers for an hour and a half. To Butts, this was the only time his players could get extra classroom help.

"You have to really get the faculty behind it. We make 'em go to their math teacher or their English teacher – their academic subjects. If they're up there and the teacher says, 'Coach, he didn't do nothing but sit up here and play around' – well he had a bad day at practice that evening. A real bad day. We're gonna run the dog shit out of you next time, and the next time we're gonna damn near kill you. The next time, you don't need to play football. And we've gotten rid of some good ones."

These efforts seemed to run counter to the media's negative opinion of E.E. Smith in the *Leandro* case. I asked Coach Butts if he was concerned about the threats to close E.E. Smith. He shook his head adamantly, revealing the activism of his days in the Black Panther Movement.

"In many ways, I'm glad the judge has drawn attention to the situation. But he needs to understand that there's no quick fix. Education deals with public money, so you're dealing with politics – a whole lot of that is involved in this thing. Judge Manning needs to ask, what are these kids like when they get to high school? If you're getting a kid who can't add or read in the 9$^{th}$ grade, then how are you gonna blame the school? Maybe this will bring some of those things to light. Put more money into the schools. Add more support. If you're going to be straddled with low-performing students from the start, you need to lower class sizes, bring in more tutors, more computers, more equipment. They need special help to catch up, and special help is not free. Let 'em keep rolling and thundering and all this if it means getting schools more money and those kinds of things.

"All 18 schools he put on that list were minority schools," Coach Butts continued, "and minority schools in most cases are your inner-city schools. There are a whole lot of problems other than the school. Here at E.E. Smith, with football, we're just gonna keep doing what we've been doing all these years the best we can. I don't know what the test scores are saying, but they walk across that stage a whole lot better than when they got here."

It was already three o'clock, and I had to leave soon if I wanted to get back to Durham for our afternoon practice. Coach Butts and I walked through the weight room one more time, and he talked with pride about kids like Jeremy Wall, who was heading up to Boston in a few days for his first semester at Harvard.

"I'll be following y'all closely this year," I said as I shook Coach Butts' hand. "But I hope we don't have to meet in the playoffs."

Coach Butts let out another one of his deep, full laughs.

"Hey, I'll be happy just to get that far again."

It was classic coachspeak. Even with Carter Sharpe gone, and another star player on his way to Virginia Tech, E.E. Smith was still a 4-A powerhouse. Milton Butts would find a way. This summer, a new group of freshman will look to Coach Butts for guidance. They could care less about the past. Their future is now. Their hope begins now.

But the Supreme Court threats were very real. In the years to come, E.E. Smith may have to say goodbye to the blue-collar streets around Seabrook Road.

In these neighborhoods of modest homes and sun-scorched grass, children of all ages can see the bright, familiar stadium lights above the trees and know that the Golden Bulls are playing at home. They'll listen for the sounds of the Friday night crowd, the muffled voice of the loud speaker, the familiar beat of the Magnificent Marching Machine. But one day there may be silence. Milton Butts will have to move to another sideline, perhaps at a far-away college, perhaps at another high school down the road. He'll continue to stress the guiding principles of faith, family, finances, and football. His players will complain about tutoring sessions and late-night practices, but they will graduate with solid GPAs and grow into responsible men.

I don't think E.E. Smith will close any time soon. The Golden Bulls make up the very fabric of Fayetteville's African American community. They stand ready to answer the call of history, of men such as Ezekiel Smith, who truly believed that both blacks and whites could reap the benefits of a solid education.

Emerson once wrote that nothing is more sacred than the integrity of the mind. I'd also say that nothing is more sacred than Man's ability to impact the exterior world. Communities are no more permanent than a field of frozen snow. They are bound by normal people who do extraordinary things. Coach Butts is an institution. His presence on the E.E. Smith sideline is an essential component to any efforts to appease Judge Manning.

As I drove home to Durham after my visit with Coach Butts, I thought about my own players. What will my legacy be with them? I'm a normal man with an average mind. My talents are far from unique. But a community's success does not depend on the actions of one individual. True power stems from a commitment to collaboration; that's where the real beauty lies.

I think I am beginning to see the heart of the matter.

# 3

# The Fire Next Time
## Jacksonville

Willie Duncan yawned as he waited for his ride to work. It was five o'clock in the morning, and most of the families along Darden Street were still asleep. Willie watched as the banks of the New River became more and more visible with the passage of dawn. Seagulls floated across the calm, dark waters flowing from Wilson Bay into the tiny downtown of Jacksonville, North Carolina.

Like most seventh graders, Willie couldn't think clearly this early in the morning. But he'd gotten used to the routine. Every morning, a manager from the *Jacksonville Daily News* would pick him up, and they would deliver newspapers to the soldiers stationed down the road at Camp Lejeune. The extra money was a big help to Willie's family. It gave him a sense of pride and ownership.

Now, more than ever, Willie needed the predictability of this job. It was the end of May, 1966, the final year of segregation in the Onslow County Schools. Twelve years had passed since the landmark decision of *Brown vs. the Board of Education*, and now, at last, the South was finally giving in to the new mandates. Rumors bounced around the black community about integration. What would happen to their beloved Georgetown High School?

Would white students go to Georgetown in the fall? Would there be violent resistance from both sides?

Willie could see the impressive roofline of the Georgetown gymnasium two blocks away. The sight was as familiar to Willie as the passing waters of the New River. Later that evening, the final graduating class of Georgetown High School would walk across the stage of the school's auditorium. Willie knew almost every one of these seniors. Some would stay here in Jacksonville, while others would go to college in such far-away cities as Durham, Charlotte, or Winston-Salem. Willie longed to visit these exotic places when he grew older. But life was just too uncertain these days.

Willie wiped the sleep from his eyes and turned to look at the high school once again.

Something wasn't right.

Willie squinted at the dark, morning sky. He saw a thin strand of smoke. Then he noticed a bright glow along the gymnasium walls.

Willie was wide awake now. His instincts kicked into gear and his heart began to race. He sprinted down the empty street and stopped at an old oak tree in front of the school. He couldn't believe his eyes; it was like something out of hell itself. The towering gymnasium and the brand new science wing were completely engulfed in flames. Explosions sent crumbling brick and mortar into neighboring yards.

There were shouts above the roar of the fire. Willie heard someone yell "...graduation," but he couldn't make out the rest. Then an old Ford Falcon skidded past the oak tree carrying four or five white men. The car was moving too fast to make out the license plate.

Willie ran to a nearby house to call the police.

Lights came on throughout the neighborhood, and families dressed in nightgowns and pajamas looked on helplessly from their front yards. Among them were Lillian Willingham and her thirteen year old son, Tyrone. Lillian was an Ivy-League educated teacher at Georgetown. She watched in horror as the high school began to implode. James Shubrick stood nearby on Darden Street. He was a cousin of Willie's, and he had just finished his ninth grade year at Georgetown. James could see bricks scattered across the road, a good 500 yards away from the school. *This was no accident*, James thought to himself.

It took six fire departments to put out the blaze. For safety reasons, all of the walls were pulled down, turning Georgetown High School into a pile of rubble. Billowing smoke filled the skies of Jacksonville well into the afternoon.

Eastern North Carolina is a mysterious place. It is a land of wide-open spaces and never-ending fields of corn and tobacco; plantation homes bleached by sunlight and sagging with neglect; tin roofs rusting underneath the weight of kudzu; towering oak trees shading the cemeteries of white-walled Baptist churches; shacks proudly displaying an unholy trinity of flags: the stars and stripes flying next to a Confederate flag and a black flag honoring American POWs.

It's like something out of a Faulkner novel. The past maintains a tight grip on the present, while the present realizes it must reinvent itself in order to survive. But if survival means losing your identity, is the fight really worth it?

My mind wandered from thought to thought as I drove deeper into the countryside of Duplin County. Cornfields and farmhouses line both sides of Highway 24 for endless miles heading east. Dirt roads cut through the fields in dusty paths, and open-air barns stretch across acres of long-leaf tobacco. As soon as I left the billboards and congestion of Interstate 40, I entered a world that had changed little over the past century, the type of place you seek out if you do not want to be found.

In the years leading up to the Civil War, slaves made up almost half of these communities. White masters were constantly afraid of slave uprisings, so they prohibited blacks from gathering anywhere other than funerals. Slaves were beaten severely for even the smallest infraction. Work days on a farm were long and brutal. Fugitive slaves often escaped north through the high rows of corn, sleeping during the day and traveling at night, reaching the Great Dismal Swamp and disappearing from the face of the earth.

For over an hour I traveled through sleepy little one-light towns like Warsaw, Chinquapin, and Beulaville, where football dominates the landscape of a Friday night more than anything else. I stopped momentarily at James Kenan and East Duplin, two high schools perched in the middle of some of the most remote farmland in the South; James Kenan and East Duplin also have two of the best football programs in the eastern half of the state. These teams play their home games in tiny stadiums made of worn wood and rusted metal, with corn fields running right up to the end zones. They routinely compete in the 1-A and 2-A state championships in Raleigh, Chapel Hill, or Winston-Salem, bringing thousands of fans from every corner of Duplin County.

I continued down Highway 24 into Onslow County. The ragged voice of Ryan Adams filled the stereo in my car. It was a voice marked by heartbreak and too many bottles of beer:

"...And in the cotton fields, by the house where I was born, the leaves burn like effigies of my kin..."

His words blended perfectly with a solemn violin and a pedal steel guitar.

"Jacksonville, how you burden my soul, how you hold all my dreams captive...How my heart goes bad, suffocating on the pines in Jacksonville..."

The words covered my final destination like a cloud.

Ryan Adams grew up along the New River in the town of Jacksonville. When he was in the 10th grade, Adams dropped out of Jacksonville High School and moved to the much larger city of Raleigh. Several years passed before he would gain international fame as a country/rock musician. Like so much of the South, his songs were a constant dance between love and hate. Adams couldn't wait to abandon the land of his youth, yet he still named his band, the Cardinals, after the Jacksonville High School mascot. Adams was bound to his past as much as anyone.

The human mind has a resilient way of finding goodness in even the darkest memories of our youth. We remember our days as a student because schooling takes up most of our waking hours as a child. A school becomes an extension of our identity. We are Cardinals, or Greenwaves, or Golden Bulls. It's just who we are. Years may pass, and a school may evolve, but the names become our own for all eternity.

Unless the school is wiped off the face of the earth.

As I made my way closer and closer to the coast, I thought about the morning of May 29, 1966. The heart of Jacksonville's black community was shattered on that day. Georgetown, a name that was dear to so many, was gone; nothing would ever be the same again. The final graduating class at Georgetown High School held a somber commencement later that evening in the auditorium of the all-white high school down the road. Georgetown's crumbling bricks and scorched textbooks were left to decompose in the city dump.

The aftermath pushed the city to the brink of disaster.


On May 30, the State Bureau of Investigation conducted a preliminary inquiry into the alleged fire bombing of Georgetown High School. Cases of arson had occurred elsewhere, and several all-black high schools across the South had mysteriously burned to the ground on the eve of integration. The evidence seemed pretty damning. Willie Duncan saw a carload of whites leaving the scene immediately after the fire; bricks and debris littered the street 500 yards away from the school, a potential sign that something more than a fire had occurred; and the two sections of the building that were destroyed – the gym and the science wing – were well-built and relatively new. Plus, it was common knowledge that many whites didn't want their sons and daughters to go to an integrated school.

The State Bureau of Investigation concluded its investigation on the same day it began. The SBI never contacted Willie Duncan, and they only interviewed a handful of neighbors. The fire was the result of "combustion," the SBI announced, not foul play. The final remaining artifacts from the school, such as band instruments, uniforms, and yearbooks from the library, were sent to a county warehouse, where they eventually disappeared.

Over the years, the Georgetown Alumni Association made repeated inquiries into the firebombing of May 29, but they reached a dead end every time. All files from the Jacksonville Fire Department were destroyed, along with the records from the Onslow County Sheriff's Department and the Onslow County Schools. The "State Insurance Agency" involved in the fire no longer exists. In a final blow, the remaining wings of the Georgetown building eventually came under the direction of the Onslow Water and Sewer Authority. The black community of Jacksonville could do nothing but simmer with rage.

In the early moments of integration, Jacksonville waited to erupt. But anger is a fickle beast. In some cities, it manifests itself in violence. In other communities, the anger festers for years and years, poisoning the interactions between rich and poor, black and white. The fuse gets lit, but sometimes the dynamite never explodes. There is no handbook or simple explanation for it.

The integration of Jacksonville's public schools was far from perfect. White students committed numerous acts of racism. And black students often felt lost in the new confines of Jacksonville High School. The building surpassed Georgetown High School in almost every way, but Georgetown was the heart and soul of the black community. Principal J.W. Broadhurst had guided the school for over thirty years, and Georgetown's teachers were educated at some of the finest universities in America. In recent years the football team had won a state championship over Jones High from Mt. Airy, a game in which big halfback Roy Hurst ran "as gracefully as the cats his team is named for," according to the *Jacksonville Daily News*. How could integration ever create the same sense of community?

Tyrone Willingham wondered about these things as he began his freshman year at the newly integrated Jacksonville High School. Tyrone would never forget the morning of May 29, when he stood with his mother Lillian and watched Georgetown burn to the ground. He also remembered riding his bicycle down to the Onslow Theatre to see *Old Yeller*, only to be sent to the "blacks only" section of the balcony. But Lillian was his inspiration. She was the first black woman elected to the Onslow County School Board. Lillian told her son that education was the key to a happy life. She said it over and over again until the message became as vital to him as breathing.

For three years, Tyrone waited his turn behind a white quarterback on the Jacksonville football team. At five foot nine and 150 pounds, he wasn't exactly an ideal replacement. But an injury to the starting quarterback gave Tyrone the opportunity he'd been waiting for; he didn't disappoint. Tyrone was a team captain and an all-conference performer his senior year, and he eventually became an All-American at Michigan State. But Tyrone Willingham truly made a name for himself as a coach. After a successful stint at Stanford University, Tyrone became the new head coach at Notre Dame, the most storied college program in the country.

But this isn't a story about college football. This is a story about community and history. Tyrone and Lillian Willingham are voices of change. They are bound by the legacies of the past, but they shed light on a much brighter future. I greatly admire the way they have responded to life's obstacles with grace and integrity.

Sometimes, however, grace isn't enough. After 21 wins in three seasons at Notre Dame, Coach Willingham was fired. Athletic director Kevin White explained the firing by saying, "From Sunday through Friday, our football program has exceeded all expectations, in every way. But on Saturday, we've struggled." It is one of the most damning comments in the history of college athletics. His words remind me why I love high school football. The teams I coach are not driven by money, or glory, or television contracts.

This is a story about people in out-of-the-way places who do great things in their own small world. Tyrone Willingham is one of many worthy figures. Another man also stands out from the rest. On that first morning at Jacksonville High School, he carried the weight of the whole school on his shoulders. Like Tyrone, he also wondered if integration could be successful in Jacksonville. And while he never gained the national fame of Tyrone Willingham, his story is just as lasting.

Phil Padgett tried not to think about his father. For three hours on a Friday night, he needed to keep his emotions together. His father would have wanted it that way. It was an unseasonably mild evening for late November, but a strong wind made the air feel crisp and cold. Phil didn't notice; his body was simply numb.

On Tuesday morning, Lenwood Padgett had lost his battle with lung disease. To Phil, the entire week was a blur. The man who had been such an indomitable force in his life was gone. While Phil grieved the loss of his father, his assistant coaches took over most of the daily preparations for the upcoming playoff game. Phil couldn't focus on football right now. The funeral was held on Friday morning, and hundreds of people from all walks of life came to Onslow Memorial Park to honor the man who had ushered Jacksonville through one of the most volatile periods in the city's history.

Lenwood Padgett was a fixture at Jacksonville High School for nearly four decades. He lived a full life, traveling much of the world as an avid hunter and fisherman. But his heart always remained in Onslow County. He was born on a tobacco farm outside of Jacksonville in Haw's Run. Jacksonville was little more than a remote village back then, and its 800 residents made a hard-scrabble living on tobacco, corn, and peanuts. At the height of the Great Depression, the economic downturn barely touched Jacksonville because no one had any money to begin with. After getting his undergraduate degree at UNC Chapel Hill, Lenwood returned home to become a chemistry and physics teacher. He loved the challenge of motivating students. Success, Lenwood believed, could only come when the mind was filled with knowledge and the heart was inspired to follow a teacher anywhere.

In 1967, the Onslow County School Board chose Lenwood Padgett to take on a job that few people wanted; they asked him to become the first principal of the newly integrated high school. Over the next 25 years, Lenwood guided Jacksonville High School with a steady hand, promoting diversity in those first tenuous years of integration and handling a difficult period in the late 1980s when several school buildings burned to the ground. Lenwood thrived on the pressures of public life, but he also loved the simple pleasures of nature, such as hand-feeding squirrels and twisting cypress branches into table legs. This interior life gave him the strength to return to Jacksonville High School year after year. In 1978 and 1988, Lenwood was named State Principal of the Year. A plaque at the front of the school honors his achievements with a picture of Lenwood etched in bronze. A calm smile plays across his face, and his dark hair curls along his forehead in thick waves.

Only a handful of hours had passed since the funeral, and Phil Padgett tried to focus on the game at hand. Perhaps his father was looking down right now, Phil wondered to himself. Then he pushed the thought aside. Coach Padgett's Southwest Onslow Stallions were losing ground quickly. A trip to the 2003 state championship was at stake, and East Bladen held a 17-6 lead deep into the second half. Nothing seemed to be going right for Coach Padgett's team; there were two missed field goals, a blocked extra point, and the offense wasn't getting anywhere. The overflow crowd was anxious. Two years ago, Coach Padgett had led the Stallions to the school's first state championship. The next year, Southwest finished in a three-way tie for first place in the East Central 2-A conference at 10-1, but a coin flip brought their season to an end. The whole team wanted revenge for such a disappointing finish.

Phil Padgett was exhausted. As much as he tried to hide it, his players sensed the burden their coach was carrying. They respected Coach Padgett. He was always there for them when things went bad in their own lives. But things were turned upside down now.

Earlier in the week, when the shock of losing his father was still fresh, Coach Padgett spoke to his team after practice and said, "Don't win this one for me. There are some things in life you can't control. Like death. Just take care of the things you can control."

His players dedicated the game to him all the same.

The turning point came late in the third quarter. Southwest was driving deep into East Bladen territory when the Stallions threw an interception at the seven yard line. The game should have been over at this point, but somehow the defensive back ran into the East Bladen end zone for a safety. With the score now only 17-8, the momentum finally shifted to Southwest.

Two touchdowns later, the Stallion faithful rushed the field and celebrated their improbable victory. Coach Padgett couldn't contain his emotions any longer. The burden fell from his shoulders, and he tried to smile. But the sadness was still there. *If only Dad could have held on a few more days.*

Phil knew his father would be proud right now.


"The good qualities I have, I got from my father," Phil Padgett said to me. He paused, then added with a smile, "The bad qualities, I developed those myself."

Coach Padgett sat at his desk in the Southwest Onslow coaches' office, while I reclined on an orange couch. The walls were covered in newspaper articles chronicling the Stallions' recent football success. Headlines such as "Horsepower!" and "Day of the Stallion" announced the 2-A state title victories in 2000, 2003, and 2004. Below the articles, rows of glass shelving displayed signed footballs, a stuffed duck, a bronze Stallion with hooves in the air, and numerous pictures of Coach Padgett's former players. There were also pictures of his wife, Cindy; his two sons, Jacob and Barry (named for the great running back Barry Sanders); as well as his daughter Stevie Grace (named for Stevie Nicks – "That may or may not be a good thing," Coach Padgett told me with a smile.)

Coach Padgett could barely sit still. He tapped his feet unconsciously and rocked back and forth with nervous energy. To him, everything in life had to be on the move. Coach Padgett always wanted to get something accomplished. He had dark, windswept hair like his father, with a mustache and goatee that made him look ten years younger than he really was. It was the same youthful exuberance that could lead a man to name one child after a football star and another after a 1970s music diva.

Padgett immediately apologized for being late to our meeting.

"My daddy was big about being punctual. You're on time, you're ready to go, you're ready to do the right thing. He really instilled that in me."

Phil Padgett picked up his work ethic from years of hot summer labor on his grandfather's tobacco farm outside of Jacksonville. He loved being outdoors, whether it was football, baseball, hunting, or fishing. Anything would do. As principal at Jacksonville High School, Lenwood Padgett would take his son to almost every sporting event at the school. Phil grew up traveling with his dad to far-away football games in Raleigh, Rocky Mount, Greenville, and a host of small towns carved into corn and tobacco fields across the eastern half of the state. Even as a young boy, Phil Padgett knew that Jacksonville was very different from these cities.

Because of its remoteness, Jacksonville was the perfect location for what was to become the largest amphibious training center in the United States military. In 1941, Congress approved the construction of Camp Lejeune on over 111,000 acres of sandy pine outside of Jacksonville. Overnight, the sleepy little community of 2,000 became a boom town of military personnel from all over the country. The area was a melting pot for all races and accents. President Roosevelt had just signed Executive Order 8802, opening the door for blacks to take on Hitler and the dark forces of the Third Reich. Thousands of black enlistees arrived at Montford Point on the northeast corner of the city. Jacksonville was a quiet town no more. Like Fayetteville after the inception of Fort Bragg, Jacksonville hemorrhaged with strip malls, fast-food restaurants, helicopter pads, cargo ships, and concrete as far as the eye could see.

Phil Padgett was stuck between the old world of Jacksonville and the ever-growing military presence in the area. As the population of Onslow County continued to surge, new schools sprung up to meet the demands. Phil followed his father to Jacksonville High School, where he played football and baseball several years after Tyrone Willingham broke the school's color barrier at quarterback. After graduating from UNC Wilmington, Phil took a job at Southwest Onslow, a school that had just opened to the west of the New River and the site of the old Georgetown High School. Phil worried that if he returned to Jacksonville High School, he would always be compared to Lenwood Padgett. Phil was proud of his father, but he wanted his own identity. How could anyone carve a space within that kind of legacy? At Southwest Onslow High School, Phil Padgett could build a program of his own.

On a typical Friday night in Jacksonville, a carload of Marines from Camp Lejeune are driving through the strip mall district of Marine Boulevard. As they cross the calm waters of the New River, they see the empty streets of downtown Jacksonville to their left. The white, one-room Pelletier House sits on a well-manicured hill above the river. It is one of the only structures in Jacksonville to survive the Civil War and the rampant fires that have destroyed so many buildings in the city.

Once the Marines reach Highway 53, they see the glowing stadium lights above the pine trees in the distance. This must be it. Veterans at Camp Lejeune say that if you want to see some quality football, you need to go to Southwest Onslow. No one in the car grew up in North Carolina, but they all love competition in any form. They also long to experience the world outside of the military. What's more American than a high school football game, after all?

A large orange moon sits high above the stadium. It's a few minutes past 7:30, and the game has already started. The soldiers find the closest parking spot a mile away from the school. They pick up their pace as they hear the sounds in the distance.

"First dowwwnn Stalll-ionnns!" shouts the game announcer, followed by roars from the crowd.

When the Marines arrive, they notice the large black Stallion at the front gates, with hooves kicking high in the air and mane flowing down to the solid brick base of the statue. Hordes of teenagers congregate around the concessions stands, and many more fans line the fence. Police officers are everywhere. Where else would they be, since the entire population of southwest Jacksonville is right here tonight?

The Marines take a seat with another group of regulars from Camp Lejeune. A Southwest student known as "Stallion Man" roams the bleachers in black tights and an orange cape. Down below, Coach Padgett works his magic with the Wing T offense. Former players stand on the sideline and offer support to the young squad.

The field is immaculate. Parents and boosters spent the previous night painting the yard markers and the trademark orange and black horseshoes. The boosters have done this for years. With an annual budget of close to $25,000, the boosters wield tremendous power. Back in the late 1980s, assistant Phil Padgett applied for the head coaching position, but it was given to an outsider. The booster club wanted Phil Padgett instead. Within weeks, the new coach caved in to the mounting pressure, and the job went to Padgett. The Stallions have never experienced a losing season under Coach Padgett, averaging ten wins a year and winning the state championship three times.

It is a perfect night for high school football. The Marines put aside their worries about Al-Qaeda and the upcoming deployments to Iraq or Afghanistan. They fall into the rhythms of a small town carnival where everyone is glad to see their neighbor, where children can play safely, and where parents fill the air with horns and whistles as they cheer their sons to victory.

A team manager knocked on the door to Coach Padgett's office.

"Are you busy?" she asked as her face peered through the cracked door.

"Yeah, I'm doing an interview. Why?" Coach Padgett cut her off before she could answer. "Get to work! I'll talk to you later!"

"What?" she asked, half playfully, half offended.

"Get to work and I'll talk to you later!"

"Alright, but if I need you –"

"Well, you'll have to wait."

Coach Padgett shut the door in her face and shook his head. I could hear laughter coming from the hallway.

"I'm getting the managers together. You can imagine what that's like."

I was beginning to get a sense of Phil Padgett's coaching style – blunt, direct, to the point. It was a balancing act, but he obviously pulled it off well.

A coach needed to be honest with his players, Padgett said.

"I've tried to be a good role model. There's a line you draw where you can't be too buddy-buddy, but there's a closeness with our kids that comes through. We've got a great relationship with them. I'm the same guy that's gonna talk to 'em about their girlfriend and laugh with 'em a little bit, and then tell 'em you ain't crap, you're not making that block.

"I've always been able to tell them the truth – even if they don't want to hear it. I'm a little bit old school as far as that goes, because you've got to tell the truth to kids. I think now we lie to them too much. We're scared to hurt their feelings; we're not supposed to tell them, 'Hey, you're not fast enough.' I'm a firm believer that you've got to tell them the truth if you want them to excel. Slow people can be faster, and weak people can be stronger. You can't make yourself taller, but there are other things you can do to make yourself a better football player."

Troy Barnett was a perfect example. In the early 1990s, Barnett was a solid but unspectacular football player for Coach Padgett. Barnett was class president his final three years at Southwest, and he earned the nickname "Computer" for his uncanny intelligence. His good grades got him into UNC, where he made the football team as a walk-on. Padgett put a good word in with the Tar Heel coaching staff, but deep down he didn't think Barnett could ever do much to help the team.

Barnett believed otherwise. He worked his way onto the traveling squad his sophomore year. His junior year, he began to get some game reps at defensive line. His senior year, he was placed on scholarship as a starting defensive tackle. The success story could have ended there. Barnett wasn't drafted, so he began the managerial training program at a McDonald's in Chapel Hill. That's when Bill Parcells and the New England Patriots came calling. For the next three years, Barnett was a starting defensive player in the NFL.

"I could not believe it!" Padgett said. "I'll never say never again."

In the NFL, Barnett's nickname changed to "Laptop." What excited Coach Padgett more than anything was the way Barnett carried himself outside of football. Barnett spent three summers working as an intern with Reebok, and when knee injuries ended his pro career, he was hired by the corporation to supervise his own group of interns. For the past ten years, Barnett has traveled the country talking to athletes about making the transition to the real world outside of sports.

"Troy didn't have the talent, but, buddy, he had the heart, and you can't measure heart. That's one thing we've always had at this school, these blue collar kids that just have a lot of heart."

Take John Davis. Davis was missing a hand, and he practiced with a prosthesis. Padgett was hard on the kid, knowing that Davis's lack of speed was as much of a handicap as his missing hand. Davis accepted the challenge, lifting weights in the off-season and working on his quickness. By his senior year, Davis was a starter on Southwest's conference championship squad.

For a school of only 770 students, Southwest High School has also seen its share of stellar athletes. The school is a blend of rural and urban, with multi-generational families from the farmlands around Jacksonville as well as a large and transient population from the military. This often translates into superior talent. Several years after Troy Barnett came through Southwest, a defensive tackle named Marcus Jones became a high school and college All-American at UNC before enjoying a six year NFL career with the Tampa Bay Buccaneers. Most recently, Kendric Burney was a starting cornerback at UNC, and Dekota Marshall was a starter at defensive back for East Carolina. The day before I arrived in Jacksonville, Burney and Marshall came back for a visit with their old coach. To Padgett, the alumni are a great motivational tool, and they talk to his squad each year about the work that goes into becoming a college student-athlete. During practice, Padgett looked over to find his two former players competing in one-on-one drills, talking junk to each other about the upcoming game this year between ECU and UNC.

These players were the heart of Padgett's success. Padgett also said that it was important for a coach to stay in one place.

"The kids want me to come back, and that makes me feel good. I think sometimes they'll work a little harder for you, because they know they're playing for somebody that does love the school and is gonna be here forever. I see no reason why I would leave here. I've been happy. Things have been good."

Winning inevitably brings mounting pressure. The team's 2006 season ended with a 9-5 record and a loss in the third round of the state playoffs. For months afterward, Stallion fans asked Coach Padgett if this year's team was going to be any good. Last year was such a downer, they said. Years ago, Padgett would have felt the same way. But all of that changed when Padgett started a family of his own.

"I've been fortunate to hold my marriage together, and I think my kids love me. When I'm gone, I hope my tombstone can say, 'He was a good coach, but he was a great father.' I've always tried to do everything I can when I'm free with my kids. I don't sit on the couch and watch TV. I'm not a guy who sits around anyway."

Coach Padgett's feet continued to tap against the concrete floor. He rocked back and forth in his chair, speaking a mile a minute, his mind wandering in several directions at once.

"Why does football matter to you?" I asked.

Coach Padgett's feet stopped twitching and his eyes focused on the ceiling. Then he leaned forward in his chair and looked directly at me.

"Football is the last great discipline kids have anymore. We've gotten rid of the draft. Kids don't work on farms anymore. They don't learn about the rewards of working hard. Football gives you that. It takes discipline to get out there in the hundred degree heat and have some coach yelling at you and cussing at you, pushing you to get better. There's just not much of that anymore as far as kids becoming men. We have babied our society so much. If we take football away, what are we gonna do?"

Padgett's feet began to twitch again.

"And let's be honest, what gets you more excited on a Friday night? People come to our football games 15 years after their children graduate. With other sports, their only interest is their child, and once their kid is gone, they're gone. Not football. They come back forever. It's a lifelong thing."

Coach Padgett could no longer keep his managers at bay. Practice was about to start. In one motion, he shook my hand warmly, answered his cell phone, and pantomimed orders to his eager helpers. As he walked away, his strong southern accent echoed through the crowded field house.

"This field will be beautiful in a few weeks," Debbie Bryan said to me as she surveyed the empty stadium. Several thick clouds dotted the sky above us and covered the metal bleachers with shade.

Debbie Bryan was in her fifth year as principal at Southwest High School. Before that, she'd been the principal at one of the elementary schools down the road. She'd known many of the kids at Southwest since they were four and a half feet tall.

"I came Saturday morning to check one more time on things. The goalposts still need to be painted. It'll look like a college field when we're finished."

Mrs. Bryan was smartly dressed in a sleeveless blouse, long black dress, and heels. At first I thought she was going to scold me for trespassing on school grounds, but her welcoming smile immediately put me at ease. I feel this kinship almost every time I walk into one of these small-town schools, as if a single look makes it clear that we are both teachers.

She asked me where I was from, and I explained to her what brought me to Jacksonville.

"Have you talked to Coach Padgett yet?" she asked.

I nodded. "Is he like that all the time?"

She began to laugh. "There's always something on his mind that we need to be working on, and there's a time line to get it done. He's constantly reminding me what that timeline is."

A few rain drops began to clink along the metal bleachers, although much of the sky was till blue.

"I get real excited this time of year," she said. "The atmosphere at these games is just awesome. When that band starts to drum, and you know they're getting ready to come through the gates – well, I've got chills right now just thinking about it."

Mrs. Bryan linked her arm with mine and demonstrated how the players enter the field. It's always very solemn, she said. A straight line. Every player enters the field the same way.

We looked at the stadium in a comfortable silence.

"Some Fridays, I wonder how I'm going to manage all these people."

"What's the typical gate for a home game?"

Mrs. Bryan thought about it for a moment, but she couldn't remember the exact figures.

"I guess Coach Padgett typically deals with that."

"Oh no. Definitely not," she said, laughing yet again.

"As the athletic director?"

"I keep that hidden as much as I can. He gets what he needs and a lot of what he wants. It's okay, because this does bring in a lot of the income. It pays for other sports, and they get what they need."

"Does that school spirit carry over into the building?"

"Definitely. When students have an athletic event to look forward to, the discipline's easy – even for the non-football players, because they know if they get in trouble, Mrs. Bryan's not gonna let them come to the game."

Academics always comes first, she told me. Coach Padgett was a firm believer in this.

"When it's interim report card day, those coaches are down in that lobby where the locker rooms are and they're waiting to tell guys they need to start tutoring immediately. Some of the assistant athletic directors keep up a tally of the GPAs. And they're very proud of that. They push really hard."

Raindrops began to fall faster as darker clouds drifted across the skyline. Mrs. Bryan paused as we walked down the slippery steps.

"I hope we have a strong team this year," she said, her mood turning serious for the first time. "We need it. I need it financially, and our whole community needs it."

Then her eyes grew bright again, as if losing was a mere afterthought. She turned her thoughts to the growing list of things that needed to be done before the first game. It wouldn't be long now.

Thousands of fans scatter like fire ants to their cars after another Stallion victory. Car horns honk triumphantly while rap music shakes the tinted windows of a nearby vehicle. Home-made noise makers and whistles fill the air. No one is in a rush to leave. The Marines weave through the bumper to bumper traffic on their way back to Camp Lejeune. After tonight, Jacksonville feels a bit more like home to them.

Years from now, they'll return to Jacksonville and wonder what has become of this remote city. They'll want to know what has changed and what remains the same. Perhaps the fires of the past will consume Jacksonville's legacy. But the spirits of Tyrone Willingham, Lenwood Padgett, and the students of Georgetown High School will never die. Effective leadership has a way of carrying a community from one generation to the next. And decency inspires future decency among people from all walks of life.

The spirits of the past speak to us often. They wonder who will step forward to lead the next generation. Who will rise up to provide hope and discipline for our children? Who will stir the fire of hope in their souls? Who will convince neighbors to gather together as one community?

Who?

# 4

## Pigskins and Politics
## Pilot Mountain

It was the smell that grabbed me. Cooked ham and grilled cheese and grease mixed together in a perfect blend.

I was sitting in a restaurant known as The Squeeze Box. The term "restaurant" probably shouldn't apply here, since The Squeeze Box is no bigger than a shed. A single counter is the only thing that separates the cook from his customers. The Squeeze Box opened in 1953, and very little seems to have changed since then. The walls and countertops are made of weathered wood paneling. There's an antique, oversized Coke bottle cap on the back wall next to several faded news articles about the restaurant. Nine chairs line the counter – the circular, red swivel chairs you used to see in every diner in the 1950s. A husband and wife stood behind the cramped counter, and their daughter worked the cash register.

"What can I get for you, darlin'?" the older woman asked me.

I looked at the menu above the grill: cheeseburger, hotdog, bologna, toasted cheese, chuckwagon.

"I'll have a cheeseburger and fries."

"Sure thing, sweetie," she said as she wrote down my order.

Her husband took out a beef patty and got to work. My stomach growled in anticipation.

I pulled out my copy of *The Pilot*, the local weekly newspaper, and glanced at the headlines. After the two hour drive from Durham, it was nice to sit back and relax for a bit.

I'd driven north on Highway 52 earlier that morning, past the industrial clutter of downtown Winston-Salem and across miles and miles of rolling hills and deep green trees. Thirty minutes outside of Winston-Salem, the bald and rounded peak of Pilot Mountain appeared in the distance. Pilot Mountain is a geological marvel of granite and sandstone rising 1,500 feet above the surrounding countryside. The Native Americans once called the mountain "Jomeokee," meaning "The Great Guide" or "Pilot." Hunters used it as a beacon through the thick forests and surrounding foothills. But more importantly, the mountain was a symbol of the "Great Spirit" that controlled every aspect of the ordered world.

I pulled off at the next exit, the town of Pilot Mountain, population 1,200. Surry County was the inspiration for America's signature TV series about small town America, *The Andy Griffith Show*. Andy Griffith grew up several miles down the road in Mt. Airy, the model for the fictional town of Mayberry. On the show, Griffith plays a local sheriff who calmly maintains order in a town full of harmless eccentrics and hillbillies. Opie, Aunt Bea, and Barney Fife have become as much a part of the Southern mystique as barbecue, sweet tea, and peach cobbler. *The Andy Griffith Show* idealized a rural world that never really existed, but the show's continued success in syndication speaks to our cultural longing for a simpler way of life. Pilot Mountain appears on several episodes as the fictional town of Mount Pilot, the rival community next to Mayberry. I was anxious to see if high school football really mattered in a town so far from the beaten path.

As I drove down Main Street, the Squeeze Box appeared to my right. I was struck by the simplicity of the old Coca Cola sign mounted in front of the restaurant with the words "Sandwich Shop" and nothing else. Beyond the light blue building, I could see the towering dome of Pilot Mountain in the distance.

I felt as if I'd stepped into a Norman Rockwell painting or a scene from *The Andy Griffith Show* – one of the early episodes, perhaps, when the show was in black and white, a time filled with nostalgia and longing. The whole town had the quaint feel of another era, with brick storefronts, multi-colored awnings, and the occasional interruption of a passing car.

An old man sat next to me at the counter of The Squeeze Box, sipping on a steaming cup of coffee and staring at the grill in front of us. He wore a pair of faded overalls and a black fishnet hat; his hands were tanned and scarred. The old man nodded my way, and I nodded back. It was still early, and the lunch crowd wouldn't be here for another half hour or so. The sounds of country music and sizzling food filled the tiny restaurant.

"You're not from around here, are you?" the cook asked as he wrapped my burger in wax paper. The lunch crowd had begun to arrive, filling most of the seats around the cramped counter.

"No sir," I said. "I'm from Durham."

"Long way off."

"Yep. I've been traveling around the state, talking to coaches about high school football."

"So you're going to see Coach Diamont?" he asked with a smile.

I nodded as I took a bite out of my cheeseburger. It was greasy but good.

"He's a good man. Coached about half this town. Taught most of my cousins, too."

By now, every man, woman, and child in the room was focused on our conversation.

"Glad you came here instead of Mt. Airy or Elkin," someone standing behind me added. "We don't think too much of them Bears and them Buckin' Elks."

The girl working the cash register told me that Pilot Mountain pretty much shuts down whenever the local boys from East Surry play Mt. Airy on a Friday night.

"You'll see stuffed Bears hanging out across the overpass with a string around their necks," she added. "People get a little crazy about the rivalry."

Surry County had three of the strongest 1-A football programs in the state. Mt. Airy and East Surry beat up on each other year after year, and Elkin – well, Elkin was in a league all its own. With an enrollment of just 360 students, the Buckin' Elks had won the 1-A state championship four out of the past five years. Mt. Airy, East Surry, and Elkin formed a lopsided triangle across Surry County, and each autumn the back-country roads were clogged with fans en route to the Friday night games.

A stocky African American man sat down beside me and introduced himself as Scott Travis. He played running back for East Surry back in the early 1990s.

"Seems like a long, long time ago," he said.

Scott Travis was wearing a black cutoff shirt, revealing a series of tattoos across his shoulders and arms. Travis crossed his arms and nodded warmly to each new person who walked through the door. He seemed to know everyone in the restaurant.

"So what's Pilot Mountain like?" I asked the small crowd gathering around me.

"It's real quiet," the girl behind the cash register said.

"Things have been kind of tough here lately," a gentleman to my right added. "Lots of job cuts down at the factories." Several people nodded. "But what's new, right?"

Over the past ten years, Pilot Mountain had lost more than 500 textile and apparel jobs. Most of the plants had moved to Mexico, where cheap labor was more profitable than community investment. For a town of only 1,200 people, the job cuts had taken a significant toll. Pilot Mountain's small-town charm stemmed from the troubling fact that nothing *could* grow or change. But for the people in The Squeeze Box, Pilot Mountain was home. It's where they wanted to raise a family and grow old.

For the next half hour or so, I talked pleasantly with the locals sitting around the counter. Mechanics and factory workers trickled in to collect their orders. The cook loaded his skillet with burgers and grilled cheese as he worked the room with good-natured humor.

Eventually, I paid my tab and thanked the cook for his hospitality. As I was walking down East Main Street, I ran into Scott Travis once again.

"You'll like Coach Diamont," Travis said to me. "He was my civics teacher back in the day. Always helped people out when they were in a fix."

"How long have you lived here?" I asked him.

"Pretty much my whole life."

Growing up as a black man in Pilot Mountain wasn't easy, Travis said to me. He was one of only 20 African Americans in his graduating class at East Surry High School. The percentage had stayed roughly the same ever since then.

"You'd think the Ku Klux Klan was dead and gone, but I remember the Klan marching down this very street back in 1990."

Travis pointed to an abandoned building on the corner of Main and Depot Street. From this rooftop, a group of his friends used to throw eggs at the passing Klansmen. It was a small act of defiance at a time when blacks often felt powerless to change the status quo. Like many rural mountain communities, the African American population in Pilot Mountain had always been sparse. Blacks preferred larger cities such as Winston-Salem, Greensboro, and Durham, where there was a communal strength in numbers. In Pilot Mountain, bigotry was more overt, and resistance came in small steps. The same year as the Klan march, three white students decided to wear KKK t-shirts to East Surry High School; a group of black students responded by beating the boys senseless. East Surry's first mascot was the Rebels, and confederate flags used to be a common sight at football games and pep rallies. In a move toward reconciliation, school officials eventually changed the name to the Cardinals.

Scott Travis pointed to another building along East Main Street.

"That used to be the Surry Drug Store. I remember when I was a kid, waiting there with my mom to get a bite to eat. They'd serve everyone else, and if there was no one else to help, they'd finally get over to you. It was pretty wild."

But Travis wasn't a bitter man. That's just the way life was back then, he said. What else could you do? Travis had a lot of friends at East Surry who didn't let prejudice get in the way. And that, ultimately, was more significant than the bigoted actions of a few backwards people.

As I drove away from Scott Travis along East Main Street, I tried to imagine the creeping horror of a street filled with hooded men.

Three teenage boys look down from the rooftops above Dept Street with a mixture of fear and indignation. They wonder who's hiding behind these masks. Could it be a neighbor, a doctor, or a police officer? The anonymity makes the Klan all the more terrifying because it could be anybody. It's the lifeblood of a racist ideology. Hate can only be fostered when humans refuse to recognize the individuality of someone else. A socially isolated community can implode at any moment, because such communities often lack the vitality to grow into something better.

Scott Travis and his friends will learn the subtle nuances of these hard truths as they get older. But for now, as they listen to the bigoted chants and the clump clump clump of boots along Main Street, they know of only one thing to do.

A dozen eggs splatter across the white robes in oozing yellow. It is a small act of defiance, but it is necessary. The boys gleefully sprint down Howard Street to their modest homes three blocks away. Sweat beads across their foreheads. Their hearts race. They are forever linked together by this moment.

David Diamont took one final look at his home and turned around with a sigh. This was supposed to be his year in the spotlight. He'd been voted student body president at East Surry High School, and he was one of the captains on the football team. Everything he knew revolved around the quiet streets of Pilot Mountain.

David's father packed the final bags in the family car. David Diamont, Sr. was an intense man who followed the Puritan work ethic: live by your actions, keep your mouth shut, and everyone will recognize you for your efforts. But David Jr. wasn't sure if this was really true. His father had been a history teacher and coach for over two decades. David Sr. had been president of the North Carolina High School Athletic Association, a Shrine Bowl honoree, and a well-respected coach of almost every sport at Pilot Mountain High School. But consolidation brought the closing of Pilot Mountain and two other small schools in Surry County. When East Surry High School opened in 1961, David Diamont, Sr. was relieved of his teaching position and his head coaching duties. Coaching had been his life's passion, even back to the years of WWII when he led the sports program at Fort Bragg. He'd passed this love of sports down to his three sons – David, Jr. and the twins, Ronnie and Donnie. Athletics had taken his family to such far-flung places as Thomasville, Statesville, Tabor City, and Pilot Mountain. They didn't want to move again, but life has a way of defying predictability.

The Diamont's new home was a mill house in the bustling textile city of Gastonia. David Diamont, Sr. got a job as the athletic director for Gastonia's YMCA, and David, Jr. began practicing with the Ashley High School football squad.

David Diamont, Jr. did his best to fit in with his new classmates and teammates at Ashley. He split time at quarterback on the Greenwave squad, and his stellar performance in school earned him an academic scholarship to Wake Forest University. David's athletic career came to a close after one year on the freshman basketball team at Wake Forest, where the legendary Bones McKinney was about to retire as head basketball coach. David resisted the urge to follow in his father's footsteps, opting instead to become a lawyer. But he loved sports with a passion that was undeniable. He took a Theory of Coaching class at Wake Forest his sophomore year, and he began to wonder if he could avoid the Siren's call of athletics.

With the onset of the Vietnam War in 1968, David Diamont made a decision that would forever alter the course of his life. He was set to train with the Marine Corps down in Quantico, just like his father had done before him. It was his duty. But David's parents urged him to give teaching and coaching a try. If he didn't like it after a year, they urged, he could head to Vietnam.

After David's senior year in Gastonia, the Diamont family had moved back to Pilot Mountain. They missed the rolling foothills and slow pace of Surry County, and David Sr. had an offer to coach at Pilot Mountain Middle School. It would be nice to have his oldest son back in the area as well. David, Jr. went with his gut and accepted a position as a history teacher at Mt. Airy High School, about 12 miles north of Pilot Mountain.

David Diamont has been coaching and teaching ever since.


The caption above the cash register stood out boldly for everyone to see: "MOUNTAINVIEW FEEDS CHAMPIONS."

I had just entered the Mountainview restaurant with David Diamont and his younger brother, Donnie. The caption was next to a team picture of East Surry's 2001 football squad, which had advanced to the state semifinals before losing to Albemarle and their star running back, T.A. McLendon, who set a national record that year for touchdowns in a single season.

"Hey there, fellas," the waitress said as she led us to a table in the center of the restaurant. The Mountainview was a bit less colorful than The Squeeze Box, but the people there were just as friendly. Greetings of "Hey Coach!" seemed to come from almost every table. Old people, young people, black, white – everyone seemed to know Coach Diamont.

When we first met at the East Surry field house, I was struck by David Diamont's unassuming presence. He was tall, with a thinning hair line and a thick, grey mustache. His younger brother Donnie was shorter and more compact, the product of thirty years as an officer with the Winston-Salem police department. David was the talker, while Donnie appeared to be more comfortable standing outside of the limelight.

All three of the Diamont sons decided to follow in their father's footsteps. In addition to being the defensive coordinator at East Surry, Donnie also coaches the Pilot Mountain youth football team. His twin brother, Ronnie, is the head football coach at Pilot Mountain Middle School. Ronnie took over the program from his father, who died of a heart attack at age 65 while he was lining a baseball field. All three brothers run the same offensive system. When a football player gets to his senior year at East Surry, he will have spent no less than ten years learning the same terminology from at least one coach named Diamont. No high school program in the state can match this level of consistency.

David Diamont ordered a salad and waved to one of his former players at a nearby booth.

"You'll wanna talk to this guy," David said to me. "Daniel's one of the best kids I ever coached."

Daniel Lynch came over and introduced himself. With a bald head and bulging neck, he looked like a WWF wrestler – and at 6'4" and 300 pounds, he'd actually won a state wrestling title in high school. After graduating from Catawba College with a degree in mathematics, Daniel bounced around several NFL mini-camps before coming back to Pilot Mountain to work as an engineer for his father's construction company.

David shook the gigantic hand of his former player and looked my way.

"I coached his dad, his uncle, his brother. His dad was one of my captains my first year. Offensive and defensive tackle."

I asked Daniel if he could tell me what Coach Diamont was really like.

"I'm gonna leave now," David interrupted with a smile.

"Nah," Daniel responded, "you can stay right here. It don't matter."

David Diamont looked my way. "He'll give you the good, the bad, and the ugly, I guarantee it."

Daniel continued: "Coach Diamont is blunt. Straight forward. He taught me a lot about discipline and the way to handle pressure. Going through college and on the professional level, there's a lot of pressure, and you lean on what you've learned from your coaches to handle it."

Daniel's voice didn't match his imposing frame. He was soft-spoken, with a lilt to his speech that turned words like *can't* to *cain't* and *nice* to *niiiice*. Every region of the South has its own unique dialect, and local residents can usually tell the difference between a Surry County accent and a down-east drawl. All Southerners may sound the same to an outsider, but we can spot the differences immediately.

"When did you try out with the Patriots?" I asked.

"Two summers ago," Daniel said. "I was playing center, and Coach Belichick (the Patriots' head coach) kept getting on me about messing up a play. He glares at me and says 'Quit talkin' like you from Mayberry and get it right!'"

The Diamont brothers began to smile before Daniel could even get to the punch line.

"So Coach Belichick comes up to me after practice and goes through this whole spiel about if I ever stop getting on you, it means I don't think you can do it. Then he says, 'By the way, where you from?' I paused a second, then said, 'Actually, I'm from Mayberry.'"

Our entire table shook with laughter.


There were times when David Diamont wondered if it was all worth it. He remembered back to that first year as an assistant coach under Alex Gibbs. Like David, Alex Gibbs was a history teacher, but he also had a doctorate in education. Years later, he would become a legendary NFL line coach and win two Super Bowls with the Denver Broncos. Gibbs demanded absolute perfection from his coaching staff, and if he didn't think David was prepared for practice, he would blast his young coach in front of the entire team. As the low man on the totem pole, David was often stuck with the grunt work. He'd drive to Winston-Salem every Friday night for the painstaking process of developing the game film, often waiting until two or three o'clock in the morning to send the eight millimeter tape back to the school. David scouted more than twenty games that first year, and for each game, Gibbs expected a written report on his doorstep by midnight. Many coaches would have folded under such demands. Football and teaching were all-consuming. There was no time for family, or romantic endeavors, or vacations. If you wanted to win, football had to become your life.

After three seasons at Mt. Airy, David decided to get his master's degree in education at Appalachian State University. It was about the time former North Carolina governor Terry Sanford was making his first bid for the presidency. Sanford was a progressive liberal with close political ties to John F. Kennedy and a reputation for fighting poverty and racial inequalities. If Kennedy had won a second term in office, many historians believe Sanford would have been his choice to replace Lyndon B. Johnson as Vice President.

David respected Terry Sanford. He'd never been involved in a political campaign before, but he found himself organizing young democrats across Surry County and the nearby mountain regions. Sanford ultimately won only ten out of the 100 counties in North Carolina, but one of those ten counties was Surry.

David had fallen in love with politics. He returned to Mt. Airy High School and immediately went to work on his own campaign for the state House of Representatives. He shaved his Fu Manchu down to a mustache and cut his long hair. He had no money and no political capital, just the naïve ambitions of a 28 year old history teacher and football coach. David crammed his way into a crowded field of four democratic candidates and miraculously won.

It was well past dinner time when Representative Diamont finally entered his Raleigh apartment. The room was cramped and bare. There was a TV against the wall, a card table, and a mattress on the floor. The TV was his one luxury; Pilot Mountain didn't have cable in 1990, but here, he could flip through fifty channels. David loosened his tie for the first time in eighteen hours and slumped onto the mattress. He looked around the one-room apartment and wondered if a committee chairman had ever lived such a modest existence before.

When David Diamont began his career in the North Carolina House of Representatives, his aspirations were modest. The House was dominated by lawyers and wealthy businessmen who could devote much of their time to state politics. But David still had to put food on the table. For the past fifteen years, he'd kept his job as a teacher and coach back in Surry County, living two very different lives.

From January to July, the months when the General Assembly was typically in session, David maintained a schedule that would kill a normal human being. He'd get up early on Monday morning and head to school to check on students and make sure everything was in line for the upcoming week. The Surry County School Board gave him an unpaid leave of absence every spring semester, but he was still responsible for creating lesson plans, grading papers, and staying on top of students and football players alike. He made the 180 mile trip to Raleigh just in time for the Monday evening session. The rest of the week, he spent every waking hour meeting with constituents and lawmakers. On Friday, David drove back to Surry County to take in a high school basketball game. Saturday and Sunday consisted of numerous meetings with constituents around the district. On Monday, he'd wake up and do the whole routine all over again. It was an exhausting schedule, but David liked to stay busy. He was his father's son, after all.

David stretched his legs and closed his eyes. His body needed rest, but his mind was alive with excitement, as well as a healthy bit of anxiety.

Recently, David had taken part in a coup to unseat Liston Ramsey from his position as Speaker of the House. It was a gamble, for sure, but something had to be done. The budget process was mired by infighting on both sides of the aisle, and confidence in the General Assembly was at an all-time low. Eighteen House Republicans and Democrats, including David Diamont, led what was later called the Mavretic revolution to replace Rep. Ramsey with Joe Mavretic as the Speaker of the House. David was popular among his colleagues, having recently been voted the most effective member of the House. As a reward, David became the new Chairman of the House Appropriations Committee. It was the most powerful committee in the legislature. The Appropriations Committee controlled state funding for roads, public safety, human services, and, most importantly, education. Millions of dollars were at stake, and perhaps for the first time in North Carolina history, a public school teacher would have a major voice in state spending.

Overnight, David Diamont became one of the most influential leaders in North Carolina. But he still had to make the 180 mile trip each week from

Surry County. There were papers to grade and lesson plans to mail back home. His $11,000 a year legislative salary enabled him to pay the bills, but money was tight. And now he was a husband and father of one child with another one on the way. On top of all this, David was entering his thirteenth season as the head football coach at East Surry High School. He was torn by equally passionate ambitions: pigskins and politics. One couldn't exist without the other.

David had built the football program at East Surry from the ground up, and he wasn't about to let a little thing like the House of Representative get in the way of his plans.

When David Diamont first applied for the head coaching job at East Surry back in 1974, he had a few basic requests. Could he film every game? Would he be able to hire an assistant coach? Could his team have pre-game meals?

No, they said. The administration only asked one question: how would he handle a player with long hair? That was it.

Needless to say, David didn't get the job. He stayed on as an assistant at Mt. Airy, but Pilot Mountain was his home. His parents lived there, and both of his brothers were back in town. He felt a deep allegiance to the place. Two years later, the head coaching job at East Surry opened yet again. David didn't ask for anything during the interview, and there weren't any questions about personal grooming this time. East Surry had nothing to lose by taking a chance on the young coach. So what if the school endured a ninth straight losing season? No one really cared about football at East Surry anyway. If things didn't work out, they could just bring in somebody else.

When David entered the East Surry field house for the first time as the school's new head football coach, he was surprised to find the locker room virtually empty. A thick layer of dust covered the concrete floor. All 35 helmets in the storage bin were outdated and uncertified. The biggest gate the year before had been $600, so there wouldn't be much support from the athletic department. David decided to hose down the concrete floor, only to discover that the drain was located at the highest point in the room. After shoveling water for two hours, he gave up on cleaning for the rest of the year. David examined the new uniforms, which were 100% cotton and included small, medium, and large sizes only. After one wash, the jerseys shrank down to nothing and had to be replaced. It wasn't exactly the start he had hoped for.

David's first squad consisted of nineteen players, all varsity. It would take a few years to get enough interest for a JV team. Donnie helped his brother whenever he could get off work, but his hours as a policeman were unpredictable. Occasionally, David took the linemen out for practice and left the backs alone in the field house, then switched the two groups halfway through practice. It wasn't ideal, but he had to make it work.

During the first game against West Wilkes, East Surry scored early in the opening half. The few scattered fans in the bleachers were stunned. One of the East Surry players ran up to David on the sideline with a perplexed look on his face.

"Gahd dawg," the boy said to his coach, "we're supposed to do that?"

After an improbable 6-4 record that first season, no one ever said those words again.


As Donnie Diamont drove us back from the Mountainview Restaurant, I marveled at the rolling hills and farmland along every bend in the road. David pointed to his brother Ronnie's furniture shop underneath a barbecue restaurant. Ronnie was a master craftsman who drew customers from all over the region. As we approached East Surry High School, I noticed the brand new press box connected to the stadium. It was a gift from Daniel Lynch's father and his construction company. The previous press box was a rickety wooden structure that could hold no more than five people and had been condemned for the past five years. It was a relic from the days when Daniel's father played for the Diamont brothers. The new press box was the Lynch family's way of saying thanks to David and Donnie for molding two generations of boys into men.

The field house looked significantly different now. Gone were the dusty floors, the sparse locker room, and any references to the Rebel mascot. David and Donnie had done much of the work themselves. The concrete walls were painted in stripes of red, black, and white. Above each locker was a hand-made, wooden nameplate. David had painted every strip of wood himself. I noticed the lockers for David's two sons; Davey was a senior linebacker, and Hunter was a sophomore linebacker. In the adjacent coaches' office, the nameplates of former players were nailed along every wall. The nameplates were a daily reminder of three decades worth of pungent sweat, ecstatic cheers, and tense pre-game talks.

I sat across from David Diamont and tried to imagine the faces that went with these crimson signs. Names like Salgado, Jessup, Galloway, Odell ... there were stories and dreams behind each strip of wood. Thirty eight years of stories, some good, some bad, some full of triumph and others dampened by heartbreak and sadness.

David leaned back in a swivel chair and stared at the walls.

"There are so many jobs out there where someone can replace you and no one even knows you're gone. But not this."

Coaches, he said, are put on a pedestal to help society blend very different types of folks. They teach kids the value of integrity and morality. For many athletes, such lessons don't come from anyone else.

"Some of our football players don't have a lot; something is missing, and this is a safe environment for them. If your child's involved in East Surry football, you know where they are for those three or four hours after school. Sometimes our kids stay in the shower longer because they don't have hot water at home. Good thing we've got the pre-game meal 'cause they weren't gonna get anything to eat that day. I remember taking a kid home to a trailer one time and he had a mattress on the floor. No one there. He had a separated shoulder when I took him home, but there was nobody there. Took another kid home several times – you know, we're not supposed to take kids home, but that's just a joke – and he would say, 'Now Coach, I want you to stop up here. Let me out to walk. Because if you go down here, they're gonna try to sell you crack, or someone's gonna try to shoot at you.' You run into that kind of stuff enough to make you realize that some kids have it rough."

Haymore, Flinchum, Griggs, Livengood ... what had football meant to each of these young men? How would their lives be different without a family of adopted brothers?


David Diamont tried to get out of coaching once before. He left the East Surry football program in 1990 so that he could spend more time with his wife, Debbie, and their young children. He also made a bid for Speaker of the House, but the bid went nowhere. For the first time in his adult life, David wasn't coaching. Sure, he loved politics, and teaching continued to be rewarding. But coaching was the glue that held so much of it together.

That's when Mt. Airy came calling yet again. Their coach, Jerry Hollingsworth, had just retired after 22 years at the school, and they wanted David to take over. Mt. Airy made an offer that David couldn't refuse: no homeroom, no hall duty, no lunch duty, no lining the field or doing laundry – all the drudgery that sapped the joy out of teaching and coaching.

Taking the Mt. Airy job would ruffle some feathers in the Pilot Mountain community, but David had a pretty thick skin. People get emotional and irrational sometimes when it comes to football. David loved to tell the story of a mother at East Surry who used to scream at him for not playing her son more, even though her son was a starting linebacker. "It's because we're Republicans!" she would scream. "That's why he ain't playing!" People like this lady would never be happy with David, no matter what decision he made.

The fact of the matter was, David needed the extra income from coaching. And he was still chairman of the powerful Appropriations Committee. The smaller work load allowed him to devote even more energy to pet issues like education, infant mortality, and social services.

In his first two years at Mt. Airy, David Diamont went 6-5 and 9-3. All the while, he continued his breakneck pace in the General Assembly. David used a pragmatic liberalism to reach a consensus in a tight budget year. The work was challenging but greatly rewarding.

Then everything came crashing to a halt.

David had just left the Executive Mansion after a meeting with Governor Jim Hunt when he noticed a pain in his chest. A week later, tests revealed that four of David's coronary arteries were blocked, and one of the arteries was 99 percent clogged. It wasn't supposed to happen this way. He didn't smoke. He didn't drink. He'd put on some weight over the years, but he took care of himself better than most of his legislative colleagues. Whatever the reason, David found himself on the operating table three days later for quadruple bypass surgery.

David was scared. What would happen to his family if he died? Who would be in charge of his funeral? If he survived, could he ever maintain a normal life again?

Luckily, the surgery was a success. Life could finally go back to normal. David returned to Raleigh for the final weeks of the legislative session, and he began a strict eating and exercise regimen. But a routine checkup revealed that two of the four arteries had already clogged again. Less than three months after the bypass surgery, David was back in the hospital again for an angioplasty to clear up the blockages.

In the operating room, a nurse asked David how old he was.

"Forty seven going on 83," he said before going under for the count.

After the second surgery, David's doctors gave him an ultimatum: he needed to choose between coaching and politics. After much deliberation, David collected his meager belongings from the one-room apartment in Raleigh and moved back to Pilot Mountain for good.


David Diamont sat alone in his living room. He was depressed. In all of his years as a coach, no loss had felt as bad as this one.

Two years had passed since David's decision to leave the House of Representatives. He'd been encouraged by the state teachers' union and other powerful figures in Raleigh to run for the office of State Superintendent of Education. With his experience as both a public school teacher and a state budget lawmaker, he was a natural choice. The only question was his health.

David had lost 25 pounds since the surgery, and he felt better than ever. He was hungry to get back into politics, too. After another year as the head coach at Mt. Airy, David left coaching yet again. With the approval of his wife and kids, David took a leap of faith and entered the race for superintendent.

Before he did anything else, David set up a meeting with Governor Hunt. Diamont knew that he could not win the election without the backing of Jim Hunt, who had become one of the most powerful governors in North Carolina history. Over the course of a 45-minute conversation, Governor Hunt assured David that his people would remain neutral during the Democratic primary. David took Governor Hunt at his word and officially announced his candidacy against Mike Ward, a former superintendent from Granville County.

David threw himself headlong into the campaign. He took a three month leave from his teaching position at Mt. Airy and drove his 1987 Aerostar van across the entire state. It was a grueling journey filled with late nights in banquet halls and hotels, shaking thousands upon thousands of hands and asking for donations from people he'd never even met before. All the while, it became apparent that Governor Hunt had made his decision in the race. At every campaign stop, David's heart sank as he noticed the Hunt supporters beating the stump for the other candidate. David was drowning, and he knew it.

Mike Ward won the Democratic primary in a landslide.

As I listened to David tell this story in the coaches' office, I could still detect the bitterness of that election.

"I was put out on a limb and got sawed off behind me," he said. "That's the way Jim Hunt operated. He helped himself, and he didn't leave any fingerprints. A couple of people told me to watch out, but it was too late. I should have known better."

David licked the wounds from his defeat and returned to Mt. Airy High School. He was chairman of the history department, the civics team, the prom committee, anything to relieve the pain of his most recent failure. But without coaching, nothing seemed to work.

When a job opened at Pilot Mountain Middle School, David jumped at the chance for a fresh start. It would be a fitting tribute to his father, who spent his final years at the school before his fatal heart attack. Like his father before him, David would get to teach North Carolina history, and the pressure, well, there wouldn't *be* any pressure to win.

David loved his new job. He could forget about the election and put all of his energy back into coaching and teaching. Some bitterness would always remain below the surface, because coaches never forget a slight. But life was too rich to dwell on the past. David's health was better than it had been in years, and his wife and three kids meant more to him than anything else in the world.

His life had a purpose. What more could he ever hope for?


A few days before my visit to Pilot Mountain, David Diamont summoned two freshmen football players into his office. He'd spotted the boys smoking a cigarette one day after practice, and it was time for them to learn a little lesson.

"Get in here, right now," Coach Diamont barked to the two freshmen.

Their eyes grew wide as they noticed a group of seniors glaring back at them with arms crossed and muscles bulging. There were two chairs in the middle of the room. Coach Diamont had placed a football in one and the two cigarette butts in the other.

David stood before the shame-faced freshmen and let an uncomfortable silence fill the room.

"Make a choice, boys. Either play ball or smoke. You can't do both."

The seniors didn't have to say anything. Their presence was enough to scare the living daylights out of the two boys below them. Both freshmen nodded and shuffled out of the office with their heads bowed.


Eight years had passed since David Diamont returned to coach the football team at East Surry. He shook his head whenever he thought back to that day in 1977 when he first walked into the East Surry field house to find a dusty floor and little else. But certain things remained the same. Teenagers still wanted to be part of something larger than themselves, despite the long hair, Afros, bell-bottoms, gold necklaces, and other cultural shifts through the years.

But it was a constant struggle, David said to me later in the week.

"If they're in love, if they're on drugs, or if they want a car, those are the three things you battle more than anything else. You can't win sometimes."

I wondered if the strain of 38 years had caused David Diamont to lose his passion for teaching and coaching. He could have retired eight years ago, playing golf all day and taking long afternoon walks through the rolling countryside. Instead, he spent his summers sweating in the afternoon sun and hoping that his heart was strong enough to last a few more years. He truly was his father's son. What would he do without work and without a purpose to guide his daily life? So many adults seemed to quicken the pace towards death as soon as they retired. But David didn't want that to happen. There was still so much to be done. A new crop of kids needed help in school and on the field. And for a community reeling from hundreds of job cuts, high school football was a shining light in a very dark time.

"I don't have a single D-1 prospect in sight on my team," David said as we walked from the field house to the football stadium. "We take what we've got, work our tails off, and make something with it. That's the fun and the challenge."

Weeds had sprouted across the visiting stands, and the concrete was crumbling along multiple rows. In the upcoming weeks, a group of parents would paint and reseal the stands. It was a yearly ritual, just one way to repay the football program for giving so much to Pilot Mountain through the years.

David admired the new press box and surveyed the land that had been his home for so many years.

"Football can be such a positive influence in a community, especially in these smaller communities. A good football program starts the school year right. It makes everybody feel good about themselves. I've got 70-80 kids that will go to school their first day, and they're gonna know each other. They're gonna smile. They're gonna feel good about themselves. And they're gonna feel good about their school."

As I drove down Main Street past The Squeeze Box, I decided to make one final detour before heading home to Durham. I've always loved the open road. There's something magical about a place that is hidden from the outside world, somewhere off the beaten path, forgotten by many and unknown to everyone else.

When I was eighteen, my younger brother and I took a cross country road trip to Alaska. As we ventured farther and farther away from civilization, we'd find a side road that looked appealing and just drive off into the unknown. Sometimes we'd see something interesting, and sometimes we wouldn't. The freedom to choose was what mattered. My journey across North Carolina has been full of such surprises. With every road trip, I discover an expansive world that would take a lifetime to explore.

I drove northward to Mt. Airy, where David Diamont got his start as a teacher and coach so many years ago. Mt. Airy looks like a larger version of Pilot Mountain, with quaint downtown streets filled with antique stores and soda shops. I understood how this place could inspire Andy Griffith to create the fictional world of Mayberry. From the highest point along Main Street, I could see the Blue Ridge Mountains twenty miles away in southern Virginia. The cobalt-colored hills blended seamlessly into the clear blue sky.

From Mt. Airy, I ventured south to Elkin. The town is closer in size to Pilot Mountain, with a sleepy Main Street and a steep terrain dotted with factories, railroad tracks, and stately homes high above the brick storefronts. Elkin High School sits on a ridge looking out over the distant mountains. Several tiers below the school, I found the football stadium nestled in the woods along the Ararat River. A life-size bronze statue of an Elk stands at the entrance to the stadium, facing the football field with antlers and eyes pointing to the heavens. Puffs of white clouds dotted the sky above Elkin and reflected the setting sun.

It was time for me to go home.

I got back in my car and took one last look at the bronze Elk statue before heading east on NC-268. The winding, two-lane road crosses the Ararat River and curves around pastures and forests for miles. I rolled the windows down and felt the warm summer breeze. The scent of earth and cattle and freshly cut grass came to me at every bend. Ancient farmhouses stood solitary at the end of long, gravel roads. I stopped several times along side streets that seemed to call to me for no obvious reason. After thirty minutes of driving, I saw the imposing peak of Pilot Mountain in the distance; shade blanketed the bald man's granite head. I let the ridge guide me homeward.

David Diamont knew every bend in this road. For more than three decades, he's driven busloads of young men down NC-268 to battle the Buckin' Elks. This year, both of his sons will play for him. He'll see them staring at the surrounding countryside with their minds focused on the upcoming game. It will make David proud. Diamont football has reached its third generation, but Davey and Hunter are only two of David's forty children this time of year.

I wonder what will happen to communities like Pilot Mountain in the future. Will they survive the plant closings and the stagnant economy? Will they maintain their unique identities in a world dominated by urban sprawl? Is the Mayberry mystique a Hollywood creation and nothing more?

I don't have many answers. Perhaps I never will. But I return again and again to the thousands of young people who have learned from men such as David Diamont.

And then I look to myself. What if I was to last 38 years as an English teacher and a football coach? How much good could I accomplish in my time on earth? How many kids could I rescue from heartache and despondency?

There is no formula for a life filled with passion and purpose, and each of us must make our own way in the world. But we all share the same dreams. On that rarest of moments, a voice will rise above the chaos to remind us of all that we have in common. The voice doesn't have to be a football coach, for sports are nothing more than a metaphor for society. But someone has to step forward.

An activity bus plods along NC-268 as dusk settles over Surry County and the rest of the East coast. An hour later, thousands of headlights will dot the back roads and highways of America to support the communities they love.

I often wish that the whole world could be like a Friday night in autumn.

# 5

# Castles on a Hill
## Asheville

On an early Saturday morning, I sat next to a ridge overlooking Asheville Memorial Stadium and the Smoky Mountains in the distance. The Asheville football field below me was bathed in warm light, with Cougar paws and a deep red "A" painted on the fifty yard line. The home stands faced the main school building on a steep slope. I was struck by the classic design of the campus. Its granite walls came from a long-ago era, a time when towns viewed the physical plant of their school as a beacon for all that was good in a community.

Danny Wilkins, the head football coach at Asheville High School, wouldn't be here for another fifteen minutes, so I enjoyed the gentle breeze and the clear blue skies from my shaded spot beneath a maple tree.

The Smoky Mountains around Asheville have always been a part of me. When my grandmother, Nan McKinnon, was a young girl living in the sweltering heat of Hartsville, South Carolina, her father used the proceeds from his general store to buy a plot of land about fifteen miles east of Asheville. She spent every summer amid the rhododendron shade and subtle beauty of these hills. Nanny loved to climb nearby Lookout Mountain and wait at the trestle path for the next train weaving its way along the ridges to Mount Mitchell and further points to the west. She placed her ears to the ground and listened for the muffled vibrations to increase. Then she dashed to higher ground and crouched with anticipation. As the box cars rumbled by, she jumped onto the train for a breathtaking ride through hidden coves and stunning views all the way to Asheville.

Nanny used to guide me along this trestle path when I was a young boy. All that remained was a flat swath of land halfway up Lookout Mountain, but it was easy to imagine those carefree days before the Depression when anything seemed possible. My brother and I would climb above the abandoned path and daydream about journeys into the green wilderness beyond.

The ancient architecture of the Smoky Mountains has always left me with a renewed sense of the natural world's majesty. But it is a majesty tempered by urban sprawl, air pollution, and rapidly evolving industries. As I grow older, I sometimes wonder if cynicism will overtake the childlike joy I take from this scenery.

Before long, Coach Wilkins arrived in a pick-up truck and parked beside my car.

"Hey Coach," he said as he stepped out to shake my hand.

Coach Wilkins had a medium build, with graying hair and glasses that made him look more like a scholar than a football coach.

"I've been having trouble with a kidney stone," Coach Wilkins said as he led me to an office next to the basketball gym.

"Sorry, Coach. We can keep this short if you'd like."

"No, no. The doctor's got me doped up on so much medicine I can hardly feel a thing." He started to smile. "But if I start squirming, you'll know why."

Coach Wilkins sat down with his arms crossed casually.

"Coach," I said, "just so you know, I'm an Ashbrook grad."

"I'm still not over that game," he said as his mood seemed to cloud for a moment. "I don't know if I'll ever get over that one."

Several years ago, my alma mater defeated Asheville in a memorable game to advance to the 3A State Championship. Asheville led in the fourth quarter by a score of 16-3, but Ashbrook stormed back for a 22-19 victory.

Coach Wilkins proceeded to narrate the final moments of the Ashbrook game in vivid detail. Like most coaches, he had an uncanny ability to remember ever play down to the exact time and distance. There were two questionable interference calls against his star defensive back. Then there was the botched exchange between a reliable fullback and quarterback that gave Ashbrook a final chance to tie the score. Ashbrook's star running back, Oreon Mayfield, ran to the right as time expired, and four Asheville defenders tackled him at the three yard line – but somehow Mayfield bounced off of the pile and ran the opposite way for the deciding score. It was an unbelievable finish to the game and a bitter end to Asheville's season.

The Ashbrook game was just the first of several heartbreaking losses for Coach Wilkins in the coming years. But he refused to let it define him. A coach's road to success is always unpredictable, he would say. Nothing worth fighting for is ever easy.

When Danny Wilkins moved to Asheville with his family, he probably didn't know that he was standing in the crosshairs of history. It was the summer of 1970, and the South was a powder keg waiting to explode. The politics of integration had taken the country by storm. Danny may have seen the horrific images of National Guard picket lines and racist agitators in places like Little Rock, Arkansas. In a few years, perhaps he would watch the television footage of neighborhood kids in South Boston throwing rocks at school buses full of African America students. But the enclosed world of the mountains likely served as a protective shield from many of these conflicts.

At the time, Danny's concerns were probably no different from any boy in the eighth grade. He was an outsider anxious to make friends in his new hometown. He also had to get ready for football tryouts. Danny was a voracious reader, and he'd devoured every book in the local library about high school football. The stories often revolved around a similar theme. The star quarterback sits in the huddle with the game on the line. His coach shouts instructions to him and waits tensely for the final outcome. The ball is snapped, the final horn blows, the climax builds to a crescendo...Danny couldn't get enough of the drama and excitement of it all.

By the end of his freshman year at Enka High School, Danny knew he wanted to be a coach. During one of the final days before summer break, Danny knocked on the door of his football coach, Bob McClellan. Danny was only 14 at the time, and as his small frame fell into a chair beside his coach, he couldn't help but feel nervous. He admired Coach McClellan greatly. Bob McClellan was an extremely organized man. He had integrity and honesty, and Danny wanted to be just like him.

"Coach McClellan?" Danny asked, "How do you get to do this for a living?"

"What's that, Danny?"

"Work with people the way you do."

It was an innocent question, and Coach McClellan gave a simple answer: Go to college and get a degree. Work your way up as an assistant. Eventually, your time will come.

From that moment on, Danny's career was set.

The whole scenario could have come directly from one of Danny's sports books. He married his high school sweetheart, and after six years as an assistant in Georgia, he got his first head coaching job at Erwin High School.

Both Erwin and Enka were part of the Buncombe County school system in Western North Carolina, and by and large, the county schools were minimally affected by integration. But the Asheville city system was an entirely different matter.

As the Wilkins family pulled into their new home on that summer day in 1970, Danny couldn't have known about the anger brewing several miles down the road. A bitter fight was being waged on the battlefields of race and community. Tensions were at an all-time high. The very identity of the city was at stake.

One man witnessed every stage of this drama. He stood on the front lines with a stubborn will and an open heart. It would take more than a decade for Danny Wilkins and this man to meet, but their histories were already entwined.

Gene Hammonds could hear the rumors all around him. He was teaching a physical education class in one of the ancient gymnasiums behind Asheville High School. The boys' and girls' gyms were stacked one on top of the other, and they retained a classically worn look from over fifty years of constant use.

Emotions had been running high throughout September, and Coach Hammonds knew that Asheville's black students had planned a walkout earlier that morning. He could hear them whispering in tense groups.

*"They had their arms locked in a straight line in front of the school..."*

*"What happened when the police broke the line?..."*

*"I didn't see anything..."*

*"Somebody said a cop pulled out a club and hit one of them upside the head..."*

*"Naw, he just threatened to. He didn't do it..."*

*"Are you sure?..."*

*"I don't know."*

As a young boy, Gene Hammonds never could have predicted that he would be teaching at the newly integrated Asheville High School. This stately granite school along a steep rise of McDowell Street had been the pride of white Asheville since it was built in 1929. It had a sterling academic reputation. And no school from Murphy to Manteo could match the beauty of its impressive exterior. The Romantic/Art Deco structure consisted of three equal wings pivoting away from the center. Its walls were made of the finest granite slabs from the nearby Smoky Mountains, and its high arching windows provided views of more than fifty acres of meadows and woodlands in every direction.

When the school's beloved principal, Lee Edwards, died unexpectedly in 1935, Asheville High School was renamed in his honor. A few years went by before the most famous son to grace the halls of Lee Edwards High School arrived. His name was Charlie Justice. Charlie wasn't allowed to play football because of a heart murmur, but he wouldn't let that get in his way. His older brother forged a consent form to make him eligible, and after breaking every major high school record in the state, Justice became a local legend. In 1946, as a freshman at UNC, Charlie became "Choo Choo" Justice and staked his claim as the most famous football player to ever wear Carolina blue.

With the onset of integration in 1969, the Asheville city school board voted to change the name from Lee Edwards back to Asheville High School. It was the first of several deliberate changes meant to ease the tensions of consolidation. But as with most cities across the South, much of the character of Lee Edwards remained, while the identity of Asheville's all-black high school fell to the wayside.

The walkout on that September morning was a direct response to these complaints. No one knew exactly what happened, but an altercation between police officers and protesting students led to a city-wide state of emergency and a nighttime curfew throughout Asheville. Tensions simmered precariously for months at a time before erupting again and again. The following autumn, a series of fights broke out between black and white gangs at an AHS football game at Memorial Stadium. Three youths were arrested for assaulting a middle school coach the same night. Later that week, a 23 year old black man was stabbed during a game between neighboring Owen and Reynolds high schools. The conflicts involved both young and old, while the students actually attending these newly integrated high schools often restrained themselves more than anyone else.

Gene Hammonds was proud to be a part of the first integrated staff at Asheville High School. Finally, minority students would have access to opportunities that had passed them by for so many years. But mixed in with this excitement was a lingering sense of loss.

The merger with Lee Edwards High School brought an end to the epicenter of black pride in Asheville. Stephens-Lee High School stood empty and condemned on a hill overlooking the downtown courthouse, waiting for a wrecking ball to wipe clean the visible reminders of its illustrious past. Gene Hammonds was an integral part of this legacy. As he watched the winds of change unfold in the early 1970s, he must have longed for the deep sense of community that Stephens-Lee fostered in his teenage years. But community building does not happen overnight. It is a product of time and history. Community building requires teachers and coaches who are willing to be surrogate parents for hundreds upon thousands of impressionable students. As the years go by, these adults become as much of an institution as the aging mortar and brick of a school.

Gene Hammonds was ready for such a challenge. He used the lessons of his own past to help a new community grow out of so much uncertainty and distrust. Coach Hammonds never forgot how far he'd come, and he always remembered those days as a star athlete and student at the "Castle on the Hill." No wrecking ball could remove this place from his heart.

It was the greatest tragedy to ever strike the Asheville schools. From the tumble-down shacks and muddy roads along Catholic Hill Avenue, neighbors could see smoke billowing out of the building, the first and only public school ever built for blacks in the city. A fire had started just moments before in the school's furnace room. Smoke poured through the central stairway, and teachers worked desperately to save as many of the 300 students as possible. Students leapt from third floor classrooms to keep from burning alive. When the flames finally turned to ash, seven students were dead, and several others were seriously injured.

The year was 1917, more than three decades since Isaac Dickson, the son of a former slave, had been appointed to the Asheville school board. The arrival of railroads in 1881 brought a tide of black workers from cities all across North Carolina and Tennessee. Dickson worked tirelessly to build new schools for this influx of black children. He helped found Catholic Hill School with a staff of three teachers and 300 pupils. Over 800 students were turned away.

From the ashes of the tragic fire of 1917 rose Stephens-Lee High School. Walter Smith Lee was the school's namesake and its first principal. Educated at Livingston College and Columbia University, Lee firmly believed in a curriculum founded on self-help, dignity, and a healthy dose of Shakespeare. The school's other namesake was Edward Stephens, a native of the West Indies and a graduate of Cambridge University in England. George Vanderbilt brought Stephens to Asheville to help build a community center for the hundreds of black laborers working on the Biltmore Estate. Stephens eventually created the Young Men's Institute, which became the heart and soul of Asheville's black community in the late 1880s. Like W.S. Lee, Edward Stephens quickly realized that the black residents of Asheville needed a public school to call their own.

The location for the new high school was obvious. A steep hill to the east of downtown Asheville had long ago been used as an "arbor school" for slaves. After the Civil War, the first school for freedmen was located there. When Stephens-Lee High School finally opened, its three floors of brick walls and high glass windows created a panoramic view across all of downtown Asheville. Several years later, the Works Progress Administration built an adjacent gymnasium that rivaled the facilities of the all-white Lee Edwards High School. Forests of deep green trees blanketed the school from above and below. It was an impressive sight, to say the least, a bit of royalty compared to the degrading conditions of the past. Thus, Stephens-Lee came to be known as the Castle on the Hill.

For decades, Stephens-Lee was the largest black high school in Western North Carolina. The school was a source of pride for citizens who were often denied access to most public facilities. Church and civic groups met there. The school was also a center for adult education, daycare, entertainment, and library use. When the only black school in Yancey County burned to the ground, its students made the four-hour trip to Stephens-Lee every day, riding in cramped and unheated buses. Black mountaineers from every cove and hilltop of Western North Carolina thought of the school with pride.

On an early spring morning, Eugene Hammonds pulls his wool sports coat closer to his body as he fights off the chill. By the time he leaves his Southside home, the sun has just begun to rise above the rooftops. He climbs the steep steps to the Castle on the Hill with the ease of a well-conditioned athlete.

Eugene is still glowing from the recent letter he got in the mail, and he finds it hard to focus on the world around him.

*What's Raleigh going to be like?* he wonders to himself.

Shaw University has just offered Eugene a full scholarship to play football and baseball. It's a dream come true, but he is frightened as well.

Other students interrupt his thoughts as he walks down the first floor hallway.

"Hey Eugene! Great job in the baseball game on Friday."

He gives an embarrassed smile and a wave.

"Congrats on the news from Shaw, Eugene!"

Many of his classmates are dressed just like him, layering a dark sports coat above a plaid or white button-down shirt. Others wear dark gray sweaters with a maroon, varsity letter "S" emblazoned across the chest. Girls swish by in full-length dresses and black heels, their hair delicately coiffed in the latest fashions of the mid-1950s.

Eugene's eyes happen upon a framed copy of the school alma mater on a nearby wall. The words are so familiar that he can say them in his sleep:

*O Stephens-Lee, dear Stephens-Lee*
*Our hearts are filled with love for thee;*
*A champion brave, thy youth to save*
*Thy children honor thee.*
*Home of truth we do believe,*
*Noble Deeds thou wilt achieve;*
*In sun or rain we shall remain*
*Faithful thee, dear Stephens-Lee*

*O Stephens-Lee, dear Stephens-Lee*

*Our hearts are filled with pride in thee;*
*A warrior bold – the right uphold –*
*Alma Mater, dear*
*When upon life's rugged sea*
*Oft our thoughts will turn to thee;*
*From day to day crimson and gray*
*Praise we Stephens-Lee.*

Eugene smiles to himself. Life has already been rugged enough. Could it possibly be any more difficult in Raleigh?

He stops by Miss Toliver's classroom to drop off an article for the school yearbook. Eugene is the sports editor; as a standout athlete in football, baseball, and basketball, the articles come to him almost effortlessly.

Five more minutes until the school day begins.

Several rooms down, Mr. Cowan puts the final touches on a chemistry lab. Eugene waves to Mr. Cowan and continues down the hall, where he catches the aroma of food before he even hears the rattling of stainless steel pans in the lunchroom. Excited voices rise above the clatter in the distance as Eugene arrives at his final destination. Before he even walks through the door, Eugene knows that Coach Moore is the source of the laughter.

This classroom feels like home.


If it wasn't for C.L. "Prof" Moore, Eugene Hammonds probably would have dropped out of school. The options for a young African-American man in 1955 were limited at best. Adults could talk all day about the value of a high school degree, but where did it really get you? What jobs could a man find besides working as an orderly at the VA hospital or doing back-breaking labor down at the railroad yards? Segregation would never allow a black man to rise above the glass ceiling of racism. That's just the way life goes, Eugene was told time and time again.

But when Eugene entered high school, "Prof" Moore opened his eyes to a world of unimaginable possibilities. Coach Moore sensed a burning competitiveness in Eugene, and he used athletics to reel the young man in.

"Clarence Moore was like a father to me," Gene Hammonds said to me on a recent Sunday morning.

Coach Hammonds was initially reluctant to do an interview. He wasn't very good at these kinds of things, he told me. But when I mentioned Stephens-Lee, his memories poured out faster than I could write them down.

"You see, at that time I had nothing to hold on to. Athletics was my initial motivation to stay eligible in school. But then the automatic pilot kicks in after a few years, and all the negativity you once had just goes to the wayside. You fall in love with the next level, and you never want to turn back."

For almost four decades, Prof Moore made this kind of impact on the young men of Stephens-Lee. He was once an outstanding athlete himself, playing semi-pro baseball in high school before enrolling at Shaw University to play football, baseball, and basketball. He coached all three of these sports at Stephens-Lee, winning a football state championship in 1957 and a basketball state championship in 1962.

Prof Moore was a sharply dressed man with piercing eyes that could appear loving and intimidating in equal measure. In the team picture for Stephens-Lee's first football squad of 1936, Coach Moore stands on the balls of his feet with his chest puffed out and his arms tucked behind his back, as if to appear larger than life. Albert Manly, the school's principal, stands in the picture as well. His hair is slicked back stylishly, and he's wearing a full-length business coat above a three-piece suit. The team looks wary and serious. Some of the players could pass for young boys directly out of grade school; others look even older than their coach and principal. There is an edge to many of their faces, a precariousness that Prof Moore must channel from anger to aggressiveness on the football field.

The picture serves as a fitting symbol. On one side is Coach Moore, who saw athletic competition as a bridge to the academic world. On the other side is Albert Manly, living proof that academic success knows no bounds. Manly would eventually earn his Ph.D. at Stanford University and become the president of Spellman College in Atlanta, one of the most prestigious institutions for African American students in the country. If Principal Manly could do it, why couldn't everyone else? And if Coach Moore spoke of a world beyond the slums and ramshackle homes of black Asheville, then perhaps that world really existed.

By the time Eugene came to Stephens-Lee, Coach Moore was an established institution. Eugene had lived his entire life in Asheville, but football opened a whole new world to him. The Bears played games in such far-away cities as Chattanooga, Gastonia, Winston-Salem, and Augusta, Georgia. On an overnight trip to play Dudley High School in Greensboro, Eugene saw a college campus for the first time. He began to imagine the very real possibility of attending a place like this, with elegant lawns and hordes of serious-minded students bustling from place to place.

What once was an impossible dream became a reality for Eugene Hammonds. He was an all-conference performer in both football and baseball at Shaw University before returning to his roots in the Blue Ridge Mountains. After coaching at two segregated schools, 9th Avenue High School in Hendersonville and the newly built South French Broad High School in Asheville, Gene Hammonds arrived at the other castle high up on a hill during the first year of integration. In a region with few minority coaches, Gene Hammonds was the head baseball coach and an assistant football coach at the formerly all-white Asheville High School for 35 years. He turned down the head football job in 1974, and ten years later he served as interim head coach for part of a season. But he never aspired to be anything more than an assistant. When Hammonds retired from teaching and coaching baseball in 2006 (after sending eleven players to the Major Leagues) he decided to stay on as the running backs coach under Danny Wilkins. The two men have worked together for the past 14 years.

According to Coach Wilkins, Gene Hammonds has taken on the role of icon in the Asheville community.

"He's been here for decades. Forty-four years of teaching and coaching experience. He's seen it all. Just a great person, loves kids, and has just been a tremendous asset to the school and program over the years. I begged him when he retired to stay on and help us with football, and I'm glad he has."

After a half-century in sports, Gene Hammonds can finally step back and see the impact of high school football on his own life and the lives of so many of his players. He doesn't regret becoming a teacher, and working with teenagers keeps him active and healthy. He doesn't have the time or the inclination to think about getting older.

"You get hooked in with two or three new guys each year," he told me, "and it keeps you young in mind. If you're not around kids, sometimes people forget how to live a full life."

The Asheville of today is a very different place from those tension-filled months in 1970. Danny Wilkins is no longer a slightly built boy of 14, and Gene Hammonds now carries the legacy of Prof Moore on his shoulders. Over the past four decades, public education has made an imperfect arc of progress and regression and then tentative progress again in the city.

William Faulkner once wrote that "The past is never dead; it's not even past." We cannot avoid the weight of history, and we learn from those who are central to our sense of place. Prof Moore is an immovable rock. Gene Hammonds is also a rock. Danny Wilkins has become a permanent fixture. These coaches are as imperfect as the rest of us, but much of their transcendent power comes from a stubborn desire to stay in one place. Communities do not simply regenerate year after year, and without constant nurturing, they can crumble at a surprising rate. Winning certainly helps. But for men like Danny Wilkins and Eugene Hammonds, the character of an individual is measured by both victories and crushing defeats. Ever since the cold night of that heartbreaking loss to Ashbrook, the AHS Cougars have understood this better than anyone.

Danny Wilkins was at the pinnacle of his coaching career, but he sure didn't feel like it this evening. The Friday night lights no longer lit up the Cougar stadium. Trash covered the grandstands on either side. In the morning, Coach Wilkins would begin the process of putting everything back in order.

Perhaps he'd watch the tape of tonight's game against Ashbrook, but probably not. The wound was still too raw.

No one could have imagined this moment ten years ago. In 1992, Danny Wilkins resigned as the head coach of Erwin High School after a dreadful 0-10 season. His four year record at Erwin was 5-34-1. The athletic program was already declining when he took over at Erwin, and everyone agreed that Erwin didn't have the athletes to compete with the bigger schools in Buncombe County. Coach Wilkins ran a clean program. His players were disciplined, and they went on to become productive members of society after graduation. But moral victories are a tough sell for a community.

Lou Fogle, the head football coach and athletic director at Asheville High School, gave Danny Wilkins a second chance as his assistant coach. It was a fresh start, and Coach Wilkins made the most of it. He worked his way up to defensive coordinator. He impressed Coach Fogle with his work ethic and commitment to academics. When Coach Fogle retired, he selected Wilkins to be the new head coach from a list of 12 other candidates. Not everyone was happy with the decision; after all, there was that four year albatross of a record to contend with. If he couldn't win at Erwin, how was he going to win here?

Lou Fogle was quickly vindicated. Going into the state semifinal game against Ashbrook, Danny Wilkins had compiled a 25-11 record as the Cougars head coach. More importantly, his players respected him, and his coaching staff was a close-knit group that put a premium on trust.

But none of that mattered at the moment. As Coach Wilkins drove home through the empty streets of Asheville, he replayed the final five minutes of the Ashbrook game in his head. It all seemed so impossible, as if the Good Lord just didn't want the Cougars to win. He had no choice but to leave the loss in the hands of a higher power. Otherwise, the pain would be debilitating.

Instead, Coach Wilkins turned his thoughts to next season. There was a good crop of kids coming back. And football was still the greatest sport in the world. Nothing compared to the anticipation of a Friday night rivalry or the afterglow of a decisive victory, that special moment when a group of individuals suddenly became a team. He tried to focus on the positives. But deep down, the disappointment of tonight's game was hard to shake off.

Fast forward one year. Asheville has won thirteen straight games since the heartbreaking loss to Ashbrook. Tonight they face South Point, yet another Gaston County team that, unlike Ashbrook, plays an old school style of Wing-T football. AHS matches up well with the Red Raiders. The Cougars have manhandled their three playoff opponents thus far, and tonight seems like a perfect opportunity to exorcise the demons from last year.

An hour before kickoff, Coach Wilkins leads his team onto the field for pre-game warm-ups. It is another bitterly cold evening, yet thousands of supporters from the tiny mill town of Belmont have already staked out their seats along the visitor's stands. The home side is filling up as well; fans have begun the trademark call and response that is as much a part of Asheville games as the smell of hotdogs and hot cocoa.

"Couuugars!" one fan begins.

"Couuuuuuuugars!" comes the answer in lingering response.

An occasional snow flurry descends upon the field as both teams finish their warm-ups early and head back to their locker rooms. Coach Wilkins is not big on rousing pre-game speeches, so this is a time for meditation instead. It is the biggest night in the lives of these young men. For some, the upcoming years will feel like a mere epilogue to this very moment. For others, the game will be a catalyst for many more achievements. The moment is different for everyone, but in a distinct way, they each share in its majesty. Away from the muffled cheers outside, a close-knit family sits together with eyes closed, hearts racing, and knees twitching with anticipation.

The clear voice of Coach Wilkins finally breaks the silence. It's game time. The old brick locker room erupts in nervous whoops and colliding shoulder pads. When the side door opens, the Cougars line up to march single file down the granite steps to the field. But there is a moment of hesitation at the door.

The sight is truly stunning. Snow is everywhere. In less than fifteen minutes, the whole world has become a winter wonderland. The ground is completely white, and the thick flakes fall faster and faster.

Gene Hammonds looks to the sky in awe. In half a century as a player and coach, he has never seen such a sight during a high school football game. The blizzard covers the stadium lights in a dull glow. Coach Hammonds spots a bird flying unsteadily above the field. The bird falters at the twenty yard line and falls from the sky, completely frozen from the unexpected weight of snow and ice.

The Cougars carefully make their way down the steps to the home side of the field, where they are greeted by a packed house of elated fans. A distant cry comes from the opposing sideline. South Point must have arrived as well, but the falling snow is so thick that no one can see much of anything across the field.

A crew tries to sweep the sidelines clear of snow, but it is a futile act. The markers are covered again within seconds.

The snow should work to the Cougars' advantage, but South Point knows how to play in sloppy field conditions. In the 3-A state semifinals last season, the Red Raiders lost to eventual state champion Winston-Salem Carver 27-6 on a field covered in more than three inches of mud. As the kickoff approaches, South Point quarterback Javar Williams stands confidently in the south end zone and bounces up and down with anticipation.

"Let it snow, let it snow, let it snow," he sings to his teammates as the snow falls all around him.

Asheville wins the coin toss and defers to the second half. On the Cougar sideline, Danny Wilkins prepares to watch his defense go to work. The Red Raiders get solid gains on the strength of several intricate plays that involve precise pitches between the quarterback, running back, and the two wing backs. The red bone offense worries Coach Wilkins. It relies on misdirection, and the snow can enhance or destroy its effectiveness.

Near midfield, or what would be midfield if the line markers were visible, Javar Williams fakes a dive to his fullback and lets the ball fly on a hot pass to his slot receiver. On the Cougar sideline, Coach Wilkins watches the release, but the ball soon gets lost in the falling snow. He knows it's a touchdown when he hears the fog horns and ecstatic cheers from the visiting stands.

This is the first of many touchdowns for the surprisingly potent South Point offense. The game quickly turns into a rout as the Red Raiders reach the end zone on 9 of their 11 possessions. Final score: South Point 57, Asheville 10.

As Coach Wilkins huddles his dejected team near midfield, reality begins to set in for the seniors. Tears of frustration blend with the sniffles of at least nine exhausted players who have battled a flu bug all week. But they hold their heads high; South Point was simply a better team tonight.

Most of the starters will be back for one final year. This doesn't feel like the Ashbrook game, where victory was so incredibly close. Things couldn't get that bad again; it just wouldn't be fair.

After three straight years, a trip to the state semifinals seems almost inevitable for Asheville High School. This time around the Cougars travel to Concord to face the Spiders and their legendary coach, E.Z. Smith. Concord is lucky to be here. Last week, they defeated Carver on a Hail Mary touchdown pass at the end of the game. Justice will be served tonight.

The Cougars dominate Concord on both sides of the ball, much as South Point did the previous year. With 5:43 left to play in the fourth quarter, star running back Johnny White scores from one yard out to give the Cougars a seemingly insurmountable 20-0 lead over Concord. But Asheville grows conservative, and the lead quickly vanishes. Spider quarterback Tommy Beecher completes a remarkable 10-of-13 passes for 221 yards in the final moments of the fourth quarter, including a seven yard score to tie the game with six seconds remaining.

In a world structured around fairness, the extra point sails wide right. The Cougars heave a sigh of relief and then trounce the Spiders in overtime. After all, no team deserves to bear the weight of such heartbreak three years in a row.

But the beauty of football lies in its objectivity. There are no charitable gifts, no moral victories on the field, no preference for color, class, or creed.

The kick does not sail wide right. For a third straight year, the Cougars go home empty-handed.

"I didn't believe it could get any worse than Ashbrook," senior receiver Evan Pappas says after the game. "But it can. This is just awful, unbelievable that we lost this game."

Veteran *Asheville Citizen-Times* reporter Keith Jarrett approaches Danny Wilkins for a comment. The coach is almost always cordial and friendly with reporters. But for several minutes, he can't bring himself to speak as he paces the field with a bowed head.

"I'm killed," he finally says. "This is awful, just devastating to these kids that played so hard."

It's the kind of moment that can destroy a football program. Players begin to question the value of unselfish play and teamwork when the only thing hard work leads to is bitter disappointment. Almost every team faces this dilemma. Thousands of athletes participate in sports each year, but only a handful will ever finish their season on the high note of victory.

Most of Danny Wilkins's starters are seniors. Sure, he has Crezdon Butler returning on defense and Johnny White at running back, but everything else is unknown. Clearly, Concord has erased the Cougars' best chance at a state championship.

It all seems to be downhill from here.


After the semifinal losses to Ashbrook, South Point, and Concord, Coach Wilkins began to wonder if his team could weather the storm of these disappointments.

"There's a lot of people in this community that know and appreciate what we're trying to do," Coach Wilkins said to me. "But there's always that small group of critics; some of them don't even have a kid in the program.

You do a little research and find out they might have played their freshman year and dropped out of the program; now all of a sudden they're experts. When you're winning 12-13 games a year, there's not a whole lot they can say, but they try to anyway."

All of that criticism came to a halt after the unbelievable 2005 season.

On another bright Saturday, this time in December, in front of thousands of fans decked in red and black, Danny Wilkins paces the sideline at Duke's Wallace Wade Stadium. Wilkins still can't believe he is coaching in the 3-A state championship game. This was supposed to be a rebuilding year for the Cougars, a time to lick the wounds of the Concord heartbreak and to come back swinging in a few years. But so much for precedent.

Western Alamance, under the direction of head coach Hal Capps, has stymied the potent Cougar offense all day long. Star running back Johnny White continues to battle through an ankle injury, but he is clearly not up to his usual magic. Nothing else seems to be working. With less than six minutes remaining in the game, Western Alamance leads by a score of 10-7.

After a Western Alamance punt, the Cougars take over on offense deep in their own territory. It's gut check time, and Danny Wilkins has been saving just the right play for this moment. The play is a gamble, perhaps, or maybe an act of desperation. But what other choice does he have?

Crezdon Butler rolls to his right on first down and gets sacked for a loss at the Cougar 30 yard line. It's now or never.

As the Western Alamance defense celebrates the sack, Coach Wilkins inserts Rahkeem Morgan into the huddle. Morgan breaks the huddle early and runs to the sideline next to his coaches, but just in bounds. Crezdon Butler and the rest of the offense take Western Alamance off guard by sprinting to the line of scrimmage.

None of the defensive backs notice Rahkeem Morgan standing off to the side.

*Snap the ball, Crezdon!* Coach Wilkins whispers to himself. *Snap the ball before it's too late!*

Seventy yards later, Rahkeem Morgan sprints to the end zone for the go-ahead touchdown. Western Alamance has fallen for the sleeper play, one of the oldest tricks in sandlot football. Danny Wilkins has rolled the dice successfully in the biggest game of his coaching career.

On the next series, Crezdon Butler makes a dazzling one-handed interception of a Western Alamance pass. The Cougar faithful are going ballistic. There have been so many close calls over the past few years. Would disaster strike again?

All the Cougars have to do now is run out the clock, but Western Alamance is not about to go down without a fight. A short run by Johnny White on first down. Then another short gain. Coach Hammonds shouts words of encouragement to his running back. In over thirty-five years of coaching, he has never been this close to a state championship.

Western Alamance calls a final timeout to stop the clock.

When I asked Danny Wilkins to describe his proudest moment as a coach, his thoughts immediately turned to that timeout.

"I got in the huddle and I'm thinking of the Ashbrook game; it's always in the back of my mind. Johnny, who very seldom speaks on the field, said, 'Coach, give it to me. I promise you I'll get those three yards, just give it to me.'"

Coach Wilkins puts his faith in the limping senior running back. Johnny White takes the handoff on an isolation play away from the power back and pounds forward for five yards.

The offense takes a knee, and a jubilant throng of Asheville Cougars rush the field. Danny Wilkins and Eugene Hammonds embrace as they are lifted into the air by numerous players. It is a joyous, improbable, ecstatic moment, the culmination of so much hope and so many dreams.

On a typical September evening at Asheville's Memorial Stadium, the leaves surrounding the field are a deep green with an occasional spot of orange and gold. The sun has fallen behind the granite school; laughter comes from the field house.

Practice is over, but two players are rolling back and forth across the game field. One of them pauses to vomit; then he continues with his punishment. Neither one of these young men will ever be late to class again.

The dreaded forward rolls are hated by everyone on the team. Coach Wilkins uses them to eliminate low grades, tardies, or any negative behavior during the school day. Even after winning a state championship, the obstacles facing Wilkins and the rest of his coaching staff are considerable. In the Asheville city schools, athletes must maintain an 80 percent average in order to stay eligible. It is a daunting standard, and one of the strictest in the state.

"It's a challenge every year," Coach Wilkins said to me from his office. "Some kids don't get it. As hard as you work, as bad as you want it for them, sometimes they don't seem to want it for themselves. You've got frustrated parents and frustrated coaches and a kid that's going to do just enough to get by in the classroom, if that. It's a lot of headaches, but at the same time, I don't think you can give up on 'em. You keep pushing, keep pulling, and hope that someday they'll wake up.

"Every year I have kids come back and tell me, almost apologetically, 'I could have done so much better. I know I really put gray hair on your head. I wish I knew then what I know now.'"

Coach Wilkins often uses his love for books to tackle the problems facing his team. The habit goes back to his days as a child, when he would devour every book he could find about high school football. This past spring, Coach Wilkins gave each of his assistant coaches a copy of Jeffrey Marx's bestseller *A Season of Life*. The book tells the inspirational story of Joe Ehrmann, a high school football coach in Baltimore who teaches valuable lessons to his players about manhood, self-respect, and love. Coach Wilkins used the book as a starting point for deeper discussions about the moral responsibilities of coaching.

"We're in a challenging community. There's a lot of poverty, social issues, the gang thing seems to be ever increasing, and then there's the lack of motivation from kids who come from homes where no one's ever graduated from high school."

While many of the students at AHS are solidly middle class, an equal number live in housing projects scattered across the city. In the shadows of the old downtown stadium – where the all-black Stephens-Lee once played their home football games on Thursday nights, followed by the all-white Lee Edwards on Friday – sits the Mountainside projects. Many of the windows in these apartments are boarded up; the front yards are full of weeds and patches of dirt. The Lee Walker Heights complex is nearby as well, and the Pisgah View Apartments are next to the city's old race track. A significant number of the Cougar football players come from these three areas.

Race plays a definite role in the ongoing tensions between the Buncombe County Schools and the Asheville City Schools. In the mountains of North Carolina, African-Americans make up only five percent of the population. This distinction becomes even more evident when you compare the demographics of the six Buncombe County high schools (which are 9% black), with Asheville High School (which is 35% black.)

According to Coach Wilkins, these tensions sometimes get magnified on the gridiron.

"There are some built-in prejudices toward Asheville. A lot of people out in the surrounding counties are a little fearful coming over here for a football game on a Friday night just because of our minority population."

I told Coach Wilkins that we deal with a similar issue back home. Durham also has an image problem, partly due to the same urban crime that plagues most large cities, but also, on some unspoken level, because the dividing line in Durham between rich and poor, and black and white, is not sharply defined.

At Asheville High School, these fears usually dissipate when an opponent finally steps on the football field.

"I remind our players every week that we're not gonna put up with trash talking and taunting; we're not gonna call attention to ourselves. It's a team sport, and they've bought into that. I've got a group of kids that if you just turned them loose, it could get ugly. But we're adamant that we're gonna win with some humility.

"We've had lots of kids over the years that don't go home to a father. It's an aunt, it's a grandmother, it's a mother that's working 2-3 jobs. Our coaching staff really tries to build close relationships with our players."

A significant number of Danny Wilkins's assistants are also on staff at the school. Charlie Metcalf and Bill Van Cleve are highly regarded social studies teachers; David Burdette is a veteran math teacher. Rex Wells and Gene Hammonds have worked together in the physical education department with Coach Wilkins for over a decade. Such visibility in the building creates a valuable bridge between the teachers at Asheville High School and the football program.

According to Coach Wilkins and Coach Hammonds, football has turned hundreds of boys at AHS into productive young men.

Michael Hines is a fitting example. The athletic receiver and defensive back came to Asheville as a freshman "with sort of that hard attitude," according to Coach Wilkins. "When he left after his freshman year, we didn't know if he'd be back. He had a lot of distractions and issues. A lot of that was probably a cover-up for insecurities. But he left here so much more mature."

It takes patience on the part of a coaching staff to see behind the mask of a troubled player and to find the core potential underneath. After graduating from Asheville High School, Michael Hines became an all-conference receiver at Western Carolina, where he blossomed academically.

Several of the stars from Asheville's state championship squad have also become successful college students. Crezdon Butler is a starting defensive back at Clemson, while Johnny White is a running back for UNC. Both of these young men serve as official tour guides for Danny Wilkins and the rest of the Cougars when the team travels en masse to learn about college life and the rigors of higher education. For many of the players, it's often their first chance to see a large university.

Coach Wilkins believes that these activities are central to the development of his football program. His players eat together every Wednesday after practice. He encourages them to trust each other and to value the worth of every person on the team, because such lessons are the foundation of a lasting community. Numerous former players visit the locker room before every game to talk to the current team. It is their way of carrying on the lessons learned from the past.

Coach Wilkins spoke with a glimmer in his eyes as he told me about these former players. They were adults now, with jobs and families of their own. Perhaps that's what keeps a coach going after 28 years on the sidelines. Or is there more to it? Can professional happiness ever be enough to fully satisfy an individual? And where does personal fulfillment come in?

As a coach and a husband, I constantly feel pulled in opposing directions. Coaching consumes countless hours of my time every week. I coach because football means so much to my players; the dual roles of teaching and coaching gives me a sense of purpose, and not many adults can say that. But I also hold a responsibility to my wife. Sometimes I wonder if our marriage can withstand three decades worth of seasons.

Danny Wilkins is a happily married father of three. Somehow he found a way to maintain this delicate balance.

As I broached this subject, Coach Wilkins leaned further back in his office chair. "You ever heard of the book *The Five Languages of Love?*" he asked me.

"No sir."

"Get it and read it. In fact, you and your wife ought to read it together. It talks about what love is to different people, and how for some people it might be giving 'em a little gift. For some people that don't mean anything. For some people it's quality time, the time that you actually spend together. For some people it's physical touch, whether it's holding hands, your arm around them, whatever it might be."

I never thought I'd be getting advice about love from a middle-aged football coach, but somehow it made perfect sense.

"And remember this," he said. "There's gonna be times where all the good intentions in the world won't make up for the fact that you're not home. It's only natural human tendency that she's going to be a little jealous and envious of your time and want you there. Even during the season, there are little things you can do to make a difference in your relationship with her. You *can* ease the pain a little bit.

"My wife's been great over the years. It takes a lot of unselfish sacrifice to be the wife of a coach, and I couldn't do it without her help. She really is the love of my life."

Later that evening, I walked hand in hand with my wife through the streets of downtown Asheville. Jenni and I had just finished a relaxing dinner in a street corner restaurant with soft, dim lights and classic jazz playing in the background. Just outside our window, tourists and homeless men mingled in a park filled with bongo drums and the throbbing sounds of heavy bass. The ambiance felt more like Greenwich Village than a mountain city in the South.

The music of the square disappeared as we made our way down narrow streets covered in shadows. The sky was still a bright blue, but the sun had dipped below the Smoky Mountain peaks surrounding the city.

I glanced at my wife and squeezed her hand. Strands of hair twirled across her face in the cool breeze. She smiled at me, and her brown eyes warmed my heart to the very core. I was deeply in love with the woman next to me; I felt completely at peace.

We crossed over College Street and Patton Avenue. At the corner of Market and Eagle Street, I noticed a tall brick structure with a sloping roof. More than a century ago, on this very corner, the Young Men's Institute first opened its doors to the black community of Asheville. The building looked very much the same as it did so many years before, down to the faded advertisements for valves and other machinery along the outer walls.

Before Jenni and I drove back home to Durham, there was one more place I needed to see.

We followed Eagle Street downhill to South Charlotte Street. Gene Hammonds and thousands of other black teenagers knew this route by heart in the years before integration. I saw a ridge in the distance, with modest homes dotting the tree-lined slope in haphazard rows. We climbed one final hill and stopped in our tracks.

This was it, the Castle on the Hill. A granite stairway rose into thin air. Crumbling stones littered the hillside. A large rat darted in and out of the rubble. All that remained of the great Stephens-Lee High School was the brick gymnasium. Everything else was gone.

Jenni and I had a panoramic view of downtown Asheville, with the sky turning pink behind a silhouette of the city. A favorite quote from Thoreau came to my mind:

*"If you have built castles in the air, your work need not be lost; that is where they should be. Now put the foundations under them."*

Stephens-Lee High School still exists. I can hear the classroom bells and the laughter in the hallways. I can feel the community fracture and reform in unexpected ways. I can see the past become present and the present become history in a never-ending cycle.

The past is not dead, after all. It's not even in the past.

A building is merely a vessel if the voices within it are forgotten. The legacy of Stephens-Lee vanishes without men such as Eugene Hammonds and Danny Wilkins to carry the load. But this is a story of many voices.

Sometimes, in the still beauty of a Friday night, the hopes and dreams of an entire community become a reality. Young men are inspired to live as they have never lived before. A community grows stronger, a family evolves, and the spirits of the past can finally rest in peace.

Ashbrook Coach Bill Eccles and the author, November 1995.

Milton Butts, facing the EE Smith scholarship wall of fame.

A typical rural scene in Eastern NC on the road to Jacksonville.

The entrance to SW Onslow's football stadium.

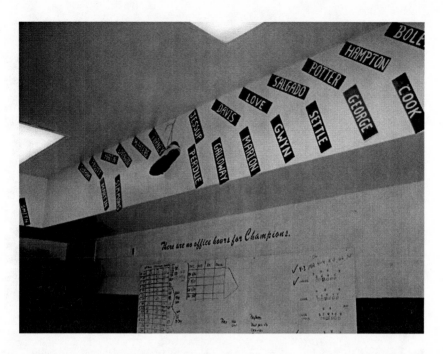

David Diamont's shrine to his former players in the East Surry football office.

The stately campus of Asheville High School, the first Castle on the Hill.

Downtown Winston-Salem, showing remnants of its days as a tobacco giant.

The Seven Clans Monument at Cherokee's Ray Kinsland Stadium.

Ed Bell, Hall-of-Fame athlete at JT Barber High School in New Bern.

The Bull, standing proud above a factory in downtown Durham.

# 6

## $100,000 Treasures
## Winston-Salem

Marine Captain Enrico Hunter fought back the urge to think of home as he performed his daily reconnaissance around the U.S. Embassy. The task demanded total focus. Almost a year had passed since the Taliban fled from the capital city of Kabul and scattered along the rocky terrain of the Khyber Pass. Some of the insurgents had been captured. A large number were now dead. But a few Taliban operatives still lurked beneath the shadows of the city in civilian clothes, just waiting for a chance to attack the American forces.

Captain Hunter knew these dangers well. When he first arrived in Afghanistan, the capital city of Kabul was in utter chaos. Afghani civilians had ransacked the U.S. Embassy in the weeks following 9/11. The Taliban police encouraged protesters to set fire to the Embassy's interior offices and to spray bullet holes across the front of the building. The trampled remains of an American flag lay next to the street. Anti-American graffiti lined the charred walls of the Embassy.

As part of the Marine Corps' security task force, Capt. Hunter made daily trips around the perimeter of the Embassy. From his gun turret above a Humvee, Capt. Hunter surveyed the gutted remains of Kabul with a watchful eye. He could see the snow-capped peaks of the Hindu Kush Mountains in the distance. Sunlight sparkled upon the Kabul River as it snaked through the rolling hills of the city. Kabul looked like one giant mass of jagged concrete. The crescent slopes of countless Mosques dotted the landscape.

Capt. Hunter steadied his fingers on the trigger of an M2 machine gun. The Humvee kicked up dust in every direction, and the peaks of the Hindu Kush Mountains faded and reappeared with every gust of wind. The dust was the first thing a Marine noticed when he arrived in Afghanistan. It was a permanent part of the landscape. The dust seeped through your clothes, your shoes, and your fingernails. It blurred your vision and muddled the rest of your senses. Capt. Hunter wore sunglasses and a mask to protect his face from the floating debris.

As the Humvee lumbered back to the Embassy gates, Capt. Hunter finally released his fingers from the trigger of the M2. He could relax now. Things weren't so bad, if you looked at it from the right perspective. Capt. Hunter didn't mind risking his life to defend America. Like so many everyday citizens, he had watched the carnage of 9/11 with a horrific sense of anger. Now was his chance to do something about it. All the struggles from his past made sense now. Everything seemed connected.

*Would they even recognize me now?* Capt. Hunter thought to himself. He was a long way from Winston-Salem, the birthplace for all those years of struggle. Even now, after four years at the Naval Academy and four more years overseas in the Marines, Enrico Hunter maintained a distinct southern accent. His voice was a little more refined now, and his diction held the crisp cadence of a military man, but the Piedmont drawl was still there.

Capt. Hunter thought a lot about Winston-Salem these days. When he wasn't driving through the streets of Kabul, and the threat of an attack was somewhat less imminent, he allowed his mind to drift back to the familiar sights of home.

Winston-Salem was a peculiar mix of blended ambitions. Colonial buildings and ancient trees lined the downtown streets of the city, which had been a Moravian settlement back in the 1700s. Winston-Salem was also home to Wake Forest University and the North Carolina School of the Arts. It was a city of culture and sophistication, but Winston-Salem was just as famous for its industrial past. When R.J. Reynolds came to Winston-Salem in 1874, he forever altered the identity of the "twin city." In no time, 15 tobacco factories were producing plug and smoking tobacco across the downtown area. R.J. Reynolds eventually became the largest tobacco company in the country. His factories dominated the Winston-Salem skyline with gigantic brick smokestacks and rusted gray water towers.

Capt. Hunter could see all of this – the train tracks running beside the factories, the black windows of the towering mills, the tree-lined streets of Old Salem. But the images grew less familiar with every year abroad. He remembered the neighborhoods north of the city much more vividly. These neighborhoods were originally built for the workers of the downtown mills, and they consisted of modest homes on slopping hills overlooking the factories and financial buildings to the south.

Life was a daily struggle for Enrico Hunter in those early years. He was a smart kid, but he had limited support at home. An aunt raised him for much of his childhood, and he regularly moved around the north edge of Winston-Salem from one home to the next. He didn't have a father, and he seemed to be heading down the same destructive path of so many young boys without role models.

Enrico's life took a dramatic turn in the summer of 1992. He tried out for the football team at Carver High School, where he began a lifelong friendship with head coach Keith Wilkes. For the first time, Enrico Hunter had a father. Keith Wilkes took the young man under his wing. Football gave Enrico a sense of discipline and accomplishment, and this mentality carried over into his classes.

When he graduated from Carver, Enrico Hunter accepted an appointment to the U.S. Naval Academy in Annapolis, Maryland. It was a difficult transition at first. Coach Wilkes talked to Enrico every week on the phone, running up tremendous long-distance bills just to lift up his former player's spirits. After a bumpy start, Enrico flourished in college. During his sophomore year, he was one of the top ten kick-off returners in the country.

He was a team captain his senior year. When he finished school, the lessons learned from the gridiron carried over to his work with the Marine Corps. After a decorated stint at the U.S. Embassy, Captain Hunter moved to Chesapeake, Virginia, where he began work as a military investigator for the Marines.

When I met with Keith Wilkes on a summer morning at Carver, he spoke like a proud father of the man everyone called "Rico."

"I was over at Rico's house last week," Coach Wilkes said, "and it's nicer than the home I've got. He's making six figures now, and he's in charge of over 500 men."

We were sitting in a small coach's office covered with team pictures from Coach Wilkes's fourteen years as the head coach at Carver. I was slightly apprehensive about meeting Keith Wilkes. Most coaches liked him, but others did not. Winning often breads resentment, and there were some hard feelings about Carver's football success. But as I learned soon enough, this resentment was as complicated as Winston-Salem's cultural dynamics.

As we talked, Keith Wilkes leaned back in his swivel chair and rubbed the whistle around his neck. Carver had their summer practices in the morning, and Coach Wilkes was still wearing his royal blue coach's shirt and black running shorts. Coach Wilkes had a large frame and a raspy southern drawl. His goatee and mustache were graying slightly, and he stared at me with intense eyes. He looked like a competitor; that much was clear to me from the very beginning. Losing wasn't a part of his vocabulary.

As a child growing up in the hard-scrabble neighborhoods of Winston-Salem, Wilkes turned to sports for guidance. He didn't have a father, so he sought out Jim Bovender, the football coach at Carver, to fill that role. Coach Bovender became the father-figure he never knew. He pushed Wilkes to do well in school, and he encouraged Wilkes to go into teaching and coaching. Keith Wilkes returned the favor during his All-American career as a lineman at Winston-Salem State University by returning to Carver every summer to help his former coach. At WSSU, Wilkes learned from such legendary coaches as Bill Hayes in football and Clarence Gaines in basketball. "Big

House" Gaines won a remarkable 828 games over his 47-year career at WSSU, making him the fourth all-time winningest coach in NCAA history. Wilkes picked up the Wing T offense from Bill Hayes, who was a master technician, and he incorporated the Wing T into his own offenses at Carver.

Keith Wilkes returned to Carver High School full-time after graduating from WSSU with a degree in education. Wilkes was Jim Bovender's line coach until 1992, when Bovender resigned to become the county's athletic director. The choice for a successor was easy.

Carver has experienced consistent success under Keith Wilkes, winning the 3-A state championship in 1998 and 2002. According to Coach Wilkes, they should have won three more. The Carver playing style was intricate and old school. Very few teams ran the Wing T anymore, but that didn't bother Keith Wilkes. The Wing T was a four-back offense based on quickness and deception. Undersized teams often used it as a way to compete with larger and stronger foes. Under the watchful eye of a skilled coach, it was a difficult offense to attack. Carver's teams were incredibly quick, but they also had great size on the offensive line. For the last fourteen years, Carver's Wing T had been a nightmare for opposing coaches.

My first encounter with Keith Wilkes and Carver High School came in December of 2002. Our team in Durham was already eliminated from the playoffs, and I decided to go see the championship games at Carter Finley Stadium in Raleigh. I was there to support my alma mater, Ashbrook, who was playing in the 3-AA final against Greensboro Dudley. As I arrived at the stadium, an elated team in blue and gold was dancing through the concourse. It was Carver. They had just capped off an undefeated season with a 34-0 throttling of Wilson Fike in the 3-A final. I was amazed at the size and strength of the Carver squad. For a school with less than 1,000 students, Carver seemed to have an endless supply of athletes. I envied Coach Wilkes. Our players at Jordan High School had just begun to understand what it took to be winners. At Carver, winning seemed to come almost effortlessly.

Carver had produced over 200 scholarship football players in the 14 years since Coach Wilkes took over the program. It was a remarkable feat. An average of fourteen scholarship athletes a year; sometimes as many as 18 players in one class. The *Winston-Salem Chronicle*, a local paper serving the city's large African American community, did a big story on the signings every year. The picture covered half of the front page – a large group of young men sitting shoulder to shoulder, pen in hand, with countless family members beaming with pride behind them. Enrico Hunter was the first of five Carver football players to accept appointments to the Naval Academy. In the past five years, Carver has sent players to UNC Chapel Hill, Wake Forest, Maryland, East Carolina, Clemson, and Tennessee, as well as to countless historically black colleges across the southeast.

The Carver High School community was proud of its athletic success, but football was a bright spot in a very precarious time. Like E.E. Smith, Carver was one of the 18 schools on Judge Manning's list of underperformers in the *Leandro* case. Carver could also be shut down without adequate increases in test scores. The parallels between Carver and E.E. Smith were numerous: both were historically black schools; both schools served students from low-income neighborhoods; and both schools were beacons of pride within their respective communities.

CHS got its name from George Washington Carver, the son of a former slave whose experiments with peanuts and sweet potatoes revolutionized agriculture in the South. The Carver School initially served the rural African-American communities of Kernersville, Walkertown, Tobaccoville, and Clemons. Like most schools across the state, integration had a profound impact on Carver. While Carver was the county's first all-black school, Atkins High School was Winston-Salem's first urban all-black school. Integration brought an end to Atkins in the early 1970s, and if it wasn't for the concerted efforts of community leaders and alumni, Carver would have seen the same fate. A new Atkins High School opened in 2005 as a vocational and technical school, but by this time the African American community in Winston-Salem had largely turned its allegiances to Carver.

The Carver school complex is an impressive series of tall brick buildings along the rural, northeast corner of the city. The school sits at the crest of a hill; the football stadium spans a level below the main building. The stadium is a large, sprawling facility with landscaped bushes around the corner of each end zone. On one end of the stadium, these bushes are adorned with a monument to Carver's two most recent state championships. On another tier below the stadium, a forest of tall hardwood trees conceals the team's practice fields. It is a beautiful setting for a high school football game. Carver consistently draws over 7,000 fans for its home games, setting most of the attendance records in the district. When Carver faces rival Parkland High School, the games are played at Winston-Salem State's Bowman Gray stadium to accommodate the capacity crowds of 17,000.

Carver's community support is not limited to athletics. In response to the negative publicity surrounding the *Leandro* case, local churches and Carver supporters banded together to form the Greater Carver Road Network for Better Education. Through this organization, churches established after-school tutoring programs for Carver students and engaged in an aggressive door-to-door campaign to get parents involved in the local Parent-Teacher-Student-Association. Church members continued the efforts of other community groups by volunteering as hall monitors during the school day at Carver. In the *Winston-Salem Chronicle*, community leader Samuel Stevens, a pastor at nearby Grace Presbyterian Church, called the *Leandro* case a wake-up call to the Carver community:

"We may, somewhere down the line, thank Judge Manning for what he has done…Some of his statements and orders have certainly inspired what we are doing."

Cheryl Jordan, the secretary of the PTSA, mobilized the Carver community for a pep-rally called SpringFest in the weeks leading up to the first day of school. Students, supporters, and parents marched from New Walkertown Road to Carver in a show of solidarity for the school's plight. Wentz Memorial Church organized a similar rally the day after school started.

Carver actively fought the school's negative image by touting the achievements of its students and teachers. Brittany Strachan was the number one student in her senior class, and she had already accepted a full scholarship to play basketball at N.C. State. Her mother, Sharon Strachan, was in charge of the school's math department and a former Teacher of the Year for the Winston-Salem/Forsyth County Schools. In recent years, Carver students had earned more scholarship money than almost any high school in the district.

But the negative perceptions persisted.

Many leaders blamed the school system's "controlled choice" plan for much of the controversy. In the Winston-Salem/Forsyth County Schools, as well as a growing number of school districts across the state, students had the option to attend their resident school *or* a number of other schools within the same zone. The following stipulations also applied: space had to be available at the new school; a student could not be recruited to change for athletic reasons; and students attending a school outside of their zone had to provide their own transportation. The intended purpose of controlled choice was to raise standards across the district through a competition of resources, i.e. students. If a student wasn't happy at a particular school, he or she could simply transfer to a "better" school, provided there was space at the other school. In theory, it wasn't a bad policy. What parents wouldn't want a say in their child's education? But the results were often far from perfect. Middle class families in the Carver and Parkland zones, particularly *white* middle class families, often used the controlled choice plan to transfer their children to more affluent schools such as West Forsyth, East Forsyth, and Mt. Tabor. The system forced parents to choose between their community loyalties to a school in their own zone and the perceived "excellence" of another high school's teachers and school resources. Opponents of controlled choice argued that schools such as Carver had plenty of good teachers and excellent facilities. In their eyes, parents were simply following the age-old model of self-segregation.

Good students want to attend schools with a reputation for academic excellence. By the same logic, good athletes are attracted to programs that consistently win games. The Winston-Salem/Forsyth County Schools specifically prohibited coaches from recruiting players from another zone. But coaches didn't have to recruit. Victories spoke louder than any underhanded tactics. Carver lost a number of good students each year because of negative publicity, but on the other hand, the school also picked up a disproportionate number of good athletes from other schools in Forsyth County.

Take the case of Matt Brim, for example. After spending three seasons at East Forsyth High School, Brim raised some eyebrows by transferring to Carver. He was a 6-foot-6, 300 pound white kid who wanted to play for a predominately black high school. Other schools cried foul. Carver may not have recruited Brim, but his motivations for transferring were not entirely academic.

"His daddy brought him here for one year, because the kid wasn't getting the right coaching over there," Coach Wilkes said. "I told him to do everything I asked of him, and in one year, he signed for $180,000 to Wake Forest; he was all-state. This kid had it locked up in him the whole time. But nobody was helping him get motivated. He couldn't see that vision for himself. I tell kids like Matt, 'I've been here long enough to *see* what you've got. I'm *telling* you what you got, and I'm telling you it's in you. I'll do everything within my power to get it out of you, but you've got to do your part.' Then they start believing you."

Winning certainly helped – who didn't want to be part of a winning team? But an athlete needed a skillful motivator to fully realize his potential.

"If you're not motivating your players to give 100%, to where they'll run through a wall for you, then you need to look at what you're doing as a coach. I don't know if it's a gift I have, but a lot of people have really prospered being in this program. That's why some of these coaches, they get kind of jealous of me because their kids will leave. You see, I don't have to worry about my kids leaving and going somewhere, but a lot of these coaches, they don't want me around their kids. Other coaches wonder how Carver gets all these kids to sign college scholarships, when other schools are only getting one or two a year. That's one of the big things I've got going here. I'm genuinely just trying to help my kids. White, black, green, or purple, they're my own; that's what makes them want to come over and play for me."

Under the competitive model of the district's controlled choice plan, Carver was simply benefiting from its own athletic success. The same could be said for schools with the highest test scores in the county. It was a slippery slope on both sides of the issue. Talent attracted even more talent, but what happened to the less athletically or academically inclined? Was the system benefiting everyone?

Either way, community support suffered under the controlled choice plan. The *Leandro* case galvanized public education across the state. Community loyalties became meaningless in the face of low test scores. But what *was* a quality education? Could quality ever really be quantified? The answers weren't simple, as I had begun to discover. Shades of gray seemed to muddle the arguments in either direction. Test scores were the logical yardstick of success. But were test scores really the best assessment? Could districts accurately measure student performance by using the same logic as a profit-driven company? And if controlled choice really did fracture the neighborhoods of Winston-Salem, why did over 7,000 people show up every Friday night to watch Carver play? Football seemed to bind the communities around Carver School Road better than any plan the district could come up with.

Keith Wilkes saw the answers to many of these questions in simple and direct terms. Kids needed hope. If a player had hope for the future, he was more likely to perform in the classroom *and* on the football field. Kids also needed to see tangible examples of dreams that had come true. Coach Wilkes created a family network of former players who came back every summer to show the current team what could happen if you stayed true to your goals and aspirations.

"We've built up a big group of kids that have already graduated and are doing real well in society," Coach Wilkes said, "and they come back and talk to the team. It's a roll-over effect now. The ones who really listen and want to make something out of themselves say, 'We've got a chance. We've got hope that we can do it too.' I tell them everyday, 'The opportunity is there for you. It's all about the choices and decisions you make.'"

Success didn't happen overnight for these former players. They all came to Carver with natural athletic ability, but what separated a good athlete from a great athlete was an *understanding* of his potential. That was the key.

"Every year I say to my players, 'You have treasures locked up in you that God places in everybody. He don't place failure in you. You've got presidents locked up in you, you've got all types of leadership roles locked up in you that you've got to get out, but you never know it's in you until you stay dedicated and focused on your dreams."

Coach Wilkes often used Chris Hairston to illustrate this important point. Last year, Hairston was an all-state lineman on Carver's team, and he was about to begin his freshman year at Clemson University.

"Chris came out here last August not knowing he had a $100,000 scholarship locked up in him. He stayed focused until December, and now look what happened. I say to the young guys, 'You put yourself in that same position. You played against him every day in practice. You know what it takes.'

"We really use the influence of our former players. We have a big group of guys who sign every year. We constantly reiterate the requirements that it takes. I bring 'em in and say, 'Son, you've got $100,000 that's gonna follow you around for four years. It's locked up in you, and you've got to do what it takes to unlock the treasure. Treasures don't come easy. God places treasures in you. In December of your senior year, you're gonna either be able to reach down and get that $100,000 scholarship, or it's gonna disappear. The opportunity's there, but if you're not ready to take advantage of it, it's gonna be gone.'"

Faith was the driving force of Keith Wilkes's coaching philosophy. To Coach Wilkes, a player was insulting God if he refused to acknowledge his God-given abilities. A coach's job was to help his players recognize and take advantage of these "treasures" locked within. In a sense, a coach who failed to motivate his players was even more to blame than a player who refused to see his God-given potential. It was a difficult scenario. Some players refused to be motivated, and Coach Wilkes knew the limits of his own success.

"You've got some kids that just don't want to be saved. Jesus couldn't save everybody either. So we do the best we can. We don't normally have a lot of them who flunk out. You see kids now with their cell phones and their video games. From a religious standpoint, I think the Devil places all of these things in there to get people off track. There are so many distractions now."

Coach Wilkes saw faith as a way to bind his players together as a family. During the season, a local pastor speaks to the team every Thursday at the end of practice. He chooses a passage from the Bible to accompany the team's goals for the week. On five Sundays during the season the team attends church services together. Collective worship brings the players closer to each other, and it also connects the young men to a larger community of believers. According to Coach Wilkes, people need spiritual guidance to survive in a world full of fighting in the Middle East and persistent poverty at home. Faith is at the very heart of a kid's ability to hope. Faith is the rock. Nothing can be realized without it.

Every season, Coach Wilkes and his staff put together a list of students with academic and behavioral problems. He tries to pinpoint the problems early on, particularly in the freshman class, because students who fall behind in school tend to stay behind. These students attend mandatory study halls before every practice. Students with good grades become tutors for their struggling teammates. Coach Wilkes holds regular parent meetings so that everyone is on the same page.

Coach Wilkes knew what could happen to struggling students if they didn't get extra help. The rest of their lives depended on these four years of high school. Graduation requirements were getting tougher. Job expectations grew higher every year. A lousy freshman year in high school could destroy a student's hopes, particularly a student without parental support at home.

After fourteen years at Carver, Keith Wilkes didn't lose many kids. His goal was to send at least 500 kids to college on academic and athletic scholarships. He anticipated this would take about ten more years.

"You think you'll ever leave Carver?" I asked him.

"Right now, it looks like the Lord wants to keep me here. I tried to get away a few times, but He kept me here. Sometimes people take you for granted when you've been in one place for so long. I've seen every high school around here have at least six coaches. It's been my philosophy to use coaching to save people's lives. I wanna win, but I also want to help people. The coaching echelon is based on great winners, but I want to be great winners with my kids. You can get all the wins in the world, but if your kids are not prospering, what good does it do? After playing for me for four years, they oughta be able to move on and go to college."

Coach Wilkes leaned forward in his chair and stared at the sea of faces on the wall.

"My biggest fear in coaching is failure. As a minority coach, we don't tend to get the opportunities sometimes. When we get fired, we get thrown back to the bottom of the barrel. I don't *ever* want to be back at the bottom of the barrel working my way back up. That's always been one of my biggest fears. That's why I'm always working, all the time, trying to stay on top of the game, because I know it could change overnight."

"How would your life be different if you never got into football?" I asked.

"I tell you…that would have been rough."

Coach Wilkes paused and shook his head slowly from side to side.

"Sometimes people don't realize their purpose. But I feel like this is my purpose. I don't know if I can do anything else. I'm no good at computers. I know my Xs and Os enough to keep me going. If I can keep motivating people to change their lives … I can't give that up."

Coach Wilkes led me through the locker room to a door overlooking the stadium. The lush green grass far below was immaculately trimmed in straight paths. The lines wouldn't be painted for another month or so, but I could imagine the stadium packed with thousands of fans dressed in yellow and blue.

The trees encircling the stadium create a beautiful pallet of red and orange and gold as the wind blows crisp and cool. Keith Wilkes marches down the sideline as the Wing T works to perfection. Proud alums such as Matt Brim and Captain Enrico Hunter cheer from the stands. I hear the collision of pads and the sounds of the high stepping Carver marching band. Everything feels right in the world.

# 7

## *Eu-stugwoe*
## Cherokee

Some people say that the trees around Ray Kinsland Stadium come alive at night. Heath Shuler wasn't sure about that, but he listened intently as his older teammates warned him about the intimidating atmosphere of a Cherokee High School football game.

Heath had just been promoted to the varsity squad of the Swain County Maroon Devils. He was only a freshman at the time, but he knew all about the rivalry between Swain and Cherokee. The Cherokee Braves were located on the Qualla Boundary – 60,000 acres of Indian reservation land crossing Swain County and neighboring Jackson County in the remote Blue Ridge Mountains of North Carolina. Cherokee boys from the Qualla Boundary often went to school at Swain, while others chose to stay at the reservation school. Swain was certainly more of a football power, winning six state championships since 1972, while Cherokee often struggled to field a competitive team with only 250-300 students in the entire school. But the rivalry was intense nonetheless.

Heath leaned from side to side as the Swain activity bus snaked along the swollen Oconaluftee River. It had been raining most of the day – not exactly ideal weather for a quarterback like Heath, but he was just excited to be on the varsity team at such a young age. Eventually the bus pulled up to the visitor stands. Five large Cherokee men stood before the gates with their arms crossed, never breaking their stare, never saying a word. Heath swung his equipment bag over his shoulders and followed his older teammates to the locker room. Heath felt the deep-set eyes of the five Cherokee men following him and his teammates wherever they went.

By the time the Maroon Devils marched onto the football field for pre-game warm-ups, the rain had finally stopped. The vine-covered trees behind the playing field seemed to move and bend with the mountain air, changing shape in the evening darkness. The vines hung like Spanish moss, only darker, thicker, resembling the thick patches of cumulus clouds before a summer storm. Gnarled faces seemed to form in the shadows. Directly behind the Swain endzone, a thick mist rolled from the Oconaluftee River onto the field. Nervous sweat began to form along Heath's neck.

Beyond the mist, Heath could hear the distinct war cry of the Cherokee football squad.

Heath Shuler would never find himself in a more intimidating environment. Not when he lead the Tennessee Vols in front of 108,000 fans in Knoxville, or at the Swamp at the University of Florida, where angry Gator students threw D-cell batteries at his mother in the stands. Not even when he played for the Washington Redskins against the Cowboys at Texas Stadium, or much later, when he became a freshman Representative in the United States Congress. Something about playing on that field at Cherokee High School just stuck with him.


I didn't know quite what to expect as I drove to Cherokee through the Blue Ridge Mountains west of Asheville. Most people don't realize just how wide the state of North Carolina really is. It takes at least nine hours to drive from the mountains in the west to the Outer Banks in the east – Murphy to Manteo, as the saying goes – roughly the same driving time from my home in the center of the state to New York, or Central Florida, or Cleveland.

In my travels across North Carolina, I've noticed that each community has its own unique flair, its own fascinating history, its own sense of place within the larger scope of American life. I've intentionally steered away from what the naturalist Joseph Krutch calls the "sloburbs," those insulated, suburban communities popping up outside of most major cities these days, where every neighborhood consists of neat, tidy yards and cookie-cutter houses, a place where culture and history and diversity are almost nonexistent. Like bacteria, these neighborhoods often multiply and swallow nearby communities whole. When one limb of an authentic community dies off, the rest of the body is forever damaged. But with the sloburbs, one neighborhood is no more vital than the rest. I'm sure that many good people live in these places, but I don't plan to be one of them.

Across authentic America, some communities defy all categories. Cherokee is one of these places. It is a nation within a nation, a town in which 8,500 residents reap the benefits of a $140 million gambling industry while at the same time attending services at over 30 Baptist churches. It is a place of both pride and frustration. While the Harrah's Casino has pumped much needed revenue into the community, Cherokee continues to deal with significant poverty, unemployment, alcohol abuse, and some of the highest rates of diabetes in the country.

Driving through the downtown streets of Cherokee, I could easily spot these conflicting dynamics. The town of Cherokee sits along the edge of the Great Smoky Mountains National Park. Peaks and rolling hills tower above the downtown area from every side, cradling the business district in a lush, green wonderland. Low wisps of clouds dot the hillsides, moving from peak to peak in the morning and then fading away as the sun grows higher in the sky – seven handbreadths in the air, as the Cherokee elders used to say. When the park opened in 1940, Cherokee quickly evolved into a popular tourist destination. Today, tourism accounts for over 65% of all jobs on the Qualla Boundary.

My car became stuck in the middle of a slow procession of RVs and vans, giving me ample time to look at the downtown shops. Some were classy, but most appeared to be tourist traps. I stopped in a store advertising "authentic Native American blankets," all of which were made in Mexico and Taiwan. Every block or so, I noticed a Cherokee Indian dressed in feathers and carrying a rubber tomahawk, the stereotypical Hollywood native ready to make a quick buck with a photo op, offering face painting to passing tourists or standing next to a multi-colored teepee, even though the Cherokee never lived in these huts. The Cherokee call this "chiefin'," a kind of hustle. The Tribe has taken steps to remove these stereotypes from the downtown area, but most of them still remain. Who can blame them? Chiefin' puts food on the table when other jobs are scarce. There are rumors of a Wal-mart coming here soon. Some people like the idea; others do not. As one local resident told me, "You either grow as a town or you die." People have been saying that about the Eastern Band of the Cherokee for a long time now.

In some ways, it's a miracle that the Cherokee have even survived in these remote valleys of the Great Smoky Mountains. In 1738, early white settlers first brought small pox to the area. Small pox had been in Europe for thousands of years, and most of the settlers possessed a built-in immunity. But not the Cherokee. The white settlers gave them blankets that were infected with small pox, and within a year, over half of the Tribe had been wiped out. A century later, President Andrew Jackson ordered the forced removal of all Cherokee Indians in an effort to free up their land for white settlers. The Cherokee were rounded up, placed in stockades, and marched on foot to Oklahoma in the dead of winter. Almost a third of the 17,000 Cherokee died on this journey. They called it the *Nunna Daul Tsunny*, the Trail of Tears.

About 1,000 Cherokee resisted the march west. They were outlaws, hiding from the federal troops in high coves and hollows that only the best of trackers could ever find. William Holland Thomas was their chief. Thomas was a white man who had been adopted into the tribe by a Cherokee chief named Drowning Bear. When Drowning Bear died, Thomas became the leading advocate for the Tribe. William Thomas used his skills as a lawyer to secure citizenship for his people, but Andrew Jackson was clear: all Indians needed to move west.

One day, federal troops captured a Cherokee farmer named Tsali and his extended family. The exact details are still open for debate, but at some point during the march to an internment camp, a soldier prodded one of the ailing women with a bayonet. Tsali and several of his sons attacked and killed two of these soldiers. Tsali fled with his sons to the hills, setting off a manhunt led by Union troops that might have gone on for months if it hadn't been for William Thomas. Thomas convinced Tsali and his sons to surrender. In exchange, Colonel Foster and the federal army agreed to let all of the remaining Cherokee stay on their land. Tsali became a martyr, a symbol of pride for the Cherokee people. Colonel Foster stuck by his word, a rarity in American's history of broken promises to the Indians, although he may not have expected to see so many Cherokee Indians come out of hiding to celebrate their newfound freedom. When the dust settled, about 600 Cherokee Indians remained in North Carolina.

For the next two decades, William Thomas used his own money and the money of the Cherokee to buy 57,000 acres of what is now called the Qualla Boundary. The Cherokee weren't citizens yet, so the land had to remain in Thomas's name. As old age began to set in, Thomas worried about the fate of his people. He eventually came upon a novel solution: if the Cherokee couldn't be citizens, they would have to be a company instead. The company could own the land. In 1889, the Eastern Band of the Cherokee Indians incorporated under the laws of North Carolina, a full 35 years before American Indians finally received their U.S. citizenship.

Here's where the fate of the Eastern Band of the Cherokee differs from other American Indian groups. The federal government's Bureau of Indian Affairs owns and operates most reservations. But on the Qualla Boundary, the Cherokee actually own their land, placing it in trust with the federal government. As a result, the land can never be sold, and as a side benefit, the federal government is obligated as "trustee" of the land to make sure the people of the Qualla Boundary receive health care, education, and other basic services. Thus, for years, the Cherokee relied heavily on the federal government for their survival. In an area where tourism was the only real industry, over half of the Cherokee living on the Qualla Boundary were unemployed. A 1970 study found that 50% of all homes were considered substandard. Nine out of ten Cherokee students were infected with roundworm, and 39% were obese. Ninety two percent of the young men who were arrested were under the influence of alcohol. The Cherokee may have owned their own land, but they suffered from the same problems that plagued inner city communities across the country.

The people of the Qualla Boundary began to gain some semblance of financial security when the Harrah's Cherokee casino opened in the mid-1990s. The casino consists of a 15,000-square-foot conference center, a 597 room hotel, three restaurants, and, most importantly, a cavernous, smoke-filled building with thousands of electric poker machines illuminated by neon lights. As collective owners of the casino, each of the 14,000 enrolled members of the Tribe receives a cut of the profits; the rest of the money goes to road construction, schools, and other services. While the Bureau of Indian Affairs still maintains oversight on the Qualla Boundary, the Tribe has finally claimed a measure of financial independence.

But what did it mean to be a Cherokee? Did one's identity come from the land, or the casino payouts, or from blood? Men were still chiefin' on the side of the road, while the blankets and rubber tomahawks came by the truckload from Mexico and Taiwan. Waves of RVs and diesel fumes filled the downtown streets of HW 441 next to the Tepee Village, the Tomahawk Mini Mall, and the Moccasin Shop. *You either grow as a town or you die.* Was Cherokee becoming just another sloburb, a Wal-mart village just like the rest of small-town America? I was about to find out.


Skooter McCoy was a seventh grader sitting in the stands on that mist-covered Friday night when Heath Shuler and the Swain County Maroon Devils played the Braves. His father had been a running back on the Cherokee football team. So had his grandfather. Skooter eventually became a standout running back and linebacker there as well, earning a scholarship to play football at Western Carolina University. But he always knew he would return to these ancient mountains. Like so many Cherokee Indians on the Qualla Boundary, this land was sacred.

The Cherokee believe that the Earth began as an unbroken expanse of water and soft mud. All the animals lived high above the sky in a land called Galunlati. This place was very crowded, so they sent the Great Buzzard to see if he could find dry land. The Great Buzzard searched and searched until he grew tired and could fly no more. His powerful wings flapped against the soft mud, creating valleys with his down strokes and mountains with his up strokes. The other animals worried that the Great Buzzard would turn the whole world into mountains, so they asked him to return. From that day until now, the Cherokee have lived among these mountains.

People often say that you can never really go back to the land of your birth, and if you do, you must reinvent yourself in a way that is foreign to your childhood self. But Cherokee is not like most other places. Skooter McCoy always knew he would find his way home again.

Skooter was a business major in college, and after graduating, he found a good job in marketing at the Harrah's Casino on the Qualla Boundary. But something was missing. Skooter found himself looking out the window of his office every day, thinking about the Cherokee football team. The program was going throw a rough spell, losing every game over a two year period. *How were the boys looking this year*? he wondered time and time again. One day he got a call from the Cherokee High School principal with a job offer. Skooter didn't know what to do. Most people on the reservation would kill to have his job at Harrah's, but it was a job, not a passion. He felt torn.

Skooter decided to talk to the one man who seemed to understand the Cherokee spirit better than anyone. Ray Kinsland had always been a second father to Skooter, as well as to countless other boys on the Boundary. He was an institution, a legend in the Cherokee community. For fifty years, Kinsland had run the Cherokee Boys Club, an organization unlike any other in America. During this time period, he had not missed a single football game at Cherokee High School. He was the PA announcer at all the varsity, junior varsity, and youth league games. He drove the activity bus on every road trip, and he kept all the stats. He also did the pre-game devotional for the football team. Five hundred straight games over five decades. The numbers were staggering. During these five decades, he also announced every basketball game, wrestling match, and track meet at the school. All of this from a man who was not even an enrolled member of the Tribe. Ray Kinsland was only the second man in the history of the Eastern Band of the Cherokee to be adopted as an honorary member. The other man was William Holland Thomas.

Skooter had sought out Ray Kinsland many times before, for advice on who to marry, what to name his kids, the list went on and on. Kinsland spoke with a deep, Appalachian accent fermented by age and experience. His measured words came out slowly and carefully. Nothing he said or did was wasteful.

"Skooter," Kinsland said. "If you enjoy your job, you'll never have to work a day in your life."

The decision was easy after that. Skooter took the 50% pay cut to become a teacher and a football coach; he never looked back.


When I arrived at Ray Kinsland Stadium, the smell of freshly cut grass filled the air. I walked toward Jess Toineeta, who was driving his lawnmower across the carefully maintained field.

"Howdy," he said as I approached the machine.

We shook hands, and I asked him if he'd seen Coach McCoy up at the school this morning. I used to plan these meetings far in advance, but I quickly learned that coaches are adaptable people. As long as Coach McCoy was around town, I knew I could find him.

"I saw Coach up there at the school a bit earlier. Not sure where he went."

Keeping with the distinct southern accent of the area, Jess Toineeta's "there" came out as *thar*, his "where" as *whar*. He looked to be about sixty five, with kind eyes and a relaxed, easy-going demeanor. He wore a well-worn hat, jeans, and workman's boots. Like many of the Cherokee residents I had already met, his skin tone was a light brown. When a Cherokee Indian leaves the Qualla Boundary, people often think they are Hispanic, or East

Asian, or biracial. But there is something about the eyes – an intensity, a history – that is entirely distinct. In every other way, Toineeta carried himself just like any normal 65 year old man from the mountains of North Carolina.

Jess Toineeta talked about the football stadium with pride. The concrete walls and press box were painted maroon, and the steps were a golden yellow. Below the press box I noticed the letters *CWY*, pronounced "Tsa-la-gi," or *Cherokee*, in English. A silversmith named Sequoyah developed the Cherokee alphabet in 1825, and every student at Cherokee High School must learn the language in order to graduate.

Jess Toineeta had worked for Cherokee High School since the current building opened in 1975. When he was a student at CHS, Ray Kinsland had been his agricultural teacher. Outside of a stint in the army, Cherokee had always been his home. His sons played football here. They also remained on the Qualla Boundary.

Toineeta wiped the sweat from his brow with a hand towel. "It's pretty special here during football season. Lots of people come out. Pretty much everybody on the Boundary."

He pointed to a sign next to the front entrance: *"No blankets or seating can be placed in stadium BEFORE 5:00 pm Friday!"*

Ever since Skooter McCoy was promoted to head coach three years ago, the excitement around the football program had grown exponentially. His first season, the Braves went 12-2. The next season, they finished the regular season undefeated. They'd won the highly competitive Smoky Mountain Conference two years in a row, something unheard of in the history of Cherokee football. They were also beating Swain on a regular basis now. Before the sign was put up, fans used to break into the stadium on the night before games so they could reserve their spot. Toineeta would arrive at the school early the next morning to find an empty stadium covered from top to bottom in colorful, hand-woven blankets.

"A lot of high schools represent their hometown or their school district, but when you play football at Cherokee, you represent a nation of people."

Skooter McCoy and I were sitting in a conference room next to the high school's main office. Coach McCoy was wearing a white Braves Football shirt with maroon shorts. His hair was shaved close to his head, and he wore glasses. He had a sizable build. McCoy was one of the youngest head coaches in western North Carolina, but he carried himself with confidence and intelligence.

"When you left for college, did you always know you'd come back some day?" I asked.

"Always."

"Why?"

"I've probably been asked that question a thousand times in my life. I don't know how to answer it. I don't want to get caught up in clichés, but there's something about living on this Boundary that calls you back. This is home, and it's been very good to us. Everybody leaves, but just about everybody eventually comes back home. For me it was about making sure that my children had the same experience that I had here.

"There's a lot of pressure having an entire nation on your shoulders. It's pride, knowing what we have to go through from time to time to put these kids on the field. There's an old adage across coaching that you should never coach in your hometown to begin with. If you have a devastating loss and you have to go to the grocery mart on a Saturday morning, it can be tough on the wife and kids sometimes. But I know what it means to be a Cherokee."

On the wall behind the conference table, I noticed an architectural rendering of the new school complex. Slated for completion in the fall of 2009, the school was the crown jewel of the Qualla Boundary. It looked like a small college campus, or maybe even a palace. Both comparisons worked. Paid for by $108 million worth of casino money, the school will house all students on the Boundary from grades K-12. At 473,000 square feet, the school will have four gymnasiums, a performing arts center, multiple gardens, and a football stadium and field house that rival any Division 1-AA college in the country. The buildings' exterior walls will be painted in traditional

Cherokee basket designs, and the entire complex will cater to an appreciation and understanding of the Cherokee culture.

The new school is a symbol of Cherokee's educational future, where culture and academic excellence go hand in hand. It's yet another testament to the resilience of a community that has been battered through the years by disease, internment, and unemployment. Some critics will probably say that this new building project is excessive. I thought so at first. But the history of the Cherokee school system is one of the most shameful stories a person will ever hear.

When Stacey Saunooke woke up, she could barely see the faint rows of cots on either side of the dorm room. She knew from the early morning light that wake-up call would be soon. At six o'clock, a shrill horn would bring the overflowing room of young girls at the Cherokee Boarding School to attention. They would march outdoors until seven, then eat a breakfast of wormy oatmeal. Stacey was only six years old, but she knew not to complain. She didn't want to get whipped with a belt like the other students who got caught speaking Cherokee instead of English. Her uncle tried to run away once, a few years before Stacey arrived here in 1912. When they caught Stacey's uncle, they dressed him up like a girl and made him eat his meals standing up. Staying quiet was the key. Obedience could save your life.

Stacey put on her blue denim dress and fought back the urge to urinate. The bathroom was in the basement, and she was too afraid to walk down to the dark, dingy room without a friend. She thought about her parents. Both of them had attended Carlisle, the nation's first Indian boarding school. If they could survive in a place like this, so could she.

For over two hundred years, white settlers had pushed Indians closer and closer to the Pacific Ocean. Whites repeatedly signed settlement treaties with the Indians, then broke these agreements when they proved financially beneficial. In the Indian Territories of what is today Oklahoma and North Texas, 15 million acres were taken from the reservations and sold to settlers. From 1880 to 1900, the white population of the Indian Territories increased from 7,000 to over one million, often resulting in bloody skirmishes between whites and Indians. When settlers finally reached the Pacific Ocean, the federal government decided to come up with a plan to assimilate Indians into the American culture. Military force just wasn't cost effective.

In 1879, a lieutenant colonel by the name of Richard Henry Pratt convinced the federal government to let him create the Carlisle Indian Industrial School in Pennsylvania. The school was a grand social experiment to "kill the Indian and save the man," as Pratt put it. Indian tribes from reservations all across the country were asked, and sometimes forced, to send their best and brightest boys and girls to learn the ways of the white man. They were taught English and math, as well as a trade such as sewing or bricklaying. Their long, braided hair was cut short, and they were given uniforms in place of their natural clothing. They had to eat lye soap whenever they spoke in their native tongues or practiced any form of religion other than Christianity. When they returned to their homes, they barely resembled their former selves.

The boarding school concept quickly spread to other parts of the country. Over the next two decades, 24 similar schools were built, housing as many as 21,568 students. Among them was Haskell, a school in Lawrence, Kansas, that is still used as an Indian college to this day. The Cherokee created their own boarding school a year after Carlisle opened. Over a forty year period, almost two hundred Cherokee children attended the Carlisle Indian Industrial School, while countless others remained at the Cherokee Boarding School until the *Brown vs. Board of Education* decision in 1954.

The impact of these boarding schools was immediate and devastating. Boarding school students learned that their previous lives were inferior, and when they returned to the reservations, their newly acquired English and trade skills did little to help them earn a living at home. They'd been taught to sit at a table with a knife and a fork, while their parents preferred to eat on the floor. They were outcasts in their own communities. But they were also resilient. Men such as Stacey Saunooke's uncle, Osley Bird Saunooke, learned to walk the fine line between the white world and the Cherokee world.

In 1937, Osley Bird Saunooke, the rebellious student who had to wear a dress after he was caught running away from the Cherokee Boarding School, was crowned super heavy weight wrestling champion of the world. He held this title for 14 years, before returning to the Qualla Boundary to become the tribe's chief. Chief Saunooke demonstrated to the Cherokee people that sports were a great way for Indians to compete against whites without bloodshed getting in the way. But wrestling wasn't the sport that quickly took the Indian world by storm. It was football.

The yearly battle between Swain and Cherokee typically happens right in the middle of October. Perfect football weather. The Great Smoky Mountains surrounding Ray Kinsland Stadium come alive with color. The air smells fresh and clean, not too cool, but crisp enough to bring out the hot cocoa and the outdoor blankets. To the casual observer, it's the kind of atmosphere you would find in most football stadiums across America. Visiting teams rarely make this mistake when they arrive at Cherokee High School. At least not anymore.

When Skooter McCoy joined the Cherokee football staff back in 2000 as an assistant coach, he began to incorporate some of the Tribe's traditions in subtle but unmistakable ways. He believed that the Cherokee had something sacred that no one else could harness. They were fighting for more than just local pride. An entire nation was watching, a history of men and women who had struggled for the right to live on this very land, to breath the crisp air of these beautiful mountains and to listen to the rush of the Oconaluftee River as it swelled from the autumn rains.

Even with the new blanket rule, the Cherokee stands on this October evening are almost completely full by 5:00 pm. When the Maroon Devils come out for pre-game warm-ups, their bleachers are packed as well. It's been a few years since Swain has made it back to the 1-A championship, but their fans are rabid nonetheless. Bullhorns echo across the valley from either side of the field. The smell of deep-fried beef and popcorn fills the air. Cars honk as they drive down Acquoni Road. The streets are practically empty, since almost every resident of the Qualla Boundary is already crammed into the stadium.

The sun has set below Thomas Ridge and the Blue Ridge Parkway. It's only a matter of time now. Swain County has the field to themselves as they go over the Cherokee offensive and defensive sets.

Without warning, tribal music begins to play through the stadium's loud speakers. The music is eerie and dark, a tune more suited to a horror movie than a family outing. When the tune ends, the Cherokee war call blasts from the speakers.

"Whewww, whewwwwwwww!" a voice shrieks.

Fans on both sides of the field begin to notice a tingling sensation in their arms and necks. The high-pitched wailing brings the anticipation to a fever pitch. From the darkness behind the visitor stands, the Cherokee football team answers the war call with one of their own:

"Whewwwwwwwww!" they scream in unison.

The war call goes back and forth, becoming louder with every response.

"Whewww, whewwwwwwww!"

"Whewwwwwwwww!"

"Whewww, whewwwwwwww!"

"Whewwwwwwwww!"

Suddenly the Cherokee Braves come out of the darkness and onto the game field, walking in pairs to their own end zone. Behind the goalpost is the Seven Clans Monument. This is another one of Skooter McCoy's additions to the pre-game ritual. A stone monument sits in the center of seven poles made of wood and stone. Wooden masks hang from each pole beneath the soft glow of solar lamps. Each mask represents one of the Tribe's seven clans, which have been passed down for centuries: Wolf, the fighters; Blue, the medicine men; Deer, the hunters; Long Hair, the diplomats; Paint, the wise men; Wild Potato, the farmers; and Bird, the speedy messengers. The circle is dark, except for the solar lamps surrounding the slab of stone in the center.

Each player places a hand on the Seven Clans Monument, and together they repeat a single phrase which is etched on the stone below them:

*Eu-stugwoe.*

In English, the phase means, "I'll play anybody."

The *Eu-stugwoe* war call has been around for well over a thousand years. It was only spoken in times of war or while playing the sacred game of stickball. Coach McCoy loves to make connections between football and the Tribe's traditional past time. Stickball combines the tactics of lacrosse, rugby, and wrestling into a sport that has clear similarities to football. Before a stickball match, opposing teams line up and face each other across the field. One team advances ten yards and issues the call, then the other team responds. They eventually meet at mid-field, the fifty yard line. At that point the drivers, or referees, pair up the opposing players by size (sort of like man coverage, Coach McCoy tells his players.) The first team to make the war call will issue the final challenge, *Eu-stugwoe.*

*Eu-stugwoe* is a prideful statement that gives the Cherokee warrior a sense of calm before every battle. It also gets an opponent's attention. When Skooter McCoy started issuing the war call back in 2001, his players took to the phrase immediately. *Eu-stugwoe* was meaningful to them alone. Other teams could say it, but it wouldn't have any power. *Eu-stugwoe* was passed to them through blood. It took a few games for the crowd to figure out what was going on, but when the elders finally picked up on it, the phrase caught on like wildfire.

As the scoreboard counts down to zero, the Cherokee Braves break the circle of the Seven Clans and run through a tunnel of cheerleaders and traditional Cherokee dancers dressed in full regalia. The crowd cheers, the air horns blare, and another evening of high school football can finally begin.

American football traces its roots to around the same time the West was won. With no more wilderness (and Indians) to conquer, football became the new proving ground for men of the Gilded Age. Four months after General Custer's embarrassing defeat at the Battle of Little Big Horn, the Ivy League Big Four of Harvard, Columbia, Princeton, and Yale founded the Intercollegiate Football Association. At first, the contests were a bloody mess of bodies thrown together in a slow-motion pile of punches to the face, heels to the groin, and teeth falling to the muddy ground. The first official college football game occurred on November 6, 1869, between Princeton and Rutgers. The primary strategy at that time was simple: kill the ball carrier. Men died regularly in those first chaotic years without referees or, for that matter, any rules. Football was more of a bar fight than a sport.

From 1880 to 1881, a Yale graduate by the name of Walter Camp proposed a series of rules that would permanently separate football from its British cousin, rugby. Camp set the number of players on each side of the field to eleven. He also created the line of scrimmage, the end zone, and the concept of downs. Referees would now be used to keep violence to a minimum, although the game was still a mass of bodies surging forward in a bone-crushing pile. There was very little strategy to it. The bigger team usually won; playing dirty didn't hurt either.

With the rising popularity of this brutal new sport, students at the Carlisle Indian Industrial School asked their principal if they could form a squad of their own. Lt. Col. Pratt hesitated at first, but he soon realized that football could be another way for the Indians to become more "white." The Indians had other motives; if they could no longer challenge whites on the battlefield, at least they could regain a sense of pride on the gridiron.

After a few years of moderate success, Lt. Col. Pratt hired a coach who would revolutionize the game of football. His name was Glen "Pop" Warner. Warner quickly realized that his Indian players weren't big enough to compete in a traditional game of football; in Warner's 13 seasons at the school, Carlisle never fielded a team that averaged more than 170 pounds. He had to improvise, and the Indians were more than willing pupils. Pop Warner created a brand of football that stunned fans and baffled opposing teams. He invented the reverse, the double wing formation, the bootleg, as well as shoulder and thigh pads to soften the blows from the much larger players at Yale and the other Ivies.

But one invention truly put the Carlisle Indian Training School on the map: the forward pass. No longer could opposing defenses simply use their brute strength to manhandle Carlisle. Football was a game played by elite young men from the finest universities in the country, but it was not a thinking man's game. All of that changed with Warner's inventions. Fans marveled at the strategy and intelligence of the Carlisle players. Perhaps Indians were smart after all, they realized. A whole litany of stereotypes began to crumble down. From 1911 to 1913, Carlisle achieved national prominence with a combined record of 38-3. Their star player was Jim Thorpe, who kicked a winning field goal in a highly publicized victory over the U.S. Military Academy and its star fullback, future president Dwight D. Eisenhower. The Indians at Carlisle, and the thousands of boarding school students across the country who cheered them on, could finally experience a small measure of pride. They'd taken a white man's game and made it their own.

The Cherokee Boarding School eventually started a football team as well. One of the early running backs for the team was Skooter McCoy's grandfather, who could trace his lineage on the Qualla Boundary back to the days when Tsa-la-gi farmers roamed the mountain coves without ever seeing a white settler. Like Carlisle, the Cherokee squads were small in numbers and bulk, but they grew to love the game of football. As the years went by, football became more than just a pastime. For many, the football team was the only family they really knew.

I followed Skooter McCoy as we walked along the empty hallways of Cherokee High School. The walls were a jigsaw puzzle of granite slabs shaped into arrows and crescent moons. The school looked clean and well-maintained, but it was no longer big enough to house both the junior high and the high school. The elementary school down the road was in much worse shape, with trailers scattered all the way to the banks of the Oconaluftee River. The new school complex on Big Cove Road would solve these space issues. It would also bring every Cherokee student together on one piece of land. The younger kids could learn from their elders, and a fractured community could begin to repair its wounds.

Cherokee is a rural community, but it faces many of the same issues that plague the inner-city neighborhoods of Charlotte, Durham, or Fayetteville. When Skooter McCoy joined the football staff in 2001 and started the *Eustugwoe* war call, only 11 of the 41 players on his team had a father. The following year, 32 kids were without a dad. Many of these men had fallen victim to diabetes, alcoholism, and drug abuse. In recent years, students at Cherokee High School have struggled with addictions to Crystal Meth, cold medicines, and pain killers such as Percocet and Vicodin. Instead of joining gangs, they choose to self-medicate.

A growing body of medical research attempts to explain why so many American Indians struggle with addictions. When a group of people experience trauma, their descendents often internalize this vulnerability over time. At first, the white settlers traumatized the Cherokee by moving onto their land and taking away their economic base of farming. Then the boarding schools forced the Cherokee to abandon their culture, their language, and their traditions. The human brain searches for a way to deal with this trauma. Some people drink compulsively. Others eat too much, leading to complications such as diabetes. It's a subconscious reaction to a problem that goes well beyond a person's own immediate history.

I pondered these thoughts as Coach McCoy led me across the lobby to the school's vocational wing. In a large classroom to my right, I noticed a work table covered with bundles of straw, a clay pot, an intricately designed wooden mask, and a life-like rendition of an elk's antlers. The Cherokee students are known across the country for their craftsmanship, and art is one of the many ways that the school tries to instill a sense of pride and tradition in its students. Football just happens to bring the community together on a larger scale.

"It's a sad statistic," Skooter McCoy said as we walked through the football locker room. "But I can probably name 20-25 kids who would not have graduated, would have ended up in jail or worse, if it had not been for this high school football program."

"Can you see yourself staying here for another twenty, thirty years?" I asked.

"If they'll have me," he said with a laugh. "I really believe in the uniqueness of my position, of being an enrolled member here. It does create a special bond. I would love to stay here."

Out of the 31 coaches in western North Carolina, only five have been at their current school for ten or more years. The same phenomenon occurs across the country. Winning opens the door to better job offers, while losing causes an administration to "go in a different direction." After back-to-back 12-win seasons to start his head coaching career, Coach McCoy began to get calls from some of these bigger schools, but he saw Cherokee as a one-of-a-kind opportunity to change the culture of an entire football program.

Skooter McCoy is the first enrolled member to be hired as the head football coach at Cherokee. For years, white coaches used the job as a stepping stone to higher-profile opportunities. The Cherokee schools have their own retirement system, with better benefits than the rest of the schools in North Carolina, but a teacher has to stay in the Cherokee system all thirty years in order to get these benefits. Teachers can't transfer their years of experience from another public school. For this reason, Skooter McCoy had as many as 16 different football coaches in his four years as a player at Cherokee High School.

It was the time-honored issue of stability. As a head coach, Skooter McCoy believed that his program could only be successful over the long haul if his players knew that he was here to stay. He also needed to create a pipeline of former players who wanted to come back and help the program. Of the four Cherokee alumni who are currently playing college football, two are getting their education degree so that they can join the staff with Skooter McCoy. A third, the salutatorian from this year's class, is on a full academic scholarship to the University of Tennessee, where he is a manager for the football team while majoring in education. Skooter McCoy was particularly proud of this player, who didn't have a home for much of his time at Cherokee High School. He lived off of the meals he received at school each day. After practice, his teammates would take him out to McDonald's and always pay the bill. For a while he lived in a tent by himself. Otherwise, he'd stay with coaches, teammates, anyone who could lend him a spare place to sleep.

"I get so attached to these kids," Skooter McCoy said. "A lot of the guys sleep on my couch or in my spare bedroom the night before the SAT, because I'm going to make sure they're in bed at a decent hour, I'm gonna make sure they've got a decent meal in their stomachs. It's become kind of a tradition."

At first, Skooter wasn't prepared for all the "daddy questions" he got from his players: *How do I shave?* they'd ask him. *How do I put on a condom? Why do I have to say "sir" or "ma'am" to adults?* Skooter didn't know if he was a coach or a psychologist half the time. The questions were never-ending.

"What does your wife think about all this?" I asked.

"You have to find that special kind of woman to make it work. I don't know how to describe it. She's there with me when it's as low as low gets, and she's there with me for the highest of the highs. We've been married for eleven years now. She knows that she's married to an idiot who's addicted to a game."

Coach McCoy opened a door to the rear of the school, sending a blinding spray of light to the dark interior hallway. A handful of teenage boys sat on a nearby bench, waiting for an afternoon workout session to begin. They wore cut-off gray t-shirts with the words "CWY Football" on the front. Skooter's wife runs a screen-printing store in town, so there's always plenty of Cherokee gear to go around.

"What's goin' on, men?" Coach McCoy said.

"Nothing much, Coach."

"You holdin' workouts today?" one boy asked. He was bigger than the rest, perhaps six foot three and as much as 290 pounds. I immediately pegged him as the class clown of the team, the type of kid who thrives on football but often gives his teachers fits.

"Coach Parks is comin' in," Skooter said.

"And he's late, again." *Laaaate, agiiiyin.* "I thought you disappeared or something."

Coach McCoy had just gotten back from a week-long vacation to Florida, leaving the off-season workouts to his assistants. It would be his final break until the football season ended in November – or December, with a little bit of luck.

We continued walking towards the football stadium.

"Those kids are freshmen and sophomores. We grow 'em big around here."

A much smaller player shuffled by us with his eyes fixed firmly on the ground."

Coach McCoy tapped him on the shoulder: "Hey, smile. They won't run you too bad today."

The boy lifted his head momentarily, then joined his teammates on the bench. He looked a lot like me when I was fifteen, so unsure of who I wanted to be in life, worrying that the older players would crush me under the weight of their massive frames. I could sympathize.

A van pulled up to us in the parking lot.

"Daddy!" shouted a three year old girl wearing a Cherokee Braves cheerleading outfit. It was Skooter McCoy's daughter.

"She'll go to sleep in that thing if you let her," Coach McCoy said to me.

Skooter's wife and two sons waved to us from the van. Both of the boys played running back in the Cherokee youth league, which had been coordinated by Skooter's father for the past 29 years. The boys wore identical Mohawk hairdos and bounced energetically in the back seat of the van.

Skooter waved back and smiled. "When I first got the head job, they told me it's not going to look right if you make your oldest son the waterboy. I said, 'I don't give a damn, I'm the head coach. I don't see my son a lot, so he's going to experience this with me.' You have to force time with them. Even if it means going against local school board, local administration, whomever. If you want to make 'em waterboys, you make 'em waterboys."

The three year old cheerleader stuck her head out the window and called to her father again.

"I tell you, Coach," Skooter McCoy said to me, "I was blessed with two very strong sons. As a football guy, everybody wants a son, I'm not gonna lie to you. I thought this was as good as it gets. I've got these two little knuckle heads; when they get out of line, I just pop 'em on the back of the head, and they get back in line. It's just great. And then that little girl came along three years ago. And son, it was no contest. I was whupped. She rules the roost now."

I waved goodbye to the McCoy family and headed to my car. My wife and I don't have any kids yet, but we hope to someday. I watched Skooter McCoy drive off with his wife and three kids. So this was what a football family could look like.

The heated football game between Cherokee and Swain County is still another month away, but tonight's match-up is no less important. This game isn't about local pride. This is the Battle of the Nations. For 11 years running, Cherokee High School has squared off against a team of Choctaw Indians in one of America's most unique high school athletic contests.

Referees in western North Carolina fight for the right to work the football game between Cherokee High School and Choctaw Central, a 3-A school located on a reservation in central Mississippi. It's a nine-hour bus trip each way, and every year the traveling team stays in a hotel next to their opponent's local casino. For the Cherokee, it's Harrah's; for the Choctaw, it's the Golden Moon. The Battle of the Nations game is the farthest trip that many of these kids will ever take. Thousands of fans make the long drive to support their team. Some of them will use their social security checks to pay for the trip, or sacrifice Christmas presents for the gasoline and hotel bills. They get there by truck, charter bus, motorcycle, whatever comes available.

After the opening kickoff, the Cherokee offense jogs to the line of scrimmage. The referees get in their proper stance and wait for the snap of the ball. Suddenly the Cherokee quarterback sees something he doesn't like. He changes the play, giving an audible call in the Cherokee language. The new play gets repeated down the line. Formations change, players go in motion, the quarterback gives further instructions in Cherokee. The Choctaw defenders react swiftly, calling out changes in their own language. Twenty two players are shouting Cherokee and Choctaw audibles to each other. The referees have no idea what is going on. Nothing in the rule book prepares them for this.

Ray Kinsland watches the action unfold from his seat in the press box. This is his second home. He remembers the fathers and grandfathers of the Cherokee football squad, generations of young men who have worn the *Tsa-la-gi* name with pride. Fifty straight years of high school football without missing a single contest. He does all the stats for the away football games, but here in the Cherokee press box, his daughter, who's an English teacher at the school, does it for him on a laptop computer. He still runs the clock and does the PA announcing.

Ray Kinsland is proud to see Skooter McCoy on the sidelines. He's proud of every young man who comes through this program. Kinsland knows all of these kids, their family stories, their successes and failures. He's not an enrolled member of the Tribe, but these are his people.

Air horns fill the air as a Cherokee running back skirts around the end of the line for a score.

"Touchdown by #24, Langston Woods," Kinsland says in a slow, understated voice. The words come out so naturally, he could do this in his sleep. But he never loses the thrill of seeing a Cherokee touchdown.

Fireworks fill the sky after every score. The sports anthem "Jump Around" by House of Pain blares from the loudspeakers. Sure, things have changed in the past fifty years, but the essence of high school football is just as pure as it once was. Ray Kinsland cups the microphone between his hands and knows that God is alive and well in this place.

I had heard so many different things about Ray Kinsland in this town that I couldn't quite picture the man in my head. He almost seemed like a figure out of a Cherokee myth. His name came to me everywhere. When I went to the local library to research the history of the Cherokee schools, the woman behind the counter just stared at me.

"You talked to Ray Kinsland yet?" she asked.

"No, ma'am."

"He's the real library. We're just the window dressing."

Skooter McCoy echoed these sentiments to me. "Ray Kinsland is the cornerstone. He'll play it down; he'll tell you he's nothing. He'll tell you he's the high school janitor. Humility is unbelievable with this man. He's the reason I'm here today."

I wondered what could drive a man to stay in a job for fifty years, to find himself among another race and feel so at home, to devote his life to a cause without asking for any credit in return. Maybe it was empathy. Maybe it was guilt. Perhaps it was simply faith.

The long fingertips of the morning mist still floated across the Great Smoky Mountains as I made my way to Ray Kinsland's office. I didn't really understand Kinsland's role in the Cherokee community, but I knew that this was a man to be reckoned with.

"Come on in, young man," Ray Kinsland said as he shook my hand firmly.

Neat, orderly file folders were stacked throughout his office. The walls were covered in Cherokee High School team pictures and plaques from various civic groups. I noticed two model school buses on top of an outdated television set. There was a King James Bible on the desk to my left, as well as a Cherokee translation of the New Testament.

Ray Kinsland sat across from me with one leg folded across the other. He looked calm and relaxed, as if he had completely tuned out the constant activity in the offices beyond his open door. He wore a navy corduroy sports jacket and khaki pants. His hair was thinning, but it was remarkably dark for a man who was well into his seventies. He looked kind, intelligent, interested in what I had to say.

Ray Kinsland grew up on a dairy farm near the Qualla Boundary. He spent much of his youth outdoors, helping out with the family farm and exploring the Smoky Mountains beyond his front door. After graduating from NC State University, he took a job as the vocational arts teacher at Cherokee High School. Kinsland's father worked for the school's maintenance department, and while his family wasn't on the official list of enrolled members in the Tribe, he knew there was some Cherokee blood in his family's lineage.

At the time, Cherokee High School was just four years removed from its controversial stint as a boarding school. In 1932, the Indian Agency (now the BIA) denied the school's petition to join the Future Farmers of America. In response, the school formed the Cherokee Farm Club. The school also organized the Cherokee Motor Club for students interested in mechanics. Ray Kinsland inherited both clubs when he joined the CHS staff in 1958, and before long, the clubs combined into the Cherokee Boys Club. The club offered vocational training and summer employment opportunities for the young men, and eventually women, of Cherokee High School. No one seems to know why the name never changed to reflect both genders.

Ray Kinsland's connection to the Cherokee football program began almost as soon as he started teaching. The Bureau of Indian Affairs placed Kinsland in charge of the school buses, and one of his first assignments was to drive the football team to an away game in Robbinsville.

"Have you ever kept football stats before?" the coach asked him.

"No," Kinsland said.

"Well, then you're our official statistician."

At the home game the following week, the coach needed someone to run the scoreboard. Kinsland volunteered to do that as well. Five hundred games later, he's still doing it.

In Kinsland's early years as a teacher, the BIA did everything in its power to convince the Cherokee students to go to the local public schools instead of the Tribal school. For several years, the BIA eliminated Cherokee's football program altogether. A few boys left CHS because of this, but most stayed. In 1964, the BIA told Kinsland to stop running the Cherokee Boys Club. The Tribe responded by taking over the organization and making it a separate, non-profit entity from the school. The initial goals of the Boys Club remained the same.

Ray Kinsland left his job at the high school to become the first director of the newly independent Cherokee Boys Club. Over the years, the Tribe asked the Boys Club to take on more and more of the services that were formerly performed by the federal government. This included social services, road maintenance, housing, and, of course, school buses. In 1990, the Tribe took over the Cherokee school system, adding yet another layer of responsibility to Kinsland's organization. The BIA continues to provide some funding for education, health, and other social services, but the administration comes almost exclusively from the Boys Club. Kinsland now has an operating budget of more than $30 million.

The Cherokee Boys Club consumes almost every aspect of Ray Kinsland's life. He and his wife live in a double-wide trailer directly behind the Boys Club. They have three daughters and ten foster children; whenever the orphanage on the ridge above the Club gets full, he and his wife take the rest of the children in as their own. In the cold winter months, he gets up at 3:30 in the morning to make sure all the roads are clear of ice. When Kinsland received his honorary tribal membership in 1968, he was also given a Cherokee name: "Di-sde-li-sgi-a-ni-wi-ni," which means "Helper of Men." In his fifty years as director of the Cherokee Boys Club, Ray Kinsland has played a role in every major policy decision for the Eastern Band of the Cherokee. Kinsland wouldn't tell me this, of course. I had to find it out from other people.

Ray Kinsland didn't own any land on the Qualla Boundary. He couldn't, since he wasn't an enrolled member of the Tribe. But that didn't seem to matter. This was his home.

I asked Kinsland if he felt closer to the Cherokee people than to the people of his own race.

"Definitely," he said. "When people tell me that Christianity is the white man's religion, I tell them – and this is the honest truth – I've learned a lot more about the Lord from some old, full-blood Indians than I have from any white preacher. They preach from the pulpit, and these old Indian couples that I've known and loved, full-bloods, they preach through their daily lives. They had all kinds of hardships, all kinds of problems, but they remained faithful. Sermons are great, but a sermon of what's in your life every day is so much greater."

Kinsland stared at the team pictures on the wall behind me. "I know I've been treated better than I deserve here."

A woman with an unmistakable resemblance to Skooter McCoy came into the office to ask Ray Kinsland a question.

"Excellent timing," Kinsland said as he introduced me to Vickie McCoy, Skooter's mother and the Administrative Manager for the Boys Club. "He's writing a book on high school football. Don't know why he wanted to talk to me."

Vickie McCoy shook her head and smiled at me. "I don't think there would be Cherokee football if it wasn't for Ray."

"Is it stressful watching your son on the sidelines?" I asked her after making small talk.

"I enjoy the games less than I did when he was playing, and I didn't enjoy them at all back then. I hardly ever see a touchdown 'cause I always have my eyes closed."

Kinsland leaned further back in his chair, then said, "You got four or five guys who holler at Skooter and the kids. I tell the boys to ignore 'em, 'cause we need their money. I remember when half of them didn't even have a ball in their hands, and unfortunately I remember when the other half of them did. Their claim to fame is sitting over there hollering at you. What makes it so bad is the ringleader is Skooter's cousin. But I told you, everybody here's related. You know it's a little worse when your relatives are bad-mouthing you."

Ray Kinsland still hated Mitchell County because it was where Skooter injured his knee his senior year, effectively ending any chances for a college scholarship at a major Division I-A school.

"The night before that happened," Vickie McCoy said, "Skooter talked to Joe Paterno for three hours on the phone. Penn State was recruiting him at inside linebacker. He already had a full offer from NC State."

Skooter went through three surgeries before doctors gave him a final choice: play football for a couple more years, or walk for the rest of your life. He stopped playing after his sophomore year at Western Carolina.

"Skooter didn't tell you about that, did he?"

I shook my head.


An hour later, Ray Kinsland walked with me to the front door of the Cherokee Boys Club. My head was swimming with information about the Cherokee Nation. Kinsland really was a library, just as the townspeople had said. But he was completely unassuming as well. He reminded me of my own grandfather. I couldn't recall much about my grandfather, since he died when I was so young. But I distinctly remember sitting with him on his favorite recliner and feeling like I was the center of the universe.

Next to the front door, Ray Kinsland showed me the framed portraits of every Cherokee Chief dating back to the Trail of Tears.

"I've worked for 11 of these men," Kinsland said. "And twenty six school boards."

The photos changed from the vibrant colors of the present to the grainy black and white images of the past. There was Chief Saunooke in his full wrestling gear, his neck bulging and his arms flexing. At the end of the row was William Holland Thomas, the white man who had been adopted by Chief Drowning Bear. Like Ray Kinsland, William Thomas had dedicated his whole life to the Cherokee. They were his family.

I shook Ray Kinsland's hand and started for the door. He placed his hand on my shoulder.

"If you love kids," he told me, "they know it. If you don't, they know it. You can fool adults, but you can't fool kids. And they don't care how much you know. They want to know how much you care."

For the first time, Ray Kinsland's voice took on a sense of urgency, as if he was afraid that I would leave this place without fully understanding what it meant to work in Cherokee, to live here, to care about a community so much that nothing could ever pull you away.

"Last thought," Kinsland said. "See, I'm 73, I've been at this a long time." He paused, considering his words carefully. "Jesus, in order to help us, had to come and be one of us. He had to leave His ivory tower. And every day in education and all walks of life, you see people who wanna help without leaving their ivory tower. Cause if Jesus had to do that, you know we have to do it more to have any hope. He didn't call us to success, He called us to be faithful, and the success is in His hands, not in our hands. We're bad about judging ourselves and judging each other on success and failure. And that's not it. It's about being faithful. And if you're faithful, you're a success."

On my way out of town, I stopped by the construction site of the new school complex on Big Cove Road. The gray sky threatened rain, but the clouds were moving fast. The sky always seemed to be moving fast while I was here in Cherokee.

An army of trucks, tractors, and bulldozers surrounded a huge collection of half-way finished buildings. The exterior of the elementary wing was already in place, creating a circle around what would soon be a network of gardens and ponds. The noise from the sight was practically deafening. I followed a bend in the road to get a better look at the new football stadium. The concrete for the home side was already in place, with 2,500 more seats than the old grandstands. The Seven Clans Monument would be the final piece added before the first game in 2009. The team was already calling the new stadium "K2" after their mentor, Ray Kinsland.

The *One Feather*, Cherokee's local paper, had just run a front page article documenting the school's progress. The whole town was talking about the project. It almost seemed too good to be true.

For years, no one thought that the Cherokee would ever own this plot of land known as the Ravensford tract. The Tribal Council had petitioned the National Parks Service for the land since 1964. At first, they wanted to build a state-of-the-art golf course. But by 1994, they were lobbying for a new school. Ravensford used to be a lumber village, but as the Blue Ridge Parkway made its way through the surrounding hills, every structure in Ravensford was demolished. The land was a prime, natural habitat now. The Tribe didn't have enough flat land to build a new school. After all, nearly eighty percent of the Qualla Boundary went straight up. The Ravensford tract was an ideal location, a mere two miles from downtown.

Despite protests from the Sierra Club and various other environmental groups, the Tribe finally reached an agreement with the Parks Service in 2004. In exchange for the 143-acre Ravensford tract, the Tribe donated a 218-acre plot along the Blue Ridge Parkway that was filled with endangered species and trout streams. The long-awaited school project could finally begin.

I stepped over construction equipment and mud puddles on the way back to my car. A circle of light blue opened in the sky, as if God had taken His fist and punched a hole in the clouds from above. Maybe He had. This land certainly seemed sacred enough.

A town that does not grow will inevitably die. That's what the people of Cherokee have said to me again and again. A town without dedicated men like Ray Kinsland and Skooter McCoy will die as well.

People sometimes ask Ray Kinsland if he's lived in Cherokee his whole life.

"Not yet," he always responds with a chuckle.

I wish that all of us could think of our communities in this way.

# 8

## Mecca of a Thousand Noble Aspirations
### New Bern

New Bern High School was about to achieve the impossible, but head coach Bobby Curlings couldn't even smile. Players and assistant coaches all around him shook hands and waved towels in the air. Along the concrete bleachers of Groves Stadium at Wake Forest University, ten thousand cheering fans decked in crimson and black were counting down the final minutes of the game. Even the security guards were cheering for New Bern. This was David versus Goliath. The little coastal town of New Bern standing over the fallen giant from Charlotte. The New Bern Bears were about to defeat the Independence Patriots for the 2007 4-AA state championship.

*It's not over yet*, Coach Curlings thought to himself. He paced back and forth along the sideline, fidgeting with his headset and waiting for disaster to strike. His Bears were playing against Charlotte Independence, after all. Heading into the 2007 season, the Independence Patriots held the nation's longest winning streak of 108 straight games. Tonight, they were playing for their eighth state championship in a row.

Patriots head coach Tommy Knotts was a legend in the state, a man hated and loved with equal enthusiasm. His supporters worshipped at the altar of "TK." To them, he was a visionary, a miracle worker – hell, he was the greatest coach in North Carolina history. His opponents thought he was a cheat. They saw him as a cocky, muscle-bound bully who would stop at nothing to win a game of football. The cries of foul play usually came from those who had taken a few of the 108 straight beatings, but that was beside the point.

Bobby Curlings stopped pacing as Independence quarterback Anthony Carruthers took the shotgun snap with less than a minute to play. Like a number of the players on Independence's roster, Carruthers transferred to Independence High School to be part of the Tommy Knotts' machine. Families moved from all over Charlotte and even far away places like Georgia and Pennsylvania to join the Independence football team. Opponents accused Tommy Knotts of recruiting. Two days before the championship game, five Independence players were suspended after Charlotte-Mecklenburg School officials determined that they had lied about their home addresses. Several weeks earlier, a starter named Dominique Walker was suspended for similar reasons.

The recent suspensions at Independence were just the tip of the iceberg. The Charlotte-Mecklenburg Schools were engulfed in the worst sports scandal in state history. Three schools had already forfeited their entire seasons. Multiple coaches and athletic directors had been suspended. So far, Independence had avoided any serious punishments, but the game between New Bern and Independence was being played under a cloud of suspicion nonetheless.

Tommy Knotts couldn't stand the accusations.

"Nobody's ever proven we recruit," he said to the *Charlotte Observer* the day before the state championship. "Our school and our record and our staff recruits itself. It's futile to sit here and deny it. No.1, people hate winners and there always seems to be some controversy around us. People naturally assume it's done unfairly."

On the New Bern sideline, Bobby Curlings could care less about the scandal. He just wanted the clock to tick faster. He wanted the Independence quarterback to make one more bad decision, the Patriot receivers to drop one more pass.

Coach Curlings got his wish. Anthony Carruthers rolled out of the pocket and threw an errant pass into the arms of the New Bern defense, bringing the game to a close. Goliath had fallen at last. New Bern 28, Independence 17.

In the ecstatic moments that followed, Bobby Curlings finally allowed the relief to wash over him. He shook Tommy Knotts' hand and then gathered the New Bern players around him. Coach Knotts stood with his bulging arms crossed. His players looked stunned; they were in elementary school the last time Independence lost a playoff game. A New Bern fan noticed the outline of a number "8" beneath Coach Knotts' game shirt. He asked Knotts if he was a Dale Earnhardt fan, then walked away cheering.

As Bobby Curlings raised his hands, the players around him grew silent. Clouds of steam floated above their sweat-drenched heads. Coach Curlings was an imposing figure, but he spoke with a quiet, measured drawl. He didn't intimidate players with his rhetoric. It just wasn't his style. Curlings used to scream at them, but it just gave him heartburn and stressed out the rest of the team. He thought a coach had to do that to win. But he wasn't being true to himself.

Coach Curlings looked at the smiling circle of teenage boys. These young men had become a part of his family, his life, his identity. So many thoughts went through his head.

"Don't let this be the defining moment of your life," he said to them. "Use this as a spring board to bigger and better things. Going to school and getting married and being a good father…" He paused, taking the moment in, making sure every eye was looking his way. "All the things that come later in life are much more memorable than this game."

The players nodded, growing solemn for a moment. An assistant coach stepped forward and led the team in prayer. Then pandemonium erupted once again. The volume from the stands grew almost deafening as the New Bern fans saluted their native sons. Black, white, rich, poor – together they created a wall of sound that drifted across the Winston-Salem skyline.

Reporters sent out frantic dispatches of the game's unexpected outcome. The Independence winning streak was finally over.

In a comfortable brick home north of Durham, a seventy year old man named Ed Bell watched the state championship celebration on his TV. He was proud of the Bears. New Bern was the town of his birth. The victory brought back so many memories of his own days as a high school football player.

*"For the first time in school history, New Bern has won a state championship in football..."*

Ed's smile momentarily vanished. The announcers were mistaken. They hadn't done their research. They didn't know the truth. All his life, Ed had been telling his story to people who listened with glazed eyes. No one seemed to care about the past. History was written by those in power, after all. What good would it do to fight the status quo?

Ed Bell remembered New Bern's first state championship victory. The year was 1956, not 2007. Ed had the letter sweater to prove it, carefully folded and framed above his stairway. Navy blue, with golden stripes and the letter "B" stitched across the front pouch. A football with a picture of an Indian warrior was stitched above the heart. Ed was the starting center and a team captain. He remembered the names of every teammate and the scores of every game. But one important detail shaped his identity as a football player and as a student.

Ed Bell happened to be black.

As I drove north from downtown Durham, I noticed an immediate change in my surroundings. I live fifteen miles away in southwest Durham, so this area was relatively unfamiliar to me. After all my travels, I was still amazed to find so many hidden places in my own hometown. I've lived in Durham for seven years now. It's finally starting to feel like home, but it will take me a lifetime to truly know this city. The industrial buildings of the tobacco district soon gave way to green pastures and gently rolling farmland as I continued north along Roxboro Road. Plantation-style mansions intermingled with modest ranch homes. Ed Bell lived in a new subdivision among these rolling hills.

When Ed welcomed me at his front door, I was surprised by his short, compact stature. Ed looked remarkably fit for a man of seventy. He had thin, gray hair, arching eyebrows, and a carefully trimmed mustache that gave his smile a mischievous, Rhett Butler-esque quality. He was wearing a white t-shirt commemorating the fiftieth reunion of his graduating class at JT Barber High School.

Ed led me upstairs to his entertainment room. A cool, spring breeze came in through an open window. A large pool table took up most of the room. The walls were covered with pictures and plaques from Ed's past. I sat in a wicker chair beside the pool table. Ed handed me a large stack of papers – football and basketball photos in black and white, newspaper articles from the *New Bern Sun Journal*, programs from dedication ceremonies – one man's entire youth stacked together in long-ago memories.

Ed talked with a faint, northern accent, the product of nearly four decades as a New Yorker. He decided to move back to North Carolina after retiring from his job as a social worker. He often made the three hour drive east to New Bern for football games, reunions, and conferences. Ed loved to talk about the past. New Bern was a very different place when he lived there. But the town had always been a part of him, even after moving away so long ago.

"So," Ed said to me, "you want to know what New Bern was like before integration."

I nodded.

"How much time do you have?" he asked with his eyes gleaming brightly.

The mud-covered streets of downtown New Bern were empty on the morning of December 1, 1922, the day after Thanksgiving. A fierce wind blew from the Trent River to the south and the Neuse River to the north, creating a tunnel of cold air that kept most of the townspeople indoors, huddled next to their coal-burning stoves.

The wind nearly drowned out the fire alarm coming from the Rowland Lumber Company on the outskirts of town. Rowland was the largest lumber mill in the state, and it was a major employer of New Bern's black community. The shrill alarm blended with the whistling gusts of wind.

Downtown New Bern was normally a busy place, but many of the white business owners had taken the Norfolk and Southern trains out of town that morning to Sanford. Central High School was playing for the eastern football state championship, bringing much of the white community of New Bern along for the ride. The caravan included a large number of firemen.

When the LaFrance pumper truck arrived at the lumber mill, flames had already spread to more than a million feet of dry lumber. Smoke was everywhere. The fire truck dashed from one pocket of flames to the next, dousing one hot stop just as a gust of wind would send the flames to another area.

On the west side of town, an eight year old girl named Dorcas Carter could hear the fire alarm in the distance, but her mom wouldn't let her go outside to look. Dorcas was doing her Friday chores with her three brothers. Beneath a blue serge dress, her feet tapped to the beat of a Bessie Smith tune. The alarm was coming from the other side of town, the white side. It wasn't her concern.

After a while, the fire alarms grew louder, closer. Dorcas looked out the window to see clouds of smoke in the distance.

"Don't worry," her mother said. "The wind's blowin' away from us. We'll be all right."

Dorcas wasn't so sure. In church, the old people were always talking about Judgment Day. *God won't destroy this world again by water*, they'd say. *He's gonna do it by fire next time.* As Dorcas looked at the darkening clouds, she began to wonder if these old people were right.

The fire whistle sounded in her own neighborhood now. Dorcas stopped tapping her feet.

Moments later, one of Dorcas' aunts burst through the front door. "Get out!" she screamed to the family. "There's a fire next door at Henrietta's house. It's blowing this way."

Dorcas ran with her mother and brothers onto Kilmarnock Street, noticing the sparks flying across their neighbor's roof. The abandoned lot next door was already on fire, and Dorcas could hear the crackle and hiss of collards. People all around them were hauling furniture into the road, desperate to save their most prized possessions before the flames spread in the gusting winds.

A fire truck arrived at the first of the burning homes, about 45 minutes after the blaze began. The firemen grabbed onto their hose, only to discover that the nozzle wouldn't hook into place. The hose was worthless now.

Dorcas carried her youngest brother for several blocks until they reached George Street. More alarms sounded from every direction. She heard the Rue Chapel AME Church bell in the distance. To her left, St. Peter's AME Zion rang as well. People were screaming and running in every direction. Dorcas covered her baby brother's head and stood transfixed by the chaos all around her.

Clusters of families gathered inside the Cedar Grove Cemetery. They crouched beneath the stone walls, hoping to shield themselves from the flying sparks. Without water to douse the flames, men began to dynamite homes in the path of the fire. A stray goat wandered near the explosions and was shot 25 feet in the air. Dorcas covered her ears and began to pray.

For weeks, the ashes slowly smoldered around New Bern. A tent city stretched across much of the town, providing temporary shelter to the 3,200 black residents who were now homeless. Church services moved to the tents as well, since Rue Chapel AME and St. Peter's AME had both burned to the ground. When white residents returned from the eastern championship football game, they were relieved to find most of their homes intact. Only 20 white families needed shelter. Dorcas and her family were lucky; instead of living outdoors, all seven of them were crammed into an upstairs room in a nearby home.

Months passed without progress. The black residents of Tent City tried to rebuild their homes, but they were told that the land was now condemned. Twenty acres near the heart of black New Bern was turned into an extension of Cedar Grove Cemetery, the white cemetery in town. Families didn't know what to do. They'd lost the land of their birth, and many were jobless, since the Rowland Lumber Company had also burned to the ground. Thousands of people decided to move North, shifting the balance of power in a town that was once over 75% African American.

New Bern had always been a center of black pride. As soon as the Union army occupied this port city during the Civil War, slaves from all over eastern North Carolina fled to freedom behind the Union lines, risking their lives by swimming across the Neuse River at night. In 1860, the African American population in New Bern was just under 3,000. By 1865, the number had grown to over 10,000. A soldier in the 44th Massachusetts militia once said of the town, "There is perhaps not a slave in North Carolina who does not know he can find freedom in New Bern, and thus New Bern may be the Mecca of a thousand noble aspirations."

Throughout much of the South, Reconstruction shifted political capital to black communities for the first time. Craven County used a black majority to elect state representatives, judges, and aldermen. Five African American schools were built during this time period. Hope was abundant.

But everything came crashing to halt with the politics of Jim Crow. The Ku Klux Klan spread its hateful rhetoric across the South, although the KKK avoided much of eastern North Carolina because of the region's considerable black majority. The Federal Government took care of the rest. Jim Crow devastated the black population of New Bern. Since African Americans could no longer vote, their political capital was gone. A New Bern lawyer and school principal named George White was the final African American Congressman to stay in the South, but he fled to the North after proposing an anti-lynching law. Congress would not elect another African American for over six decades.

In the coming years, New Bern residents were split along a racial divide that ran roughly through the center of town. Blacks lived to the west of George Street in narrow shotgun houses built so close to each other that neighbors could often pass food from one window to the next. On the other side of town, Tryon Palace dominated the landscape. The large, brick mansion was the governor's home in the years before the Revolutionary War. To the east of Tryon Palace, colonial homes steeped in Neo-Classical, Georgian, and Italian architecture created an insulated world for New Bern's white elites. The only blacks who were welcome in this part of town were day laborers and maids.

Despite New Bern's racial divide, the Great Fire of 1922 created a momentary influx of goodwill from several unexpected places. On the Sunday after the fire, thousands of travelers ventured into the city to provide food and clothing for the homeless. Fort Bragg sent 1,000 tents. The American Red Cross helped to secure new home sites for the victims. In a mass meeting, townspeople collected Christmas money for the homeless. Even the Ku Klux Klan sent money from two of its branches.

But for much of the black community in New Bern, the aid wasn't enough. Dorcas Carter was sad to see so many of her friends move to Chicago, Philadelphia, and New York. Her family was staying behind. New Bern was the only home they had ever known. Their identity was tied to this land, even if it lay buried beneath ashes and crumbling black shingles. Somehow they would find a way to put their lives back together again.

Dorcas realized that Judgment Day hadn't come here after all.

As a teenage boy living in New Bern, Ed Bell didn't think much about race. The boundaries were pretty clear. Whites never came to his neighborhood, and he rarely entered theirs. Occasionally he would gather up a group of friends to pick fallen pecans from the streets along the Trent River, but it wouldn't be long before a white man would scold them for hanging out where they didn't belong. Ed knew better than to walk inside the downtown Kress's or to stop for a bite to eat at Clark's soda fountain. These places were off limits. But Ed didn't have time to feel bitter. Life was moving fast enough already.

Ed came from a large and rambunctious family, the 12th child out of 13. His mother worked as a maid for some of the wealthiest families in New Bern, giving the Bell family a slightly higher social standing in the black community. Ed's father drove a delivery truck for the Ives Oil Mill on the west side of town. Ed liked to tag along when his father drove outside of town to pick up Nazi POWs to work at the oil mill. Ed sat with the prisoners in the bed of the truck, unaware that these men wanted to create a world that was entirely blond, blue-eyed, and white. On other days, Ed ran errands for the white men at the mill, or for the trainloads of American soldiers who made pit stops down at the train depot.

At night, Ed and his friends liked to steal cast-away cucumbers from the pickle factory and sweet potatoes from another factory down the street. Black New Bern came alive after dark. Ed would hitch a ride to a waterfront club across the Neuse River in James City, where rhythm and blues favorites such as Ruth Brown sang on a regular basis. Locals came out to sell pork chop sandwiches, potato salad, chitlins, and white lightning moonshine. Back in New Bern, juke box music could always be heard down in Frog Pond, where a social club occupied the second floor of the Royal Dry Cleaners. And then there was the intersection of Dodge City and Duffyfield, where gun shots mingled with the sounds of juke joints at all hours of the night.

New Bern was an exciting place for a boy like Ed. It was also a very close-knit community. Ed was a rebellious child, but he knew better than to push the limits too far. When he got in trouble at West Street School, he'd get a whooping from his teacher, who'd then take him home to get a whooping from his mother. Later on, he'd get a whooping from his father and any other adult who happened to be in the neighborhood. All the teachers at West Street School lived nearby; they also went to church with their students. Parents respected these teaches because they had a personal connection to them.

No one embodied this commitment more than Ed's fifth grade teacher, Miss Carter. She was a rail-thin woman of steel, and her students feared and admired her in equal measure. Miss Carter was a stickler for proper speech, discipline, and manners. She was highly refined, having been educated at Boston University soon after the school was integrated. Miss Carter knew that the South would follow suit before too long. Her students needed to be prepared for that glorious day. Miss Carter lived for these moments to help her community. It's why her family stayed behind after the Great Fire of 1922, and it's why Miss Carter – Dorcas Carter – loved being a teacher.

"Honey, dinner's almost on."

"In a minute, baby," Ed Bell called down to his wife.

Over the past two hours, the afternoon sunlight had faded to dusk, casting the room in a soft, dim light. I could smell grilled chicken from the kitchen below, mixed with the faint hint of garlic and basil. My stomach growled. I'd lost track of time; my wife would be expecting me home for dinner soon.

I looked down at a faded, black and white picture from Ed's senior year in high school. He's leaning against a trophy case with his hands in his pockets, smiling confidently, wearing khaki slacks and shiny black loafers. His letter sweater is buttoned over a plaid shirt.

The man sitting before me looked remarkably unchanged from this teenage boy, despite the passage of fifty years.

Ed showed me a team picture of the JT Barber football squad. For two years, Ed attended West Street School before JT Barber High School opened in 1955. West Street School had served the black community of New Bern since 1905; it was now an elementary school. The new high school was named after the legendary Mr. Barber, who was the principal at West Street for 39 years.

Ed Bell grew up at a time when high school football was king in New Bern. Thousands of fans packed the stands at Kafer Park on Friday nights to watch star players such as George Slaughter and Bud "Preacher" Parker lead the all-white Central High School. Joe Caruso was the imposing coach for the Central Bears, guiding his team to a string of winning seasons in the 1950s. On Thursday nights, the black community of New Bern came out to watch the mighty Warriors of J.T. Barber High School, under the direction of Simon Coates. Coach Coates was a 300 pound bear of a man who would be an institution in New Bern for decades to come. One of his assistants, Grover Fields, eventually became principal at the newly integrated high school in 1970.

Ed Bell was captain of the 1956 J.T. Barber football squad. Another prominent member of the team was Walt Bellamy, a lanky, 6'11" end who went on to fame as an All-American basketball player at Indiana, an Olympic gold medalist, and an inductee into the NBA Hall of Fame. The Warriors trounced opponents from as far away as Elizabeth City, Durham, and Raleigh. When they returned home after each win, a bell would toll across Duffyfield and the rest of black New Bern, sending hundreds of people into the streets for an impromptu celebration.

Each Warrior victory was a powerful statement against the inequalities of segregation. There was no such thing as "separate but equal" in the New Bern public schools. The textbooks and desks at J. T. Barber were secondhand castaways from the all-white Central High School. When Central High School ordered brand new electric typewriters, J.T. Barber was stuck with old-fashioned, manual typewriters. Dorcas Carter and her colleagues at West Street Elementary taught geography lessons without a globe, while the white elementary schools had extra globes gathering dust in a storage room. The basketball teams at the all-black school played in a gym with a dirt floor and no roof. Central High School had its own gym, but it was off limits to the students living west of George Street. The football equipment at J. T. Barber was also inferior. Players didn't have rib pads, and their facemasks looked flimsy and brittle compared to the newer, Central High School equipment. Ed Bell and his Warrior teammates wanted to play against Central High School, to prove once and for all that they were just as good as the boys from the other side of town. Central head coach Joe Caruso was intrigued by the idea. He admired Simon Coates's innovative offensive schemes, often attending J.T. Barber's Thursday night games to borrow concepts for his own squad. But the ruling class in New Bern wasn't ready for a football game between whites and blacks. At least not yet.

J. T. Barber finally won the attention of white New Bern with a 13-12 victory over High Point in the 1956 state championship at Kafer Park. No team, black or white, had ever won a state championship in New Bern before. Ten years later, Simon Coates led J. T. Barber to another state championship. Four more decades would pass by before New Bern could even think about winning a state championship again. The coming years would forever change the social fabric of the town. Integration was here at last, years after the landmark *Brown vs. Board of Education* decision.

"Miss Cardah?" a young boy said with his hand raised high in the air.

"Miss Car-Ter," Dorcas Carter corrected him. "Use proper diction when you speak, young man."

"Yes, ma'am." The boy tried again. "Miss Car-Ter, what they doin' out there?"

Dorcas Carter looked out her window to see hundreds of high school students marching passed West Street School in the direction of downtown New Bern. Dorcas Carter didn't know quite what to tell her fifth grade class.

For the past three days, students at J. T. Barber had staged a series of sit-ins at the Kress store and at Clark's soda fountain downtown. Twenty nine students had already been arrested, including Ed Bell's younger nephew. Earlier that Friday morning, a group of at least 200 protesters left St. Peter's AME Zion church to picket both stores again. Six weeks had passed since the fateful day of February 1, 1960, when four college students first sat at a Woolworth's lunch counter in Greensboro, about 180 miles west of New Bern. The sit-in movement had exploded across the South, prompting demonstrations in at least fifteen cities and nine states. That evening, Martin Luther King was planning a rally at Rue Chapel AME Church. Dorcas Carter was anxious to see the charismatic young preacher again, after meeting him years ago when she was in graduate school at Boston University.

As Miss Carter watched the protesters march by her classroom window, she could faintly hear the sounds of "We Shall Overcome." Her stomach tightened. She felt apprehensive, but lingering just below the surface was an exhilarating sense of pride.

"What they doin' out there?" the boy asked again.

"You'll see soon enough," Miss Carter responded, before resuming her lesson at the chalkboard.

A decade later, Dorcas Carter took her class on a field trip to Tryon Palace. So much had changed since that December day in 1922 when she watched her neighborhood crumble into ash.

"Where we going, Miss Car-Ter?" a little boy with blond hair and bright blue eyes asked his fifth grade teacher. The boy held a much darker hand in his own. Dorcas Carter insisted on this. Her classes marched together two at a time, a black student always paired with a white student. Other tourists at Tryon Palace might stare at her class in disbelief, but she didn't care. It was the right thing to do.

Miss Carter's class marched in a straight line to the Tryon Palace gardens. In the early morning sunshine, the blend of colors must have been truly stunning.

On a spring morning many years later, I drove down Walt Bellamy Drive along the Trent River. The Trent Court housing projects appeared to my left, a maze of drab, brick apartments where over a thousand low-income residents of New Bern lived. Long clotheslines stretched between the buildings, with t-shirts and jeans flapping in the breeze coming off the river. The bright clothing provided the only color in the area. In the distance, I could see the stately rooftop of Tryon Palace, my final destination.

I had only been to New Bern once before. In 2002, our team in Durham played against the Bears in the first round of the state playoffs, arriving long after darkness had fallen over the sandy pines. We were competitive for a half, before folding in the third quarter. New Bern went on to play Independence for the state championship that year, the first of four such meetings between Independence and New Bern over the next six years. Independence won the first three contests with relative ease, but the 2007 state championship was a different story.

New Bern was still in a state of euphoria from that victory back in the fall. I felt jealous of their success. We'd never won a state title at Jordan High School. I didn't know what it was like to end a season without the feeling of heartbreak. Sure, we won plenty of games, but like most teams, a state championship was still out of reach.

I pulled into the parking lot at Tryon Palace, where Sharon Bryant, the African American outreach coordinator at Tryon, soon greeted me at the visitor center. She had agreed to take me on a tour of New Bern's black community.

Sharon Bryant was a stylish woman in her forties with sharp eyes and an intense, thoughtful demeanor. She grew up in New Bern and attended segregated schools until the 5th grade. Later on, she was a cheerleader at the newly consolidated New Bern High School. Sharon eventually married a military man and lived for a number of years overseas and in Houston, Texas. When her marriage ended, Sharon returned with her three young children to New Bern. Despite its many imperfections, New Bern was her home. She wanted her children to be raised here.

I rode with Sharon down Broad Street to Kilmarnock Street, where the Great Fire of 1922 first took wind at the home of Henrietta Bryan. Row after row of identical brick apartments dominated the blocks north of Kilmarnock Street. This was Craven Terrace, the other low-income housing complex in New Bern. Craven Terrace was even larger than Trent Court, housing somewhere between 2,000-3,000 black families.

From there, we headed east through Five Points, Frog Pond, and Dodge City.

"We're going deep into the African American section now," Sharon told me.

Sharon knew the history of every street corner, church, and business in the heart of black New Bern. The past came alive as we drove for over an hour through neighborhoods that had seen better days; clapboard houses with chipped paint or no paint at all; churches that were built by their congregants brick by brick, then burned to the ground, then rebuilt again with a painstaking attention to detail; funeral homes, dry cleaners, recreation centers, and aging schools. I felt the pulse of this community in all of its unvarnished beauty.

We drove through a section of Duffyfield with ranch homes and carefully tended lawns.

"In this area right here, there were nothing but school teachers," Sharon said.

We passed Dorcas Carter's home, then the home of Dorothy Bryan, whose daughter Gwendolyn was one of the first four students to integrate New Bern High School. J.T. Barber's large brick house soon appeared to my left.

It bothered Sharon that so many students in New Bern knew nothing about their own history.

"To me, if I live in an area, I should be able to tell you something about that area. History is repeating itself here. Ask kids about slavery, and all they know is what they *may* have seen in a picture. *'Oh yeah, we came from Africa.'* You didn't come from Africa. Some of your forefathers may have come from Africa, but you didn't come from Africa. Everything has been swept under the rug or sugarcoated, but when you talk about slavery, the ugliness of it comes out, and they can't deal with it. That's why we need to put history back into schools because our kids are going to be lost. They don't know it."

"So first, you have to acknowledge all the skeletons in your closet?" I asked her.

"Exactly. You have to acknowledge everything that has taken place, digest it, accept it, *and move on*! And once you do that, this world will be a better place. You have your uppity whites, you have your uppity blacks. Each side has the same thing. So what's keeping us from living together?"

I asked Sharon if she thought that integration had helped the black community of New Bern. She considered the question carefully, her brow furrowing as she thought about the complicated history of race in these neighborhoods.

"Some people say the love in our community is not there anymore."

"Do you agree?"

"I don't know," Sharon said, shaking her head. The brick gates of Tryon Palace appeared in the distance. "Integration opened doors that could have stayed closed forever."

Sharon stared out the window as we drove through the Trent Court housing projects.

"But we have to find a way to bring back our community."

New Bern High School looked very different in the light of day. Night time has a way of distorting our perceptions and exaggerating our insecurities. Shadows are always larger than the objects they reflect. Sounds take on a distorted quality, playing tricks on the mind. Our football players must have felt this way when we drove down here five years ago to play the Bears. Perhaps it was just a sense of awe, since New Bern was a legitimate football powerhouse.

Skip Crayton pulled into the parking lot next to New Bern's football stadium and grabbed another stick of gum from the pocket of his sailing jacket. When I told Skip I was planning a trip to the New Bern area this spring, he gladly volunteered to introduce me to Coach Curlings. Skip had shaggy white hair and a tanned, windblown face. He was a real estate agent in town. He also wrote a weekly column for the *Sun Journal*, where he often shared his childhood memories of New Bern, the land of his birth and the only place he had ever wanted to live.

"If I had a choice," Skip said to me when I first met him, "I'd make this area the 51$^{st}$ state in the union."

Skip was territorial about his home town. If someone had a problem with that, he really didn't give a damn. When neighboring Kinston started bragging about its bustling growth, Skip wrote a column comparing Kinston's downtown streets to a bombed out section of Baghdad. He loved every piece of hate mail that followed.

The New Bern football team was just finishing an afternoon workout as we walked into the weight room to meet with Coach Curlings. He was sitting at a desk in the corner of the room. Piles of college letters and other paperwork cluttered every free space around him. For a man who had just derailed the nation's most prominent football dynasty, I expected something a bit more regal. But that didn't mesh with Coach Curlings' personality.

Bobby Curlings came to New Bern as an assistant coach in 1997 to work under Chip Williams, a legend in his own right who ultimately compiled a 132-55 record in his 15 years at New Bern. When Coach Williams retired in 2005, he reapplied for the head coaching job, only to find that a member of the school board had blocked the principal's recommendation. Despite protests from the community, Chip Williams was not offered his job back. Months of uncertainty hovered over the program before Coach Curlings agreed to take the job.

Bobby Curlings led the Bears to a respectable 9-3 record in his first year as the head coach. But the season ended with two blowout losses. At the age of 37, Bobby Curlings felt the weight of the entire community on his broad shoulders.

The following season took on a scope that was far beyond the hopes of one small southern town.

I love the purity of high school football. Perhaps this makes me naïve. I sometime wonder if anything in this world can ever be free from the cancer of our own human weakness. For this reason, I'll narrow my focus to the football field alone. Corruption seeps in when you start to include the sports boosters, sponsors, college recruiters, ESPN producers, and all the unrequited dreams of families living in poverty.

2007 was a bad year for high school football.

Let's start with Miami's Northwestern High School, 6-A state champions and the #1 football team in the country for 2007, according to ESPN. The previous year, star running back Antwaine Easterling, an eighteen year old senior, was caught having sex on a locker room floor with a fourteen year old girl. Later on, two of his teammates joined Easterling for sex with the same girl on school property again. When Northwestern principal Dwight Bernard was informed of the incidents, he swept the matter under the rug. Easterling was charged with a felony sex crime three months later, just days before Northwestern's state championship game against Lake Brantley. Principal Bernard let Easterling play anyway, and the star running back tallied 157 yards in the team's 34-14 victory. A grand jury eventually charged Bernard with a felony for covering up the sex crime. In the aftermath, twenty one employees at Northwestern lost their jobs, included the principal, the athletic director, and the entire coaching staff.

The grand jury concluded its investigation by saying, "The consequences for the little girl included attempted suicide and life in a residential psychiatric facility. The consequences for the school included a state football championship, the possibility of a nationally televised high school football game for the team, increased exposure for the players and coaches, and perhaps most important, an image of success for a school that was failing in nearly every other way."

In spite of the scandal, ESPN televised Northwestern's highly anticipated game against Southlake Carroll in Texas the following year.

Not to be outdone, Alabama's Hoover High School cast a similar black eye on the sports world in 2007. The Hoover Bucs were the subject of MTV's highly-rated TV show *Two-A-Days*, a behind-the-scenes look at the team and its controversial head coach, Rush Propst. At the end of the 2007 season, Propst resigned from Hoover in the wake of an eligibility scandal that forced the Bucs to forfeit five victories. Propst also admitted to fathering a child outside of his marriage, although he denied accusations by *The Birmingham News* of alleged affairs with an assistant principal and several other women at the school.

Perhaps the most bizarre scandal of the year involved a lineman named Kevin Hart from the rural town of Fernley, Nevada. On National Signing Day, Hart stood before a packed assembly of students and announced his decision to attend UC-Berkley on a full athletic scholarship. As the news cameras looked on, Hart's classmates and teachers gave him a standing ovation. The 6'5", 300 pound Hart certainly looked the part. But there was one small problem: the coaches at Cal had never heard of him. As Hart's story began to unravel, he claimed that a professional recruiter named Kevin Riley had duped him into thinking that he was offered a scholarship. When local police investigated, they discovered that Kevin Riley did not exist.

Finally, Hart admitted that the whole story was a hoax. "I wanted to play D-I ball more than anything," he said through a statement. "When I realized that wasn't going to happen, I made up what I wanted to be reality."

All across this country, high school athletes (and their families) have similar dreams of college stardom. Many athletes believe that they have to play for the right coach or the right program in order to get the "exposure" they deserve. They want a five-star rating from the recruiting web sites that make their money by exploiting the dreams of impressionable teenagers. Some coaches feed into the problem, but the vast majority of coaches do this job because they love working with kids.

That hasn't stopped parents from moving across district, county, and state lines to get their kid in the "right" program. More often, they'll simply lie about their home address. In large cities, where high schools are sometimes less than a mile apart, college recruiting has become a multi-headed beast. Why stay at your neighborhood school when you can simply transfer to another school down the street?

On numerous occasions, I've been told by parents, and even a few administrators, that it's our job as coaches to keep kids happy, no matter what.

*Go ahead and try to put my son on the bench,* these parents seem to be saying. *We'll just send him elsewhere.*

All of these complex issues came to a tipping point this past season in Charlotte, North Carolina. By the time Independence battled New Bern for the state championship on December 8, 2007, the Charlotte-Mecklenburg Schools were at the climax of the worst sports scandal in state history. New Bern didn't have to worry about student transfers, since they were basically the only show in town. But Independence was part of the largest school district in the state. Charlotte-Mecklenburg has at least 20 high schools, while Craven County only has three.

As with any gripping story, the main characters in this drama were never quite what the media made them out to be. It's not fair to simply call New Bern the good guy and Independence the bad guy. The truth lies somewhere in the gray areas.

There was more at stake than just a state championship on that cold night in early December. The very concept of community was also being put to the test.

The Charlotte-Mecklenburg Schools scandal began in much the same way as Watergate, with a petty crime that ballooned into something totally unexpected. Instead of a hotel burglary, the setting was a drunken high school party.

The scandal began in Union County, a rapidly growing suburb to the south of Charlotte. Early on the morning of September 13, 2007, Union County police officers learned that a 15 year old student was reportedly missing after stumbling into the woods during a party. When police arrived at the scene, they arrested a number of Providence High School students on alcohol-related charges. Two of these students, including the teen who hosted the party, were standout players on the Providence football team.

As news of the incident came to light, reporters at the *Charlotte Observer* began to wonder why a student living in Union County was enrolled at a high school in Charlotte. Was this legal? Would Providence have to forfeit all of their games? Charlotte always had rumors going around about ineligible players, but few of these rumors were ever substantiated. Providence eventually removed five football players from their team after the incident. The story appeared to reach a dead end after that.

Down the road at South Mecklenburg High School, star quarterback Jey Yokeley read about the Providence arrests with a certain degree of interest. After all, his team had an important conference game against Providence in a few weeks. But Jey had more pressing matters to deal with. His mother, Sheila Yokeley, had been fighting a rare form of breast cancer for the past three months, suffering through painful treatments and the eventual removal of her breasts. If it wasn't for the football team at South Meck, Jey didn't know how he could deal with it all. His teammates wore pink ribbons on the back of their helmets in honor of Jey's mother. For weeks, they delivered get-well cards and food to her front door. Jey finally felt at home here, after attending three different high schools before his senior year. Jey lived with his grandparents in the South Meck district while his parents tried to sell their home in Union County. Jey's mom was feeling better, and the Sabres were in the middle of their best season since 1994, the last year they made it into the state playoffs. Things were looking up.

Several weeks later, a young *Charlotte Observer* reporter named Ryan Basen wrote an article about a star football player who transferred from a private school in Charlotte to a public high school in Union County. The head coach hoped that this player's success would convince other Union County students to stay home rather than transferring to Charlotte schools.

The next day, Ryan Basen received a tip from a youth league coach who had read the article in the *Observer*. The coach gave Basen a list of other Union County players who were currently attending public schools in the Charlotte-Mecklenburg district. None of these players should be eligible to play, the coach said.

Jey Yokeley was one of the more prominent names on this list.

Basen and a handful of *Observer* reporters began an extensive investigation into football eligibility at CMS. They made house calls, checked public records, and contacted coaches about player eligibility. Basen soon realized that he had stumbled across a problem that was much larger than a handful of Union County players.

On a Thursday evening, November 1, a separate football incident dominated the state-wide news channels for over a week. Independence was playing Butler for the junior varsity conference championship. Tommy Knotts coached both teams at Independence, and the junior varsity Patriots had not lost a game in over seven years. Earlier in the season, the varsity's streak of 109 straight victories had ended with a loss to Cincinnati Elder, a powerhouse program out of Ohio. Both the junior varsity and varsity teams at Independence had rolled through the rest of the season. Butler was their biggest rival, the one team in Charlotte with a legitimate chance to dethrone the Patriots.

The Butler/Independence JV game was a back-and-forth slugfest, ending in a Hail Mary pass from Independence that fell short of the goal line. Butler had stunned the Patriots by a final score of 15-14. Butler's fans broke into a wild celebration after the game, vowing to end Friday's varsity contest in exactly the same way.

Tommy Knotts gathered his players at mid-field to begin his post-game talk. He wasn't used to this feeling. He didn't want his players to get used to it either. Over the sound of their coach's voice, the players heard an Independence fan heckling Tommy Knotts from the stands. The man was a 42 year old father who had driven down from Pennsylvania to see his son play in tonight's game. The parent was angry at Coach Knotts for his play-calling down the stretch.

"That's enough!" Knotts yelled at the man.

The cursing continued.

Finally, Tommy Knotts snapped. He approached the chain link fence separating the two men and slammed the fence into the heckler's face, splitting the man's nose open and sending him sprawling backward.

Knotts was given an indefinite suspension while CMS officials considered whether to charge the coach with simple assault on the

Independence parent. In the meantime, Butler lived up to its Thursday night boasts by defeating the varsity Patriots, 21-20. Ultimately, Knotts was reinstated to the team the following week, and the Patriots got their revenge on Butler in the second round of the playoffs, winning 20-7 in the rematch. But the dark cloud surrounding Independence would only grow larger.

Down the road at South Meck, the Sabres were excited about their first playoff appearance in thirteen years. Jey Yokeley had led the team to a 7-4 record, and they were traveling to Central Cabarrus for the first round of the state playoffs. South Meck students hadn't shown this much school spirit in years. The whole community was behind the team.

Just minutes before the Sabres boarded their bus for the game, their coach gathered the team into the weight room. He had terrible news. They wouldn't be traveling to Central Cabarrus tonight. The team had to forfeit all of its wins.

The *Charlotte Observer* discovered that although Jey Yokeley lived with his grandparents in the South Meck district, his grandparents did not sign the necessary paperwork to gain legal custody of him. By a North Carolina High School Athletics Association rule, student residence and athletic eligibility were two different things. The South Meck AD and head football coach should have known that Yokeley was ineligible, the NCHSAA said.

The devastated Sabres walked around the locker room in a daze, some crying, others shouting in frustration. Jey Yokeley stumbled to the top of the football bleachers and placed his head in his hands. *How could this happen?* he wondered between sobs. Surely this was some kind of nightmare.

Ryan Basen, the lead reporter for the *Charlotte Observer* investigation, received threatening phone calls and emails from all across Charlotte. How could he break the hearts of so many teenage boys, people wondered, not to mention the entire South Meck community? The timing was awful, Basen knew, but there was nothing he could do about it. South Meck was just the tip of the iceberg.

In the upcoming weeks, the integrity of the Charlotte-Mecklenburg Schools began to fall like a house of cards. The *Charlotte Observer* investigation turned up ineligible players at a growing list of schools: Vance High School forfeited two wins; North Meck forfeited one; Berry Academy forfeited two; and Waddell forfeited four (although one of the wins came against Berry Academy, creating a bizarre double forfeit in which neither team got credit for the win.)

The bombshells continued with the two most prominent programs in the city. The *Observer* reported that Independence starting cornerback Ranzell Watkins had used the address of a long-time Patriots football supporter living in the Independence attendance zone. Watkins was immediately removed from the team, although South Meck fans cried foul when Independence didn't have to forfeit any games. The NCHSAA ruled that a school couldn't be punished if a student lied about his address. By the time Independence and West Charlotte squared off for the state semifinals on November 30, both teams were embroiled in controversy. West Charlotte suspended its star receiver, Nicholas Mata, after the *Charlotte Observer* reported that Mata had used an address that belonged to the West Charlotte athletic director's in-laws. On the eve of the game, Independence suspended another defensive player for providing a false address.

Independence defeated West Charlotte the next day by a score of 10-8, but the ongoing eligibility scandal overshadowed the victory. CMS scrutinized the addresses of all 99 athletes on Independence's playoff roster, turning up five more ineligible players as the team headed to Winston-Salem to battle New Bern for the state championship. New Bern sat back and watched the madness unfold. They wanted to beat Independence fair and square. A forfeit win just wouldn't have the same meaning.

The last of the New Bern football players filed out of the weight room as I sat beside Head Coach Bobby Curlings and Skip Crayton.

"You know, Coach," Skip said to Bobby Curlings, "after that game, I'm sitting up there with two judges and two businessmen in town, and we're all just bawling our eyes out."

"Really?" Coach Curlings asked.

"Oh yeah. That win meant so much to the people in this town."

Bobby Curlings smiled. He'd heard this sentiment a lot here lately. Sure, people were happy now, but what would the Bears do for an encore? After a week of backslapping and congratulations, he'd turned his attention to the upcoming season. Curling's son would be a freshman football player at New Bern this year, so he could no longer separate the pressures of work from his family. But that was just fine. New Bern had already become one big family to him anyway.

About 280 miles to the west, things weren't so rosy in Charlotte. After the 2007 season, West Charlotte forfeited all thirteen of its victories, fired head coach Maurice Flowers and one of his assistants, and returned $16,000 in ticket sales. East Mecklenburg also forfeited all nine of its wins after CMS determined that an assistant coach had blatantly recruited three players. East Meck head coach Greg Hill was suspended until September of the following year, and the school paid a $7,038 fine to the NCHSAA.

After a five month, $96,000 investigation, CMS officials concluded that Independence was not guilty of any recruiting violations. It was time for everyone to move on, officials said. Tommy Knotts remained bitter about the whole ordeal. Opposing fans were equally disappointed that CMS couldn't find any evidence to punish the Patriots.

The whole scandal was deeply troubling to me. Charlotte's coaches and parents were systematically destroying the last remaining threads of their community. Parents had the right to want what's best for their children, but they didn't have the right to lie in order to get the best results. Maybe this was inevitable. Some people will say that it isn't reasonable to expect a growing city like Charlotte to maintain its ties to a local community. I disagree. When families lose their sense of loyalty to a neighborhood and its schools, they are more likely to become disconnected from their neighbors. A village can't raise a child if the villagers don't even know, or care, who the child is.

In many ways, Charlotte and New Bern are as different as night and day. Despite New Bern's checkered history of race, football has bridged the gap between two fiercely independent groups of people. It *is* possible for this phenomenon to carry over to a large urban district like Charlotte. But it will take coaches and parents who are willing to value community over championship rings, teambuilding over college exposure, and goodwill over selfish ambitions. A whole paradigm shift has to take place.

Charlotte must replicate the kind of excitement that existed in New Bern at the beginning of the Civil War. At that time, New Bern was a "Mecca of a thousand noble aspirations." Slaves could find freedom and opportunity here. When the black community burned to the ground in the Great Fire of 1922, many families followed their dreams to the North. But others stayed behind, just as they did in Asheville five years earlier when a fire destroyed the largest black school in the Appalachian Mountains. They also remained in Jacksonville when the beloved Georgetown High School burned to the ground on the eve of integration.

These communities survived because everyday men and women decided to stick it out. They created a larger family by convincing others that they shared the same basic aspirations: a decent education, a steady job, a place to call home. They simply wanted a fair chance.

Happiness, it seems, can only be fully realized when we share it with others. A football team is successful when all eleven players work together. Likewise, the hopes and dreams of a community are inextricably tied to cooperation. Citizens have to feel invested in the welfare of their neighbors.

I can think of no greater aspiration in this world.

# 9

## Bull City Lockdown
## Durham

Downtown Boston looked beautiful against the backdrop of a rich, blue sky. I took in the view as I settled into the top row of the visiting bleachers. It was a Saturday morning in September, and Boston English was taking on O'Bryant High School. O'Bryant was one of the three exam schools in Boston, and it shared a small wing of a four-story fortress with Madison Park High. The school complex was a uniform gray, with hardly any windows facing the football field. Chicken wire surrounded the building on all sides.

This was not the Boston I knew from postcards and history. Nothing about this area resembled Beacon Hill or the South End or the Boston Common. I was in Roxbury, the hidden Boston. Roxbury was the city's answer to Harlem and the Bronx. It was a place full of abandoned row houses and crime.

When I first moved to Boston, I was amazed by the degree of segregation in the city. Boston was an enlightened place, I was told. It was a stronghold of liberalism and tolerance. *Up here, you're not gonna see racism and ignorance like you do in the South.*

This view of Boston turned out to be a total lie.

I had just started teaching 10th grade literature at Boston English High School. English High was in the Jamaica Plain section of the city, about two miles south of Roxbury. I'd come to several conclusions after three weeks on the job. First, this was the line of work for me. I loved teaching from the very beginning, and I accepted the challenge with open arms. The second conclusion: I didn't need to worry about getting mistaken for a student because English High was almost entirely African-American and Hispanic; sadly, my skin color gave me credibility as an adult. I also realized that the word "community" was almost nonexistent up here.

Boston English is the oldest public high school in America. Founded in 1821, English High moved several times around the city before landing at a former gas factory in Jamaica Plain, or JP, as the area is often called. The school building is a cramped structure with rooms divided by partitions. Designed for 700 students, English High typically enrolls more than 1,100. Boston's school choice plan allows students to move seamlessly across a home district of multiple schools. In one of my 10$^{th}$ grade classes, only three of the 30 students actually lived in JP. The rest were from neighborhoods such as Dorchester, Mattapan, and Roxbury. Gentrification was slowly seeping into the area, but most of the neighborhoods south of downtown Boston continued to struggle with high rates of poverty and violent crime.

I did a quick sideline count. The visiting Bulldogs of English High carried 26 varsity players. O'Bryant didn't fare much better with 31. I was one of only 24 fans on the visitor side. There were 45 fans on the home side, including a small student section. I didn't see a single English High student at the game. The eight Bulldog cheerleaders chanted throughout the game to the empty metal bleachers. The English players wore ragged uniforms with navy and light blue stripes along the shoulders. The mismatched jerseys were carryovers from several decades.

When I arrived at the end of the first quarter, I sat behind Oscar Santos and John Canty, two veteran teachers who were strong supporters of the English football program. John Canty informed me that English was already up 14-0. The broken scoreboard looked as if it had been caught in a machine gun drive-by. Huge pockets of dust clouded the field with every tackle. Weeds had long ago replaced the grass, and the yard lines were barely visible.

There were no yard markers. I soaked up the familiar sounds of a high school football game, but the purity of it seemed hollow and false.

I looked at the clear blue sky above me and wondered if the world would ever be the same. Tuesday had begun like any normal day. I was out the door by 6:00 a.m., heading east on the subway's Red Line. The dark underbelly of Cambridge gave way to a startling sunrise as we crossed the Charles River into downtown Boston. *It's going to be a beautiful day*, I thought to myself. I switched to the Orange Line at 6:25 a.m. and rode south through Chinatown, Roxbury Crossing, and finally to the Green Street stop in Jamaica Plain. The early autumn air felt refreshing and clean as I walked the final three blocks to English High.

Several miles to the north, a plane arrived at Logan International Airport from Portland, Maine, carrying two sharply dressed men on board. I started teaching around the time these two men, Mohammed Atta and Abdulaziz Alomari, boarded American Airlines Flight 11 bound for Los Angeles.

The horrible news came to us two hours later.

What do you say to a group of high school students as they watch their innocence go up in flames? Do you shield them from the sight of bodies falling through the sky? One tower collapses; then another. All that remains is dust and rubble and shocked silence. The tears begin to flow as you hear sirens on a TV screen and watch with a feeling of utter helplessness.

Four days had passed, and the sky on this Saturday morning held the same beauty as that fateful Tuesday. Tragedies like 9/11 cause us to look inward. We think about family and home, and we long for the past. It is a natural response. As children we push further and further away from our parents, only to retreat into their comforting arms when danger strikes. At some point the scenario flips, and we become parents to our own fathers and mothers. There were no protective arms for me and for millions of other Americans after 9/11. But I felt a calling all the same. *Return to the land from whence you came.* The voice was faint, but it was there.

I watched a number of English High football games that fall, and each one pulled me homeward to North Carolina. There was nothing noble about this feeling. I taught some amazing students in Boston, and they cried out for love and hope. They desperately wanted to feel some sense of ownership in their school. They craved community, but the system almost always let them down. Even I let them down, in my own small way.

English High played only two Friday night games all season. The other eight games took place on Saturday mornings or immediately after school. City officials thought the games were unsafe otherwise. Late in the season, I traveled to see English play one of these two night games against Malden, a suburb of Boston that was relatively free from the risk of gang violence. The Malden stands were filled with students, parents, and community supporters. Five of us sat on the visitor side – three parents, John Canty, and me. The cheerleaders chanted to the empty bleachers once again.

Part of the problem was systematic. Boston required its students to maintain a C- average in order to be eligible for athletics. In most of the suburbs, athletes only had to maintain a D average. In Boston, the head football coach earned up to $8,500 for the job, and one assistant earned $6,000. But that was it. Funding for equipment and travel was almost nonexistent. O'Bryant's football stadium may have been substandard – and I use the term "stadium" rather loosely - but the stadium at English High was just plain pitiful. It looked like a relic from ancient Rome, minus the historic distinctiveness. A concrete slab ran the length of the home side, and a series of boulders formed a natural curve at the goal line. The boulders and slabs of concrete were covered in graffiti. Janitors regularly painted over the graffiti, but it came back like urban kudzu the very next day. Football games took place on the baseball outfield, and the turf was little more than dust and mud. As the weather cooled in the early weeks of September, the dirt hardened into New England permafrost. Games often turned into chaotic scrums as players on both sides fought through the dust and barely visible sidelines and yard markers. The scoreboard was falling apart and unusable.

Keith Parker had been the head coach at English for 22 years, and Barry Robinson was his top assistant. Robinson left North Carolina in 1984 to coach at English. Coach Parker and Coach Robinson ran the football program almost entirely on their own. Winning consistently was a major challenge, especially with a talent pool that was either ineligible or worked long hours after school. I admired these two men for their dogged commitment to English High, but they needed help in a major way.

High school football in Boston, like many inner-city communities across America, is a microcosm of society's larger problems. White students do not play for the Bulldogs or even attend English High because white families have long since abandoned neighborhoods like Roxbury and JP. This is the city where Paul Revere once made his gallant trip to the Old North Church and where the battle at Concord first ignited the American Revolution. Not far down the coast is the town of Plymouth, where the earliest Europeans landed with hopes of a better world. I was living in the enlightened age of a new century, yet the world seemed to be reverting further and further away from these hopeful visions.

So I did what many other whites have done before me; I abandoned the city. I'm not proud of it, but this wasn't my home.

There comes a time when each of us must go beyond the familiar boundaries of all that we know. Distance gives us the clarity to see the past for what it really is. It crystallizes our purpose in life, and it deepens our moral code. Distance is the perfect irony, the greatest lie, and the most effective teacher. I never really understood the allure of North Carolina until I no longer lived there. The "grass is always greener" phenomenon has a definite inverse, for we must leave home if we are to truly understand the beauty of home.

Leaving the South was a necessary step for me, and Boston certainly had a magnificence all its own. I loved the crispness of autumn in the Northeast, the roar of the subway train beneath Fenway Park, the soft crunching of snow along the Charles River at night, the bagpipes lining the streets of Southie on St. Patrick's Day. I loved the dogged toughness of my students in Jamaica Plain. Their optimism defied logic and challenged me to see education as an avenue for social change. My students desperately wanted a second family at English High. This family could evolve from a poetry club, a dance competition, ROTC, a sport, job training – each activity held the power to create a real community.

Living in Boston definitely shaped me, just as each day adds one stitch to the fabric of our lives. I returned to the South with a newfound appreciation for North Carolina and the struggles of its people. I wanted to foster a sense of community in my own small way. But how? People often say that they want to change the world, but how many of us actually do anything about it? Paralysis always seems to seep in. The problems are just too big. And how can a change ever be lasting? I started thinking about Coach Eccles and my father and all the other people who have been molded and shaped by athletics. Maybe I could be a coach and a teacher. I could teach kids that sports and academics are not mutually exclusive. I could do something I love and actually get paid for it. Today, the goal is still very clear to me. Never again will I stand by and watch the disintegration of a community without trying to do something about it.

The world is full of chance, and mere chance led me to the center of North Carolina. Durham is about seven miles east of Chapel Hill, so I was vaguely familiar with the city from my college years at UNC. My general perception of Durham was that it was dirty, gang-infested, and, perhaps most prominently, it was home to the hated Blue Devils of Duke University. For now, Durham would have to be my new home. Northern Durham High School had the one true powerhouse football team in the area, so I naturally wanted to teach there. I also interviewed at Jordan High School before flying back up to Boston to finish the school year. Jordan called first, so I took a job there as an English teacher and assistant football coach.

If I knew the history of Jordan football when I was hired, I probably would have taken a job at McDonald's instead.

On September 19, 1997, the Jordan High School football team accomplished something truly monumental. The moment seemed greater than the slaying of Goliath and more awe-inspiring than the D-Day assault at

Normandy. It was the product of years of hard work, dedication, sacrifice, and suffering. A glorious cascade of Gatorade fell on the shoulders of head coach Jimmy Weekman as the Falcon football players danced all the way home to Durham.

For the first time in four years, the Jordan Falcons had won a football game.

I couldn't believe it at first. Thirty seven consecutive games without a victory. The old saying goes that it's not whether you win or lose but how you played the game, but how do you write off thirty seven losses in a row? You have to throw the old clichés out the window with that figure. Even the streak-busting game was somewhat fitting. Jordan defeated Southeast Raleigh, a first-year school with no seniors and only one junior. In reality, one of the longest losing streaks in state history ended with a victory against a jayvee squad playing a varsity schedule.

Northern Nash was Jordan's opponent the following week, and the Falcons came to practice on Monday with an extra hop in their step. They could finally walk the halls at school without the constant jokes and taunts from their classmates. To top it off, this week was Homecoming, and Northern Nash entered the game winless at 0-4. Plus, the enormous weight was gone. The scarlet *L* for loser still felt like an eight ton chain, but everything seemed possible now.

On Friday, this newfound optimism ended with a 56-7 massacre at the hands of the lowly Northern Nash. The Falcons fell back on their losing ways for the rest of the year. It took another three seasons for Jordan to finally manage a winning record, something they had not done since 1973. It was only the second time since the Eisenhower administration that the Falcons had even gone to the playoffs. A forty year period of mediocrity. But it went beyond mediocrity. Even the worst athletic programs have occasional pockets of success. Mediocrity, by definition, means neither good nor bad, and Jordan was just plain bad.

Soon after I took the job at Jordan, I decided to leaf through the press clippings from those dark days of the mid-1990s. In a 1996 *Durham Herald-*

*Sun* article, dejected lineman Darryle Jackson said of the streak, "We are tired of feeling low; feeling you are no good. [A losing streak] is not as bad as losing a loved one, but when you go out and lose, you feel like you lost something you wanted and you didn't get to where you wanted to be." Quite the understatement. The following year, with the streak still very much alive, senior Eric Aikens had this to say in the *Talon*, Jordan's yearbook: "It takes a big man to be able to have played here these past couple of years. Sometimes we take a lot of abuse from not only the media and other teams, but from our peers too...Anybody who has played here these last couple of years must have had a tremendous amount of heart."

Words like heart, pride, perseverance, and adversity appear throughout these articles. Athletes often cloak the agony of defeat behind such platitudes in order to soften the blow and dull the pain. But the inalienable fact was still there – 37 straight games is a hell of a lot to lose. Even some of the yearbook captions tell the story: "Jaye Middleton runs for his life from the Northern defensive backfield...Tempers rise as Michael watches intensely from the bench." The 1996 *Talon* sums up the team's season with the following opening: "Winning isn't everything. The Varsity Football Team learned that well this year."

What was it, I wondered, that made Jordan football so bad for so long? Each article had the feel of an obituary, and every loss was like the death of an anonymous man. I felt no grief and no remorse after reading these stories. Death is a fact of life. May the Falcons rest in peace. Perhaps the Falcon players felt that way too. You have to insulate yourself from these things. The teenage mind is a fragile thing, and a crushed spirit can be irreversible. You dull the pain by not feeling anything at all. What's one more loss in the larger scope of life, right? Winning isn't everything. We gave it our best shot. We played as a team, etc, etc. This thought process is personal and unspoken, because no one wants to admit that they don't really care anymore. What is life without the ability to feel anything, after all?

So I read these articles with detachment. But I had to ask myself if I was really above the fray. What if I had been a member of that coaching staff?

Would I have moved on to a stronger program, abandoning Jordan just as I had abandoned Boston? I looked at these yellowing pictures of young men in agony, and I tried to figure out what could have been done differently. Perhaps nothing. Perhaps everything.

No one knows the suffering of those years better than Mike Briggs. When Coach Briggs reminisces about Jordan football in the 1990s, he sounds like a Vietnam veteran lamenting the horrors of battle. But there is a hint of triumph at the mere survival of it all. The soldier dreads the violence and daily drudgery of war. He longs for the simple life of a quiet town with a girlfriend pressed against his arm as he drives down the empty streets on a Friday evening, the gentle wind swaying in the trees, the cicadas singing their nightly songs. The soldier dreams of this other world, but the suffering somehow gives him life. When the brutality comes to a close, the soldier is a new man. The cicadas sound more beautiful than ever before. The barren streets of his rural town are alive with energy. The word *home* takes on a deeper meaning. Mike Briggs went through such a war. The losses piled higher and higher until winning seemed like an impossible fairytale. But he stayed in the bunker and fought. When the victories finally came, everything felt all the more glorious.

Mike Briggs endured the pain of those awful years because Jordan was an undeniable part of his identity. Briggs graduated from Jordan in 1988 and played football for Elon University. After Elon, Briggs coached down east for three years before returning to his alma mater as a junior varsity coach and teacher. Briggs suffered through the 37 game losing streak and most of the other losing seasons of the 1990s. He cringed, he struggled, and he survived the worst of the storm. Jordan's fortunes began to turn when Rick Brown became the head coach in 1998. With Briggs as his offensive coordinator, Jordan exploded for a 12-2 record in 2000 and reached the third round of the state playoffs. The following season, Briggs became the head coach.

Ignorance is bliss, so they say, and I was ignorant of Jordan's past when I joined the staff in 2002. I love working at Jordan, and I don't see myself leaving anytime soon. The drudgery of those losing seasons is largely absent from the school these days, and only a few veteran teachers remember how bad Jordan football used to be. But the change did not happen overnight. Coach Briggs instituted a rigid weight program. Off-season conditioning also became a vital key to his success. Above all else, Coach Briggs convinced his players that football success and personal character were forever intertwined.

Winning is important. No coach can deny it, and if he does, he can proclaim the value of character all day long from the unemployment line. Defeat isn't tolerated in our culture, and all the virtue in the world cannot rescue us from this simple fact. But winning doesn't have to be an isolated accomplishment. Winning stems from an insistence on community in its purest form. A true teammate abandons his name, his face, and his ego. Something greater and more lasting fills the void, but it is not an easy transformation. The ego constantly screams for approval; jealousy is as natural to Man as breathing, and team unity often gives way to instant gratification. Every community is different, so the dynamics of a team have to be weighed accordingly.

No city embodies this give and take between personal glory and collective action quite like Durham.

We call it the Bull City Lockdown.

It's an easy gesture to teach. You make a fist with each inverted hand, and then you raise the opposing thumbs into horns. That's the Bull City part. Then you pound your fists together several times in a forceful and intimidating fashion. That's where the Lockdown part comes in. You can use the "Bull City Lockdown" on any number of occasions – a vicious hit, a touchdown run, or a mere sign of confidence at the beginning of a game. It doesn't matter when you use it, as long as you carry the swagger that comes from being a Durhamite. The origins of the Bull City Lockdown run as deep as the city itself.

In April of 1865, an exhausted Confederate General named Joseph Eggleston marched to the outskirts of Durham and surrendered his 88,000 troops to General Sherman and the Union army. The surrender was inevitable, since Lee and Grant had already begun the process two weeks earlier at Appomattox Courthouse. During the negotiations, soldiers from both armies looted a nearby tobacco factory owned by John Ruffin Green. Union soldiers had never sampled the sweet, bright-colored tobacco before, and when they returned to the North, they immediately wired John Green for more. Word traveled fast; soon, Durham's brightleaf tobacco was the product of choice for smokers across America.

John Green wanted a distinctive symbol for his new product. Colman's Mustard used a bull's head in its marketing campaigns, and since that company was based out of Durham, England, the bull became an obvious choice for Green. The success of Bull Durham Smoking Tobacco was unprecedented in the post-war economy of the South. The bull logo was plastered across the world, from newspapers and playing cards to a giant banner on the Great Pyramid in Egypt. Other entrepreneurs tried to cash in, including a poor, hard-nosed farmer by the name of Washington Duke. "Wash" Duke slowly made a name for himself by selling tobacco from the back of his wagon, but John Green's Bull Durham tobacco reigned supreme.

The whole market changed when Washington Duke's son, Buck, took over his father's company. Buck was a brilliant workaholic with the business acumen to conquer the tobacco market. He gambled on the untested technology of cigarette-rolling machines, and before long, the "Duke of Durham" cigarette brand was outselling all the rest. Buck Duke had the ruthlessness of a Rockefeller, and by the age of thirty-three, Buck bought out his Bull Durham competition. Duke's American Tobacco Company wiped out 250 smaller companies and put Durham on the map as the leading tobacco producer in the world.

Durham quickly grew into a thriving working class town sprinkled with giant mansions for its tobacco and textile magnates. A buzz began to circulate across the region. Durham was the place to be for the working man. It was the Chicago of the South, a magical city, a place where the sweet smell of brightleaf tobacco mixed with the even sweeter smell of new money. In downtown Durham, a forty-by-fifty foot sign lit up the night sky with multi-colored lights that proclaimed, "Durham: Renowned the World Around." Other Southern towns, such as my hometown of Gastonia, gained similar prosperity with their own mills, but it was the two-headed monster of tobacco and textiles that truly put Durham on the map.

Then there was the issue of race. Most of the South's industrial wealth stayed in the hands of the white upper crust, while African Americans continued to struggle under Jim Crow. But Durham was different. In 1898, a handful of black men forever altered the racial dynamics in the city when they founded North Carolina Mutual Life Insurance. John Merrick, a former slave and owner of several barber shops, ignited the growth of NC Mutual, followed by Aaron Moore and C.C. Spaulding. NC Mutual allowed thousands of black families to become homeowners for the first time, and black businessmen seized the opportunity to open stores in the downtown district. White insurance companies saw black customers as a financial risk, but men like Merrick, Moore, and Spaulding ripped that theory into shreds.

Durham was no longer just the Chicago of the South. It was Harlem as well, replete with a bustling downtown culture of restaurants, theatres, and nightclubs that made Durham the closest thing to a Renaissance anywhere outside of upper Manhattan. Outsiders quickly took notice. Booker T. Washington and W.E.B. Du Bois visited the city at the height of its booming success, and while the preeminent black scholars could agree on little else, they each praised Durham as a model for racial advancement. Durham was a beacon of hope for the common man, the outcast, the downtrodden, and the oppressed.

But the reality of Durham did not always gel with its public persona. There was still the thorny dilemma of class. A new aristocracy seized the tremendous profits of the tobacco and textile markets while the laboring poor continued to grow exponentially. With the success of NC Mutual, the black community of Durham saw a parallel split along economic lines. Two Durhams existed: Black Durham and White Durham. Both communities were lauded for their financial successes, but they were also a case study of the haves and have-nots. In the 1950s, urban renewal led to the destruction of much of what was called Hayti, a black enclave of Victorian homes, carefully manicured gardens, nightclubs, and businesses near the downtown area.

Durham was not a magical city, as some had called it. Racial tensions bubbled to the surface as they did in every Southern community. Economic class lines remained stubbornly intact. But a spirit of pride remained, and Durham citizens clung to the essential goodness of their community with uncommon zeal. *This is the Bull City, damnit. There's a cloud of tobacco smoke hovering overhead, but it's our cloud of smoke. We're rich and poor, black and white, educated and unrefined. Our flaws are out there for everyone to see, and that's how it's gonna be.*

Durham was a city of contrast. One side possessed the prosperity of Duke University, NC Central University (the first black liberal arts college in America,) American Tobacco, and North Carolina Mutual. On the other end of the spectrum was the West End, East Durham, Braggtown, the South Side, and other communities struggling to find a place in the city. Durham was a glass container overflowing with competing voices. The tension was messy, but it was a fascinating mess.

Jordan High School embodies the evolving nature of Durham. When Jordan was built in the 1960s, the surrounding area consisted of farms and wetlands. Today, Jordan is a motley blend of the old and the new. The school is part rural, part inner-city, half-white, and half-black. Since the integration of all-white Durham High and all-black Hillside High in the early 1970s, Durham has struggled to maintain a sense of community within its public schools. Students can transfer from one school to the next with relative ease, and to a degree, the concept of neighborhood schools seems like a thing of the past. This fluid nature is not unique to Durham. Most large cities face similar obstacles to community building, and the Federal No Child Left Behind legislation encourages the practice of competition between schools. Teachers and coaches continue to struggle onward despite these obstacles.

The most successful students in any district are the ones who feel a distinct, familial tie to their school. They see their school community as a refuge from the chaos of the outside world. Students want structure, whether they admit it or not, and a good school provides all of these things and more. It is a truly daunting task, but the very fate of our society depends on the success of public education. There are many ways to create this kind of school climate. Football is just one small effort, but it is particularly effective in a community like Durham. Jordan High will never bring out an entire town for a Friday night game, but it is in places like Durham where football can truly make a difference.

The four of us were an unlikely group. When we arrived at Jordan to coach football, our histories and backgrounds could not have been any more different. We mirrored the racial diversity of Jordan High School (Chris Starkey and LaDwaun Harrison were black; Tim Bumgarner and I were white), but the physical similarities ended there. Coach Starkey was the shortest, but he was powerfully built after years of heavy lifting. Coach Harrison was a bruising former running back who reminded me of Jamie Burris from my own playing days. Coach Bumgarner was at least 6'4" with a bald head, mustache and goatee. He resembled a WWF pro wrestler, and he had a booming voice to match.

I was the oddball of the group. All three of these coaches played football in college, and there was no way I could match their imposing presence. But a strange phenomenon happens with athletics. Personal differences grow obsolete next to a higher goal, and competition reveals the true character of an individual. All four of us loved football, and we cared deeply about helping kids. That's what really mattered. From this point of view, our personalities were remarkably similar. There are few people in the world I respect more than these three coaches. They are devoted fathers, loving husbands, and skilled teachers.

Coach Starkey was our head jayvee coach that first year. It was a season of highs and lows. Jordan High School no longer had the worst football program in the state, but ripples from the past still persisted. We didn't reach every kid that first season. As a coach, perhaps it's unreasonable to hope that you *can* help everybody, but that was our goal.

Several freshman athletes seemed utterly beyond our reach. One of them was a 6'6" 360 pound lineman who terrorized students and teachers alike. He moved to Detroit in the middle of our season after being kicked out of Jordan, but his problems persisted; the following year, he was arrested for assaulting his dad. Another freshman encountered even graver legal problems that season. He was a tremendous punt returner for us and a solid student. But a rage bubbled just beneath the surface, and we struggled to keep him out of trouble. The young man was sent to Durham's alternative school after stealing a teacher's wallet; his downward spiral continued from there. Before long, he had stolen a car, kidnapped a college student, and raped her at knife-point. I remember staring at the police mug shot of our troubled former player and wondering if we could have done anything to prevent this awful crime.

Another freshman player dealt with demons of a different sort. He'd been moved to a foster home after getting beaten with the blunt end of an axe by his father, and he struggled with schizophrenia. The rage would appear out of nowhere. Usually we could channel it productively by sending him to the defensive line with instructions to destroy the ball carrier. At these moments he became a standout player. But more often than not, the rage exploded into disaster. After an early season loss, he threw his helmet to the ground and charged the winning team while they sat in their post-game huddle. We restrained him before any damage was done. The following week, after another disappointing loss, he threw his helmet to the ground again and went after the referees. Once again we were lucky to prevent any damage.

These three young men were far from the norm. We had a large number of success stories, but it was the troubled players who kept us up at night. Our mission was to help these young men develop into productive citizens, and jail time did not constitute success by any means. Perhaps we should have recognized the demons earlier on. Maybe we could have saved these kids from themselves. I don't know for sure. As coaches, we never wanted to lose a kid like that again.

Our 5-4 record that first JV season improved to 6-4 the following year. Then there was the glorious, 2004 undefeated season in which Antonio Smith's miraculous touchdown catch ended Garner's 55 game winning streak. The varsity team saw similar improvements under the steady direction of Mike Briggs, going 5-6, 7-6, 7-6, 10-4 and then 9-4. The victories were nice, but winning was merely a byproduct of other successes. Our players started to see Jordan football as a program instead of a team. We worked tirelessly to keep kids eligible; we provided tutoring for students on the brink of failure; we disciplined students who misbehaved in class. In short, we did everything possible to connect personal character to athletic performance. Varsity offensive coordinator Jason Luck dove into the complicated world of college recruiting, spending countless hours making highlight tapes to help kids earn scholarships. The results were immediate: we had nine college signees in 2004 and nine more signees in 2005. We saw lower failure rates and increased parent involvement. Coach Starkey joined the varsity staff, and the Falcon defense solidified its reputation for smash mouth football. Coach Harrison took the helm of the junior varsity team and continued our program's success. Through it all, we tried to shape all of our players, regardless of their ability or background, into productive members of society.

I have a deep and abiding respect for my fellow coaches at Jordan High School. We coach because we love the game of football and because we love working with youth. We relish the excitement of a Friday night football game, and we think of these players as our own children. Football profoundly shaped our own identities as teenagers, and somewhere down the line a coach gave us the confidence to stand up for what we knew to be right. We paid them back by going into coaching ourselves.

For men like Coach Starkey, football was the key to a better world. Chris Starkey was born in a Brooklyn housing project along the East River. He was too young to remember being taken by his grandparents to live in Farmville, a rural town in North Carolina founded on tobacco farming and little else. Starkey still had a thick, down east accent, and he was the unchallenged comedian of the coaching staff. Like many rural North Carolinians, Starkey often spoke in outrageous comparisons. A football player was never simply weak. "That boy is softer than drugstore cotton," Starkey would say. An athlete with limited speed? "He's slower than a government check at the end of the month."

Coach Starkey got away with these sayings because he understood poverty on a very personal level. Growing up in Farmville, "if you didn't play football," Starkey said, "you weren't nothing. Tobacco was all we had."

Starkey grew up working in tobacco warehouses, but his grandfather refused to let him toil in the fields. His grandfather was a strict disciplinarian who didn't want Chris to live the difficult life of a tobacco farmer. The black community in Farmville was largely the product of slavery, and Starkey's extended family lived in eastern North Carolina long before the days of the Civil War. As a kid, Starkey sometimes heard the shouts of Klansmen riding through the back roads of his town at night. Like my own hometown of Gastonia, a railroad track physically separated whites from blacks.

Football and church were the primary ways for Starkey to get out of the house. One evening, Starkey came home from practice and grabbed a bite to eat in the kitchen. When his grandfather discovered the empty cupboard, he immediately stormed into his bedroom and started cleaning his gun. Starkey hid in his room as his grandfather threatened to shoot him if he ever ate all of his food again. The frightened boy didn't know if his grandfather was serious, but he wasn't about to find out.

Football was Starkey's ultimate ticket out of Farmville. His competitiveness and speed landed him a scholarship as a defensive back at Elizabeth City State University, where he majored in Psychology.

After college, Starkey did everything possible to simulate competition. He even tried bodybuilding for a time.

"I'm sick," Starkey said. "I gotta have that competition."

Coaching became a natural outlet for Starkey's fierce competitive streak. He moved to Durham and completed a master's degree in special education while teaching and coaching at a local middle school. Defense was Starkey's forte, and when he joined the staff at Jordan, he carried the hard-nosed tradition of the Bull City Lockdown with him. Football was Starkey's competitive outlet, but coaching also proved to be a good way to create a close-knit family.

"As a coach, I don't like finger pointing," Starkey said. "If one guy's fighting, you better be in there to fight too. You stand up and support each other, like a family's supposed to. You look out for your brothers during school and after school."

To Starkey, competitiveness on the football field equaled success in the real world.

"When you look out for a teammate like he's a family member, you learn how to win, and you take that into the workplace. If you are competitive on the football field, then you'll be competitive to get that job."

If Chris Starkey was the fiery bulldog of the coaching staff, then Tim Bumgarner was his giant, Caucasian brother. Coach Bumgarner brought the same level of intensity to coaching. He struck an intimidating pose, with a booming voice that echoed across southwest Durham whenever he got excited in practice. And he was almost always excited. Coach Bum, as we affectionately called him, was the team's unofficial preacher, partly for his ability to talk the ear off of almost anyone, and partly for his strong religious convictions. Coach Bum always said what was on his mind; he simply had no internal censor.

Tim Bumgarner originally came to Jordan High School because his son, Robert, was a rising ninth grader on the football team. Bum had coached Robert in the peewee leagues of the Durham Eagles and at Githens Middle School, but he swore he wouldn't follow his son to high school. That conviction didn't last very long. The next four years proved to be his most rewarding time as a coach.

Coach Bum loved many things about coaching. His favorite story was about Chris Miller, one of his offensive linemen. It was classic Bum; the man couldn't talk about his players without launching into an elaborate description filled with so much passion and enthusiasm that the listener inevitably came along for the ride. Coach Bum loved to work with guys like Chris. Bum was a fan of the underdog, the undersized lineman who used his intellect and a superior work ethic to beat his bigger and stronger foes.

"Chris was having trouble with pass protection," Coach Bum would say to anyone who would listen. "Guys were getting behind him. Then one game our quarterback, Eric Weaver, takes a deep snap, and I'm keying on Chris, and Chris is doing everything right. He's sliding his feet, he's got his hands engaged, the guy starts to flank him and Chris rides him right by the quarterback, and Weaver steps up and hits a 60 yard bomb for a touchdown. I didn't see the throw, and I didn't see the touchdown. All I saw was the pocket form and I saw a kid apply something that I taught him. I get chills just thinking about it."

Coach Bum is usually floating off the ground by this point in the story.

"When I saw that it was a touchdown, I ran onto the field during the game and grabbed Chris and hugged him, and I said, 'That's how you do it! That's exactly how you do it!' And of course the official comes running over and says, 'Coach you're gonna have to get off the field,' and I said, 'The hell I am! Did you see what my kid just did?!' I was so excited for him, because when I went up to grab him you could tell by looking in his eyes that he had done something special."

Coach Bum spoke with a rising intensity, and he moved his arms a mile a minute to simulate the triumphs of his long-struggling linemen. Bum was happiest when he told these stories. The world was as it should be, and these successes convinced him that football was more than just a game.

For the Bumgarner family, football had always been a way of life. Tim's father was an All-American lineman for Duke in the 1950s. Dwight Bumgarner never forced the sport on Tim, but football was simply in his son's blood. Tim became a Shrine Bowl lineman at High Point Central, and from 1979 to 1982 he played under Steve Spurrier at Duke. Coach Bum picked up his appreciation for offense from Coach Spurrier, who had just begun to make a name for himself in the coaching world. In 1982, Tim was a starting offensive lineman at Duke while his younger brother, Billy, was a starting defensive tackle for UNC.

"It nearly killed my mother," Coach Bum said. "She couldn't bear to watch."

Coach Bum's son was about to become the next family member to join the college ranks. Robert accepted a scholarship to play tight end for Presbyterian College, and his father couldn't have been more proud.

For the first time, Coach Bum would not be by his son's side.

"When Robert graduated, it left a tremendous hole in my heart," Coach Bum said. "But we're called to raise these guys up. They're on loan from God, and we have to let them go. I can't tell you how proud I am of him. I remember after we lost that final game, I just stood there and hugged him. I told him, 'It's been a tremendous honor for me to coach you all these years.' I told him he's in my soul. Whether he decided to play football or not, it really didn't matter to me."

Coach Bum cherished these special moments between a coach and a player. Before every game, he gathered his linemen in a circle of prayer. His starting center last year was Jewish; his right tackle was a Muslim; all faiths converged in these private moments before battle.

To Tim Bumgarner, coaching was a calling from above. He even toyed with going into the ministry before realizing that God wanted him to work with teenagers instead.

"I think we don't pray enough as a society, and you sow what you reap. We've turned our back on God in a lot of ways. We're called as Christians to give back, and this is one of the ways that I can do that. I love these kids. They're so pounded down. The world's beating on them and peer pressure is beating on them and in some cases, unfortunately, their parents are beating on them, and when they come out here, there should be no doubt that we love them."

When one of our seniors was kicked out of his house, Coach Bum and his wife were the first to take him in. They treated him like a son and helped him to get into a good college. They are his family now.

After Robert left for college, Tim Bumgarner couldn't stop coaching. New kids seemed to arrive every week, and many of them couldn't get in a stance or run a lap without passing out. If you drive down Garrett Drive in the sweltering heat of a summer evening, you can still hear Coach Bum's booming voice from the practice fields. It may sound like a revival sermon, and in a way it is.

I admire men like Chris Starkey and Tim Bumgarner for the energy they bring to coaching. They are much older than I am (although Starkey still claims to be eighteen and refuses to reveal his true age), yet they retain the childlike passion for life that eludes so many adults. They know how to balance humor and discipline as they coach, and when they tear down a player's ego, they are quick to build it back up in an appropriate fashion.

No one has mastered this careful balance between humor and discipline quite like LaDwaun Harrison. He is considerably younger than Starkey and Bumgarner, but he carries the wisdom of a much older man. When Harrison became the head jayvee coach, I had the unenviable task of taking over his offensive coordinator duties. Harrison is a brilliant tactician. He is an innovator, and he is not afraid to take risks on the football field.

According to Coach Harrison, our success as a football staff has everything to do with mutual respect.

"All of us are just real good people, and it's easy when you get around other good people to relate to them and form bonds, and we all just formed that kind of bond from the start. We look out for each other. We know what our own strengths are, and we play off of that. We just became friends. We came in together, so it felt like it was all of us against the world."

As a standout football player at Durham's Hillside High, LaDwaun Harrison treated every opponent as if he was a personal enemy. His focus before games was so intense that he rarely said a word to his teammates. Harrison obsessively visualized the defender in front of him. He hated him and despised him. He wanted to run over and through him until the defender surrendered every last bit of restraint. When the game started, Harrison went about his business with the steady calm of a silent assassin. No need to trash talk. Let the pads speak for themselves. Harrison's intensity carried over to the classroom, where he was a one of the top students in his class. He piled up over 2000 yards rushing and receiving as a senior, earning him a full football scholarship to Wake Forest University.

After graduating from Wake Forest, Harrison married his high school sweetheart, a striking and intelligent woman who attended the rival school down the road. Fellow Hillside graduates still can't forgive Coach Harrison for joining the football staff of his wife's alma mater. The Jordan-Hillside rivalry may not have the history of other great North Carolina clashes, but it is bitter nonetheless. A five minute drive separates the two schools. District lines run together in a seemingly haphazard fashion. Players and fans spend each summer taunting the opposing side. Everyone marks their calendar for the annual Falcon-Hornet football game.

Coach Harrison hated to lose, and he saw a direct connection between losing and a lack of discipline. To Harrison, every player had to understand that there was a right way and a wrong way to do things.

"You have to learn to respect people," he said, "and most importantly, you have to respect yourself. We force them to do more than they think they can do sometimes, and we don't take a lot of BS and excuses. We have a high standard, and we hold everybody accountable to that. We're all competitive, and we hate to lose, period, whether it's grades or anything else. We instill that in our kids. It's not okay to lose. When they leave us, they have that winner's attitude, that little edge that some people may consider cocky, but it's that chip on your shoulder that helps you get through the tough times."

Coach Harrison believed that one of the keys to our success was not playing favorites.

"We give everybody an opportunity. It's easy to have a good relationship with a great athlete. It's the ones that aren't the great athletes that we do the best job with. We've always found a way to get all the guys on the same page, the team page."

Like Coach Starkey, Coach Harrison thrived on the competition of coaching. He hated to lose games, but he also hated to lose kids to eligibility issues. Academic performance turned into yet another form of competition. Harrison knew the cruel realities facing these kids if they didn't get an education. It pained him to see so many players struggle with grades. *What can we do differently?* he asked himself over and over again. Academic failure became another defender staring at him across the goal line with sharp teeth and devilish eyes.

The answer was simple. We needed to do everything possible to create a community within our football team.

"Whoever you come in contact with, that's your community," Coach Harrison said. "We try to make sure they have the academics to do other things down the road. We all want to win, but we know that the most important thing is to get them into college. If you have a team that's doing well academically and they listen to you, that transfers onto the field. It all adds up."

When Antonio Smith made his miraculous catch to defeat Garner, I sprinted across the field with three men who have become a family to me. The moment was magical for any number of reasons. But above all, it was a communal experience. We achieved something lasting in the world without making shortcuts or moral compromises. These boys were growing into winners; that much was clear beyond a shadow of a doubt.

Every player on our team has a story. The plots may vary from one athlete to the next, but the lessons remain the same. Great stories invite us to find a bit of ourselves in the hopes and dreams of a main character. If the protagonist triumphs, so can we. I could tell hundreds of these stories, perhaps thousands. But two will suffice.

Kinney Rucker looked like a giant next to the wide-eyed boys in front of him. The campers sat in a shaded corner of the Jordan High School practice field, drinking Capri Sun pouches and eating pepperoni pizza. Sweat poured from their faces and dripped onto the dirt below.

It was the final day of our annual youth football camp. At the end of each session, a former Jordan player gives a motivational talk to the campers. Today it was Kinney. He stood confidently in front of the group and spoke about staying in school and following your dreams.

The smallest boy in the group tentatively raised his hand to interrupt Kinney.

"Why did your dream come true?" the boy asked.

Kinney smiled. "There's going to be something in your life that motivates you, whether it's your mom, your parents. Mine is my family, and making my family better financially."

Five more kids raised their hands, and Kinney answered the barrage of questions with patience and wisdom.

Patricia Anne Rucker would be proud of her grandson at this moment. When Kinney came to live with her in Durham, his world was falling apart. Kinney grew up in the tough New York neighborhoods of Brooklyn, Bed-Stuy, and Hempstead. His father left when Kinney was only five, and his mother did everything she could to raise three sons on her own. But Kinney's older brothers fell into the wrong crowd, selling drugs and getting arrested again and again. The legal fees began to add up. Their power was cut off. Their house went into foreclosure. Kinney began to wonder if his destiny would be the same as his two brothers.

That's when Patricia Rucker stepped in. At the age of 11, Kinney packed up his few possessions and headed south to live with his grandmother in Durham, North Carolina. Patricia Rucker was an extremely devout woman who, despite losing both legs to diabetes, was an indomitable force in the Rucker household. Kinney immediately responded to her compassion and grace. For the first time in years, he let go of the fear that had plagued so much of his childhood.

Then everything fell apart. Two weeks after Kinney's 12th birthday, Patricia Rucker passed away. Kinney was devastated. His grandmother was the one person who truly believed in him. She constantly encouraged Kinney to rise above the obstacles in his life. Now she was gone.

Kinney attempted suicide at least four times. When his grandfather found him cutting his wrist one day, he urged Kinney to see a psychologist. But Kinney refused. He knew what was wrong. What more was there to live for?

Two events halted Kinney's downward spiral.

"I believe that there's an afterlife," Kinney said to me, "and I believe that people come back sometimes. I'll never forget what happened when I was 13. It was my first Christmas without her. Some people believe what I'm about to tell you and some people don't, but it got real cold in the room and I smelled her perfume. I just knew that she was with me, and it gave me another chance to go out there and do what I know I could do."

After this epiphany, Kinney never attempted suicide again. His grandmother would always be there, no matter what challenges lay ahead.

Soon after, Kinney decided to try out for football. He had always been a good athlete, but on the city streets of Long Island, basketball was king. It wasn't until his sophomore year in high school that Kinney began to realize his athletic potential.

Kinney was a student in one of my most memorable English classes. The class was full of loud and obnoxious eleventh graders who seemed to thrive on making my life a living hell. Kinney kept me from going insane. He sat at a table up front, with his long legs sprawled in every direction and his mind focused on becoming a better writer. He never joined in the chaos all around me; for that, I will be eternally grateful. I almost quit my job after that year, but Kinney, and a few other students like him, inspired me to return.

The following season, Kinney accepted a $180,000 scholarship to play football at Duke University. His dream was now a reality, thanks to a resolute faith, the love of Patricia Rucker, and the support of his teammates on the Falcon football squad.

In his first week as a freshman at Duke, Kinney didn't say a word in class. He had never been so intimidated in his life. But as he talked to me about these initial fears, I could sense the confidence of a young man who truly belonged at such an elite school.

"Duke is a private school, predominately rich white kids. New Jersey and New York, that's basically it. I didn't say much at first, but then, I was hearing what some of the people said, and I was like, I've got the same answers, I'm thinking the same things. I realized that these kids aren't any smarter than me. I could compete with them on an academic level."

Kinney decided on an African American Studies major with a minor in cultural anthropology. After graduation, he wants to go to law school and eventually open up a firm to help prisoners who are unjustly accused of a crime. Kinney believes in doing things the right way. It's one of the core values he picked up from his days as a player for Coach Briggs and the rest of the football staff at Jordan.

"To play for Coach Briggs you've got to have character. It's been a blessing; there's just so many people I love through this program. It's taught me how to work with people. I love Jordan football because it's given me so many intangible things that I can't even name. It's a big family, and we all have the same purpose, the same goal."

Kinney was a man now. I realized this as I watched the campers hang on his every word. If Kinney could achieve his dreams, then why couldn't they?

As the camp came to a close, I walked with Kinney across the Jordan practice field.

"When you pray these days, what do you tell your grandmother?" I asked him.

"I just tell her thank you for believing in me. There's been so many times when I laid my head down not knowing what I wanted in life when she passed away. But she led me in the direction of God. Even while she was in a wheelchair, if someone needed something, she would always be there."

Kinney paused, deep in thought. "She had the biggest heart. When no one would help me out, she was there."

On the first day of his senior year, Siddiq Haynes entered my Creative Writing class with a swagger to his step and a smile on his face. This was nothing new; Siddiq always seemed to be smiling these days. Several students looked skeptically at the 300-pound senior as he shook my hand and took a seat in the front row.

*What's a football player doing in here?* they wondered. *This is supposed to be a writing course.*

I'd waited five years to teach a class like this. The room was packed with thirty-four students, and several of them were sitting in temporary chairs or on the floor. Siddiq pulled out a pen and some loose-leaf paper. His knees turned awkwardly as he maneuvered his massive frame from side to side beneath the desk. I was familiar with this routine. Siddiq had been one of my best American Literature students the year before. He wasn't afraid to take intellectual risks in class, and he'd slowly grown into a confident writer. Siddiq decided to sign up for Creative Writing after receiving an A- in my English course. But what were his Creative Writing classmates to think? This was Siddiq, the hulking Muslim bear of a man, the football star, one of the most popular students in school, and he *chose* to take a class like this? Siddiq's nickname was the Beast, not the writer. He didn't fit the mold. Within two weeks, every student in the class knew why Siddiq was so happy to be here. It all made perfect sense.

Siddiq Haynes was born in the Edenwald Projects of the Bronx. It was a place filled with poverty and danger, and when Siddiq was four, his family decided to find somewhere safer to live down South. They had relatives in Atlanta, but an even bigger factor was the city's large Islamic community. More than twenty years ago, Siddiq's father converted to Islam while he was in prison. Mr. Haynes had been in jail for four years when a Muslim prayer leader, an *Imam*, began teaching him about the Prophet Mohammed. Everything changed. When the prison sentence was up, Siddiq's parents got married and began a new life structured around the discipline of the Qur'an. The Haynes family drifted from Atlanta to Macon before finally settling in Durham when Siddiq was in the 5$^{th}$ grade. By this time, Siddiq was well-acquainted with the soul food of the South, and his frame grew larger and larger. He attended a local Islamic school next to Durham's primary mosque, where he wore a uniform every day and attended Friday evening prayers.

In the 8th grade, Siddiq switched over to the local middle school. He didn't know a soul, but at least he could play football now. The first people he met were Bruce Rosell and Andrew Blaylock. The three boys would later become the captains of Jordan's 10-4 playoff squad in 2005. But the journey began on that first day of practice back in 8th grade.

When Siddiq came to Jordan as a freshman, he was short, out of shape, and weak. He couldn't bench more than 95 pounds, and he weighed well over 300 pounds. Before one of our games that year, I remember walking into the locker room to find Siddiq dancing on top of a wooden bench. He immediately lost his balance and fell to the floor with a thud, breaking the foot of the schizophrenic kid who liked to go after referees and opposing teams. Siddiq looked at me with innocent guilt. It was a look that freshman athletes seem to master so well. *Don't blame me for being an idiot. I'm just a freshman. I don't know any better.*

This bumbling, uncoordinated freshman eventually grew into a talented football player. Siddiq never missed a workout, even during the month of Ramadan. He fasted and suffered through the heat of practice without water and without complaints. He grew dizzy from the lack of food, but his devout focus prevailed during these difficult times. Siddiq soaked up the family atmosphere that football provided, and the sport allowed him to release the anger that sent his father to prison so many years before. His older brother was serving a thirty year sentence for the accidental death of a friend during an armed robbery; Siddiq wondered how things could have been different if his brother had just joined a football team.

Now it was time for Siddiq to move on to college. Neither one of his parents had a college degree, and Siddiq was extremely proud of his upcoming future at the University of Delaware. It was far from home, but he didn't seem to mind. His world had been chaotic at times, but what good would it do to complain? Football taught perseverance. It taught you to meet challenges head on. I was happy for Siddiq, but I knew I was going to miss him.

We were in the middle of summer workouts when Siddiq came by for one final visit. It was the dog days of football, those humid afternoons before the season really kicks into gear, when the sweltering heat saps every last bit of energy from the air. Siddiq gave me his customary handshake and bear hug that swallowed me into his enormous frame. The smile was there, as always, but I sensed a restlessness as well. It was time for him to be on his own. We walked through the halls of Jordan and dodged stacks of books and cleaning equipment, all part of the typical chaos of summer renovations at the school; the building took on a surreal, post-Apocalyptic atmosphere this time of year.

I asked Siddiq if he remembered the day four years ago when I found him dancing on the locker room bench. He nodded his head and laughed. Everyone knew Siddiq's laugh. It was high and shrill and full of life. Surely that dancing freshman was some other boy named Siddiq, because this was not the same person at all. Siddiq scanned the quiet hallways.

"You think you'll miss anything about this place?" I asked him.

"Just suiting up," Siddiq said, "putting on those nasty shoulder pads, the jersey. As strange as it sounds, I loved it because I looked forward to coming to practice, just to get that feeling. It gave me a drive. I'll miss how close we were – that's why we won so many games. I'll just miss the feeling of having a family on the football team."

I wanted to know why football was so important to him. I've asked this question countless times, but never to someone as close to me as Siddiq. He paused momentarily to think. Siddiq was serious now, introspective, deep in thought.

He looked at me candidly as he spoke: "When you play football, the attention to being good in school is always there, because without grades in school there will be no football. And I learned about a family outside of my immediate family. They say blood is thicker than water, but this football team actually felt like blood. It taught me that there's always a family out there if you need it. If you've got problems at home, then you can come to your coaches or your teammates and just talk about it. Football teaches you how to live. Instead of putting your anger out there in whatever else and getting in trouble, you can just hit somebody on the field and be good. A lot of people see football as a way to relieve tension and stress from doing anything that they're not supposed to be doing."

Siddiq leaned on a stack of textbooks, then thought better of it.

"I appreciated y'all staying on top of us, making sure we're good in classes. Y'all teach us about discipline and how not to talk back to grownups because there are punishments on the field and off the field. Y'all teach us about respect and about comradery and to trust everyone else around you because that affects how the play – or how life – is gonna go. You showed us how to be men on and off the field, because they're parallel to each other. Football taught me not to quit, because with quitting comes nothing but more quitting. It just helps you look at everything in a different way."

"Dang, Siddiq. When did you start talking so much?"

"Come on, Coach," Siddiq said with a smile.

"They're gonna lock us in here before too long."

Siddiq's laughter echoed across the hallway.

I grew serious once again. "So what else does a coach have to do to be successful?" I asked.

"They have to stay on top of players. They have to stay in their ear no matter what, whether they're throwing up or they wanna quit. Then at the end of the day, you have to tell them it's gonna get easier and all of this hard work will pay off, because it will, and it has for me. It'll teach them how to have a family on the field, because when you trust your teammates, then the team will be a thousand times better. I think that's why we succeeded so much this year, because we were all like brothers, and so we listened to each other. We had our fights like any family, but at the end of the day we hugged each other, and we went out on Friday night and we won those games."

"Is a family the same thing as a community?"

"A community is the people or things around you that make a whole," Siddiq responded. "You can have a community in school. Some people say a gang is a community, and you can have a gang and not be negative. You can have a gang of friends who write together, and you can call that your writing community, or you can live on a block that makes up ten houses and everybody knows each other and that's one little community. A community is a group that's together in one set place in time and has the same ideas. Sometimes a community can drift you away from what you want to do, and sometimes it can help you.

"That's where school comes in. Education is a platform to succeed in life, because with education you learn, and you're not illiterate about the world around you. It gives you something to be proud of."

We eventually wandered back to the locker room, and Siddiq asked me about the creative writing curriculum for next year. Over 150 students had signed up for my class, and many of them were football players recruited by Siddiq.

"As a freshman," Siddiq said to me, "I didn't talk a lot, and even when I started talking, I don't think anyone actually knew me as a person because I kept to myself. I kept a poetry book, and when I was mad, or when I wanted to get some words on paper, I would write poetry. My words translated into my feelings. When I heard about your writing class, I jumped on it because my feelings would be on paper. I never thought I could write a story, and when you would give us prompts like 'The smell of rainfall and gasoline...' I was the one at the beginning of class saying, 'Oh, we can't write about this!' But when I started writing, ideas just started to pop up and pop up, and when you said stop, I had a page and a half written down. I was amazed, and it was good because it all came from feeling."

I opened the door to the practice field, and we shook hands one final time. My eyes squinted against the sun; the humidity seemed to fill every pour of my skin. Siddiq's massive frame swallowed me up yet again, and I remembered another embrace seven months before. We had just lost in the third round of the state playoffs. The temperature was well below freezing that night, and my fingers were numb from the biting wind chill. I grabbed Siddiq by the shoulder pads and patted the top of his helmet. High school football was over for him. It seemed impossible, but it was true. We stood on the empty football field and cried together just as I had cried into the arms of my own football coach so many years before. It was a never-ending cycle.

The future Siddiqs of the world are practicing on fields of bone-dry crab grass at this very moment. They are wide-eyed freshman with little coordination and uncertain footsteps. One day they will grow into men with the heart and the character of Siddiq. That's how a community works. The welcoming arms of a family grow wider and wider with every new son. These sons eventually become fathers and teach their own sons the value of a close-knit community. A young boy realizes that someone cares about him, and one day he becomes a man filled with compassion for others. But there has to be a guiding light.

Somewhere in North Carolina, a child is growing up in a community of love and support. He is smiling, because life is beautiful. He is part of a family. Hope exists. Everything is possible.

# EPILOGUE

My story does not end perfectly. That only happens in Hollywood. As a teacher and coach, I want to save every student I come in contact with, particularly the ones who desperately cry out for guidance. But sometimes I feel like I'm banging my head against a brick wall.

In the movie version of that junior varsity game against Garner, the lights fade to black as we dash to the endzone following Renard Edwards' Hail Mary pass to Antonio Smith. As the credits scroll down the screen, we see homemade videos of each player in their graduation robes, proudly walking across the stage and pumping their fists in the air. Every player on the team goes on to achieve great things in the world. They become lawyers, senators, teachers, family men. Some of them even go into coaching themselves. They return home to thank us for transforming their lives.

Did everything really turn out that way? Sort of.

On that junior varsity squad, over 90% of the players went on to attend a four year college. Thirteen of them are still playing football. Josh Dorfman, the stoic center from that team, plays for Butler. Wide Receiver Antonio Smith began his career at North Carolina Central and is now playing for Louisburg College. Tight End Clark Richards is at Elon. Delson McAdams, our leading running back, is a student at North Carolina Central.

The story of Renard Edwards is a bit more complicated. After leading our junior varsity team to an undefeated season as a freshman, Renard's grades began to slip. He got suspended twice for fighting in the cafeteria. He joined a local gang. We had conferences with him and his mom, interventions with some of his teammates, signed contracts in which he promised to do the right thing. Nothing seemed to work.

Three games into his sophomore season, Renard received a week-long suspension after fighting a rival gang member. We had no choice but to remove him from the football team. Tears streamed down Renard's face as he turned in his shoulder pads and walked off the practice field.

It wasn't safe for Renard to stay in Durham any longer. He'd made too many enemies at the school. So he moved in with his father in Orlando, Florida. I thought about Renard from time to time, but no one knew how to get in touch with him. It was as if he had vanished from the face of the earth.

Fast forward to last summer. I opened my email one morning to find the following message:

*Long time no hear, coach, i really miss things there. I wanted to ask you a question. If i was to come back to Jordan will i be accepted by the coaches and the team? I know we considered ourselves a family and you all continuously put yourselves out there for me and i left you hanging. I'm sorry for breaking my contract, I'm sorry for breaking the trust and bond of the family i should have been interacting with the whole time i was there. Pretty much i let everyone down. I honestly want to come back and be a Falcon, a teammate, and a family member to the great group of coaches and players. I worked hard to catch my grades and credits up. I am busting my behind now because i made a bed and now i got to lay in it. My last memory as a Falcon was Coach Briggs telling me i was no longer able to be on the team. I want my last memory as a Falcon to be playing in the playoffs, showing that i belong on the field and not the streets. I guess what I'm saying is I'm sorry. May i please have a second chance?*

*Sincerely,*
*Renard Edwards*

When I saw Renard two weeks later, I almost didn't recognize him. His long, braided hair was gone. He looked lean, almost fragile, as if the past two years had done a number on his body. Renard had been taking classes from seven in the morning until nine at night to make up his lost credits. He'd been in a couple of fist fights with his father; he'd even been homeless for a little while. But he was here.

Renard hesitated as he reached the locker room door. What if his old teammates didn't want him back? Where would he go from here?

The locker room door opened, and a line of players came out to hug Renard. The whole team, one by one.

Five minutes later, I happened to see Renard at the other end of the hallway, leaning against the wall and crying silently to himself.

Renard was our back-up quarterback this past year. He passed all of his classes, although he still had a few bad habits. He often came to school late. In my Creative Writing class, he'd be a model student one day, then fall into a comatose state the next. Renard could be moody. But writing became a great way for him to release all the pain and frustration that had built up for so many years. In his poetry, Renard was the quintessential romantic, gushing over a new crush one moment and then bleeding out the sorrows of lost love the very next week. He was a rollercoaster of emotions.

On June 8, 2008, Renard Edwards walked across the stage at Duke's Cameron Indoor Stadium to receive his high school diploma. He was heading to Savannah State University in the fall. The path wasn't straight, and it wasn't easy, but Renard made the most of his second chance. It's been an honor to watch him grow up along the way.

I wrote the bulk of this book over three consecutive summers. Writing is a privilege that few teachers can afford during the school year. Every time I tried to get back on the computer, a mountain of ungraded essays always called to me from the living room. During the football season, coaching and teaching are an all-consuming, 80-hour-a-week task. Therefore, some of the teams profiled in this book have changed more than others since I first wrote about them.

At **Ashbrook**, Bill Eccles retired this past year after 38 years of coaching the Greenwave football team. His son, Jake, continues to be the head junior varsity football coach. Jake is also the head wrestling coach. Bill Eccles now volunteers as his son's top assistant. I've lost touch with most of my high school teammates, including Nick Sherrill and John Butler, although I've heard that Jamie Burris is happily married and living in Charlotte. The Mullinax twins are also doing well. I still see their father whenever I go home for an Ashbrook football game. Both of his sons have good jobs and are living in Charlotte.

After removing Carter Sharp from the **E.E. Smith** squad, Milton Butts coached the Golden Bulls for one more year before returning to Westover, the first school to hire him when he originally came to Fayetteville. Before Coach Butts took over at Westover, the program could barely field a varsity team; now, the team looks to contend for a conference championship. Carter Sharpe left Hargrave Military Academy after one game and enrolled at Trinity Christian in Fayetteville, a school so small that the team plays in an eight-man football league. After two games, Sharpe abruptly dropped out of Trinity as well. The following year, Sharpe played running back for a new postgraduate program in Charlotte called North Carolina Tech, where students pay $2,500 to play football and have the option to work on their high school diploma. Carter Sharpe carried the ball 47 times for 325 yards at NC Tech before leaving the team near the end of the 2007 season. He is now working toward his high school diploma at a community college. No one seems to know if he will ever play football again.

Down east in Jacksonville, Phil Padgett still coaches the **Southwest Onslow** Stallions. Last year's team lived up to Debbie Bryan's hopes for a good season by finishing 10-3 after losing to cross-town rival Northside in the playoffs. Expectations will no doubt be high for the upcoming season.

At **East Surry**, David Diamont's football team had a respectable 10-3 record last year. Diamont coached his son, Davey, in the East-West All-Star game at the end of the year. His younger son, Hunter, is a talented junior linebacker for the Pilot Mountain school.

Danny Wilkin's **Asheville** Cougars ended this past season with a 9-4 record, a year after another heartbreaking loss in the state semifinals. I ran into both Wilkins and Eugene Hammonds at the annual North Carolina Coaches Clinic this year. Coach Hammonds still works with the running backs after nearly forty years at the school.

In March of 2008, Keith Wilkes left Winston-Salem **Carver** to take the head coaching job at Shiloh High School in Snellville, Georgia. "I have been here close to 20-some years, and I feel like I want to try something new, and now is the time," Coach Wilkes told the *Winston-Salem Journal.* "My mom has been laid off and struggling down there, and I hope to get down and help her out a little bit." In 25 years at Carver, Wilkes won two state championships and had an overall record of 139-62-1. At Shiloh, he will take over a team that has only won four games in two years.

Despite losing a talented senior class from the 2007 season, **Cherokee** reloaded the following year to finish 11-3. All 8,500 residents on the Qualla Boundary High have closely monitored the construction of the brand new Cherokee school complex. Called "the Cadillac of public schools," the K-12 facility will open in the fall of 2009. Skooter McCoy and Ray Kinsland plan to continue their work with the football team for years to come.

In **New Bern**, expectations were extremely high for Bobby Curlings' squad to repeat as state champions, even with the loss of 26 seniors. Throughout the off-season, Tommy Knotts' future at Independence seemed to be in doubt. His offensive coordinator left to become the head coach at beleaguered West Charlotte. Knotts was linked to several jobs in the Charlotte area and around the South. But Tommy Knotts decided to come back to Independence. Almost every newspaper in the state picked the Patriots to reclaim the state championship this year.

Here in **Durham**, LaDwaun Harrison and I continue to coach the junior varsity football team. Chris Starkey works with the varsity now; his son CJ is a freshman wide receiver on Campbell University's inaugural football team. Tim Bumgarner also works with the varsity; his son Robert caught two touchdown passes as a freshman tight end this past year at Presbyterian College. Kinney Rucker is now a junior defensive tackle at Duke University, where he maintains a 3.0 GPA. He still plans to go to law school when his playing days are over. Siddiq Haynes started one game as a freshman defensive lineman at Delaware. I watched him on ESPN as the Blue Hens played Appalachian State for the Division-1AA National Championship. Appalachian State won, but Siddiq made an impressive goal-line tackle in the game. This past season, Siddiq lived the dream of every lineman by rambling 31 yards on a fumble return against nationally-ranked Furman. Siddiq is majoring in journalism, with plans to become a television news anchor after college. He earned a 3.2 GPA his first year at Delaware.

When a new class of freshmen arrives at Jordan each year, I never know what kind of impact they will have on my life. They always seem so desperate for guidance, so scared of the unknown. For many of them, joining this football team will be one of the defining moments of their teenage years. They'll never be able to look at family and community in the same way.

What will their story be? Who will they become? Their chapter is only just beginning.

# ACKNOWLEDGEMENTS

This book would not have been possible without the guidance and support of a small army of people. All of the coaches profiled in these pages were profoundly gracious with their time and their candid answers to my persistent questions. I am truly inspired by the positive impact they have made on the lives of thousands of young men across North Carolina.

Rick Strunk and Bland Simpson helped me to frame the original concept of this book. I am also indebted to the following individuals for their help along the way: Tamara Holmes in Fayetteville; Ray Kinsland in Cherokee; Skip Clayton, Ed Bell, and Sharon Bryant in New Bern; and the public library staffs in Jacksonville, Pilot Mountain, Asheville, and Durham.

Staff writers at various newspapers across the state provided valuable insights into the communities I profiled. Richard Walker's multi-part series on the "Ghosts of Gastonia's Football Past" in the *Gaston Gazette* includes some of the finest sports journalism I have ever read. I am also indebted to the work of Keith Jarrett at the *Asheville Citizen-Times*, Earl Vaughan at the *Fayetteville Observer*, Ryan Basen at the *Charlotte Observer*, and Langston Wertz at the *Charlotte Observer*. In addition to newspaper archives and oral histories, the following books were also very helpful in my research: *The Greatest Sports Heroes of the Stephens-Lee Bears* by Johnny Bailey and Bennie Lake; *The Eastern Band of the Cherokee Indians, 1819-1900* by John

Finger; *The Real All Americans* by Sally Jenkins; and *The Best of Enemies* by Osha Gray Davidson.

My fellow coaches at Jordan High School are some of the most passionate advocates for youth I have ever known. They include Paul Atkins, Brent Blaylock, Mike Briggs, Tim Bumgarner, Ngozi Collins, Shawn Davis, LaDwaun Harrison, Antonio Garner, Antonio Hill, Matt Holway, Jason Luck, Mike Mangili, Brett Moseley, Dan Richards, Brent Rogan, Kenneth Sloan, and Chris Starkey. The dedicated faculty and staff at Jordan make this school a special place to work, and the students I have taught and coached over the years have inspired me to stay in this job for years to come.

I am grateful for the love and encouragement of Lou Pearson, Joe and Lil Summerville, Bill and Sharon Eccles, Mary Layton, and my brother Rob and his wife Molly. My parents, Nancy and Alan Albright, have given so much more to me than I have ever deserved. Finally, I would like to thank my wife, Jenni. You are the love of my life, my best friend, and the most beautiful woman I will ever know. This book would not exist without your constant support.

# ABOUT THE AUTHOR

STUART ALBRIGHT is the author of *Blessed Returns*. A native of Gastonia, North Carolina, he earned his B.A. in English and Creative Writing from UNC Chapel Hill and his M.Ed. from Harvard University. He currently teaches English and Creative Writing at Jordan High School in Durham, NC, where he also coaches football. In 2008, Albright received the Milken National Educator Award, dubbed the "Oscars of Teaching" by *Teacher Magazine*. He lives with his wife in Durham.

LaVergne, TN USA
08 April 2010
178624LV00004B/183/P